ENCYCLOPEDIA OF HISTORY

ENCYCLOPEDIA OF
HISTORY

Consulted by Philip Steele

Miles Kelly

First published in 2015 by Miles Kelly Publishing Ltd
Harding's Barn, Bardfield End Green, Thaxted, Essex, CM6 3PX, UK

2 4 6 8 10 9 7 5 3 1

Publishing Director Belinda Gallagher
Creative Director Jo Cowan
Editorial Director Rosie Neave
Design Manager Simon Lee
Image Manager Liberty Newton
Indexer Philip Steele
Production Elizabeth Collins, Caroline Kelly
Reprographics Stephan Davis, Jennifer Cozens, Thom Allaway

ISBN 978-1-78209-863-8

Printed in China

British Library Cataloguing-in-Publication Data
A catalogue record for this book is available from the British Library

Made with paper from a sustainable forest

www.mileskelly.net
info@mileskelly.net

Contents

Prehistory 14–45

Civilization 46–101

The Ancient World 102–185

The Medieval World 186–293

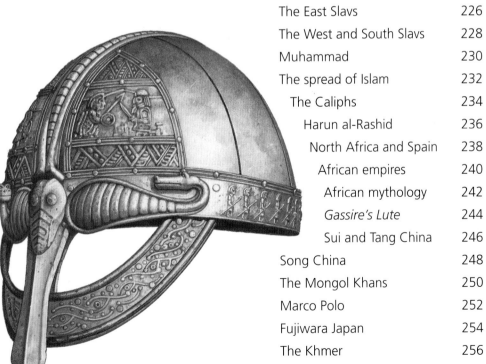

Age of Discovery 294–365

Industry and Empire 366–427

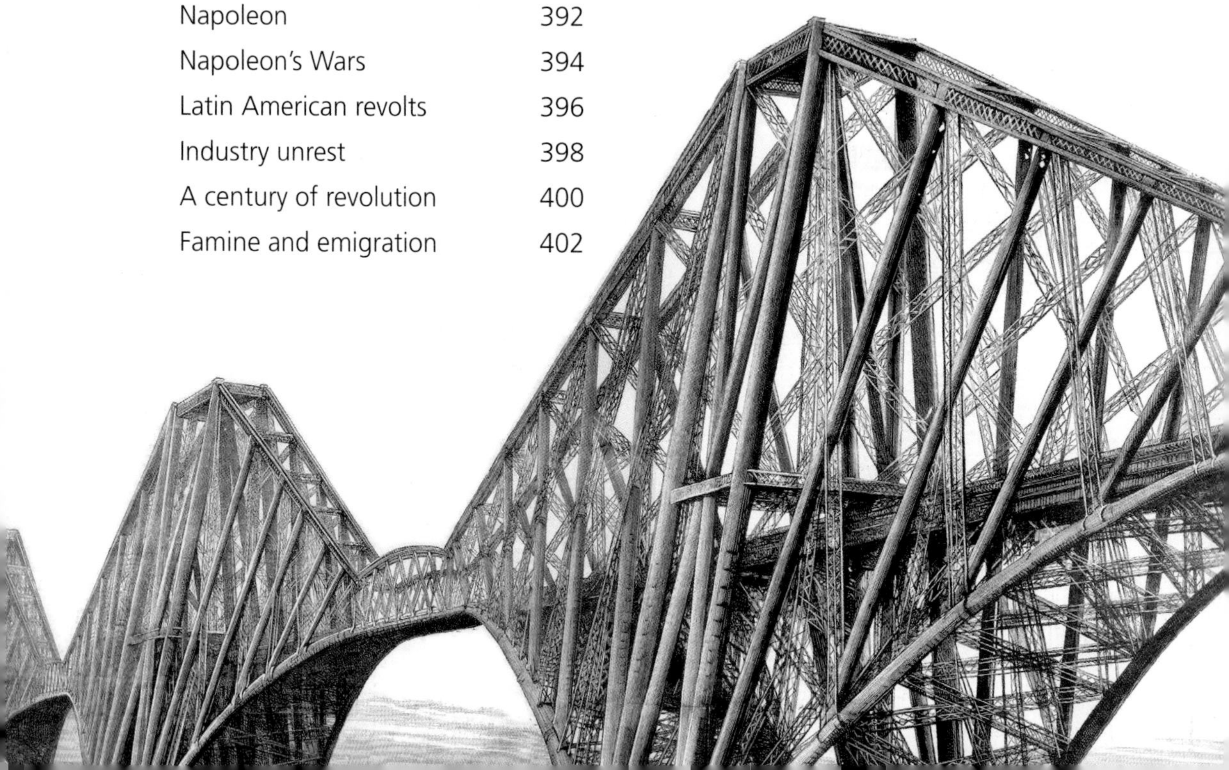

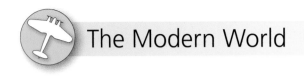

The Modern World 428–487

What was the world like before humans learned how to write down the story of their lives?

AFRICA

c.25–23 million years BP
Proconsul living in East Africa, possibly a common ancestor of apes and humans.

c.4–2 million years BP
Australopithecus ('southern ape') species are walking on two legs.

c.2.3–1.4 million years BP
Homo habilis ('handy man'), an early member of the human family, is able to make tools.

c.1.8 million–143,000 BP
Homo erectus ('upright man') evolves in Africa and spreads into Asia.

c.200,000 BP
Earliest fossil evidence of modern humans (*Homo sapiens*, 'wise man') shows they were living in Ethiopia.

c.125,000 BP
Homo sapiens spreads from Africa into Western Asia.

c.100,000–75,000 BP
Bone tools and shell necklaces at Blombos Cave, South Africa.

c.8500 BP
Rock art in the Sahara, then a fertile region of North Africa.

EUROPE

c.500,000 BP
Heidelberg Man, probably an ancestor of humans, living in Europe.

c.200,000–39,000 BP
Neanderthal people, closely related to modern humans, live across Europe.

c.110,000–12,000 BP
The last of the great ice ages freezes northern Europe.

c.45,000–30,000 BP
Cro-Magnon people (modern humans) spread across Europe.

c.40,000 BP
Rock paintings in El Castillo cave, Spain.

c.10,000–5000 BC
The Palaeolithic (Old Stone) Age gives way to the Mesolithic (Middle Stone) Age cultures of northwest Europe.

c.8500–3000 BC
Climate change brings rising sea levels and changes in vegetation.

c.6500 BC
Farming reaches southern Europe's Balkan peninsula, from Asia.

ASIA

c.1.8 million–40,000 BP
Homo erectus living in Asia. Important finds in China and Java.

c.120,000 BP
Neanderthal people living in western Asia.

c.120,000–60,000 BP
Homo sapiens spreads around the Indian Ocean and through Asia.

c.73,000 BP
Massive volcanic eruption of Mount Toba causes global climate change.

c.22,000 BP
Greatest area of northern Asia affected by the Ice Age. Low sea levels.

c.12,000 BP
Earliest known pottery in the world, Xianren Cave, China.

c.9000–7000 BC
Domestication of animals and development of farming across the Middle East.

c.9000 BC
Oldest remains at the city of Jericho, Palestine.

c.7500 BC
Start of large housing settlement at Çatalhöyük, Anatolia, Turkey.

Prehistory

NORTH AMERICA

c.16,500 BP
North America's Ice Age reaches its greatest extent.

c.15,000 BP
Settlement of North America by Paleo-Indians, either by way of a land bridge from Asia or by water.

c.13,000 BP
The 'Clovis' culture, tools of flaked stone, bone and ivory.

c.10,500 BP
Ice sheets retreat. Hunting of big game.

c.9000–c.8000 BC
The 'Folsom' tradition of central North America, bison hunting.

c.8000–c.2000 BC
The 'Archaic' stages, widespread hunting of smaller animals and gathering of plant food and shellfish.

c.7000 BC
Crops grown in Tehuacán Valley, Mexico.

c.3500 BC
Log-built housing in North America.

CENTRAL AND SOUTH AMERICA

c.32,000 BP
Possible date (disputed) for artefacts at Pedra Furada, Brazil.

c.14,800 BP
Settlement at Monte Verde, southern Chile.

c.7000 BC
Manioc grown in the Amazon River basin.

c.6300 BC
Potatoes grown in the Andes mountains, Peru.

c.4000 BC
Pottery made in Guyana region.

c.3500 BC
Cotton grown in southern Peru, used to make textiles and fishing nets.

c.2800 BC
Villages and horticulture in Amazonia.

c.2600 BC
Temple mounds built near the coast of Peru.

OCEANIA

c.50,000–40,000 BP
Ancestors of Aborigines reach Australia, migrating from Southwest Asia

c.25,000 BP
Aborgines spread to southeast Australia and Tasmania.

c.20,000 BP
Flints are mined at Koonalda Cave, southern Australia.

c.18,000–16,000 BP
Increasingly arid conditions in Australia.

c.10,000 BC
New waves of settlement in Australia.

c.7000 BC
Cultivation of bananas and taro in New Guinea.

c.5000 BC
Coastal flooding. New Guinea and Tasmania become islands.

c.3000 BC
Introduction of canines (dingos) to Australia.

Discovering the past

▲ *Archaeology is a very painstaking process. Diggers work with immense care to avoid overlooking or breaking tiny, fragile relics.*

- **If we are to understand** the present and future, we must understand our past. Recent history offers us clues from books, photographs, films and buildings, but for more ancient evidence we may need to search beneath the ground or the sea.
- **Palaeontology is the science** of evolution and fossils. Archaeology is the scientific study of remains left by humans, from old bones to ancient temples.
- **Aerial photographs** or satellite imaging often reveal where archaeologists should dig. Crops and grass will grow differently if the soil is affected by a buried wall or filled-in ditch.

- **Geophysical surveys** involve using metal detectors and other electronic probes to pick up features underground. Field-walking involves exploring the site on foot, carefully scanning the ground by eye.
- **Archaeologists dig down** through layers of soil. They note exactly where every relic was found. The deeper a relic is buried, the older it is likely to be.
- **Archaeologists work** with different kinds of experts to help them interpret finds. Forensic scientists may help to reveal how someone died long ago, based on their skeleton.
- **Radiocarbon dating** is a way of dating the remains of once-living things from their carbon content. This is fairly accurate up to 50,000 years ago. Potassium argon dating helps to date the rocks in which relics were found.

◀ *Archaeologists have found many remains of Roman life. Roman pottery was beautifully made and designed, while statues give an idea of how Romans looked. Oil-burning lamps have been unearthed, and we know that the Romans loved beautiful jewellery.*

Human origins

- **Humans and apes** have so many similarities – such as long arms and fingers, and a big brain – that most experts think they must have evolved from the same species in prehistoric Africa.
- **Our common ancestor** may be four-legged orangutan-like creatures called dryopithecines, which lived in trees from about 23–10 million years ago.
- ***Ardipithecus ramidus*** is known from 4.4-million-year-old bone fragments found in the Afar depression, Ethiopia.
- **An evolutionary breakthrough** occurred when hominins (human-related species) began to live on the ground and walk on two legs.
- **Many very early hominins** were australopiths ('southern apes'). *Australopithecus anamensis* lived in Kenya and Ethiopia from 4.2 million years ago.
- **Footprints of three hominins** from 3.7 million years ago were found preserved in volcanic ash at Laetoli, Tanzania.

▶ *Experts once thought humans had evolved in a single line from australopiths, through* Homo habilis *(1),* Homo erectus *(2) and 'Neanderthal man' (3) to humans (4). They now realize there were many evolutionary branches.*

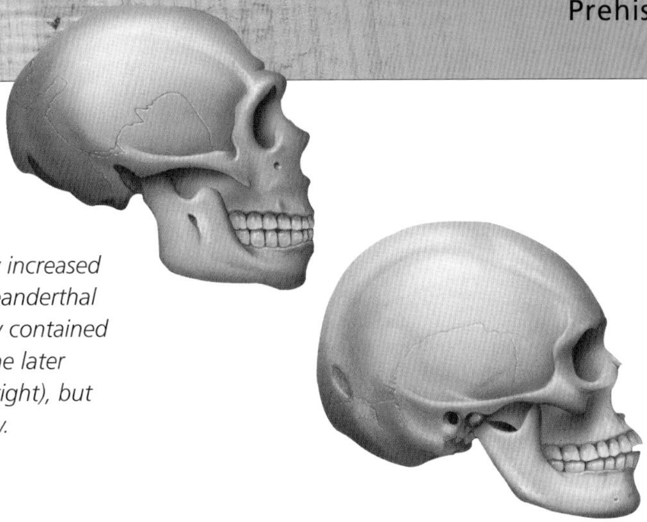

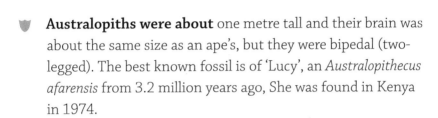

▶ *Brain size generally increased over the ages. The Neanderthal skull (top left) actually contained a bigger brain than the later human one (bottom right), but it served a larger body.*

Australopiths were about one metre tall and their brain was about the same size as an ape's, but they were bipedal (two-legged). The best known fossil is of 'Lucy', an *Australopithecus afarensis* from 3.2 million years ago, She was found in Kenya in 1974.

Lucy's discoverers – Don Johanson and Maurice Tieb – called her Lucy because they were listening to The Beatles' song 'Lucy in the Sky with Diamonds' at the time. Lucy's skeleton shows that hominins learned to walk upright before their brains got bigger.

Clever creatures

- **The first really human-like hominins** appeared around 2.5–1.8 million years ago. These are all given the genus (group) name Homo, which is shared by ourselves.
- **The best-known early examples** are *Homo rudolfensis* and *Homo habilis*. These were taller than the Australopiths and had bigger brains.
- **Australopiths had originally** been plant-eaters. These hominins ate more meat, perhaps because the climate warmed up, reducing the amount of plant food that was available.
- **Brains need a lot of food**, and eating meat gave these creatures extra nourishment
- **The first hominins** in the genus Homo lived for a million or more years alongside 'robust' (bigger) Australopiths such as *Paranthropus boisei*.

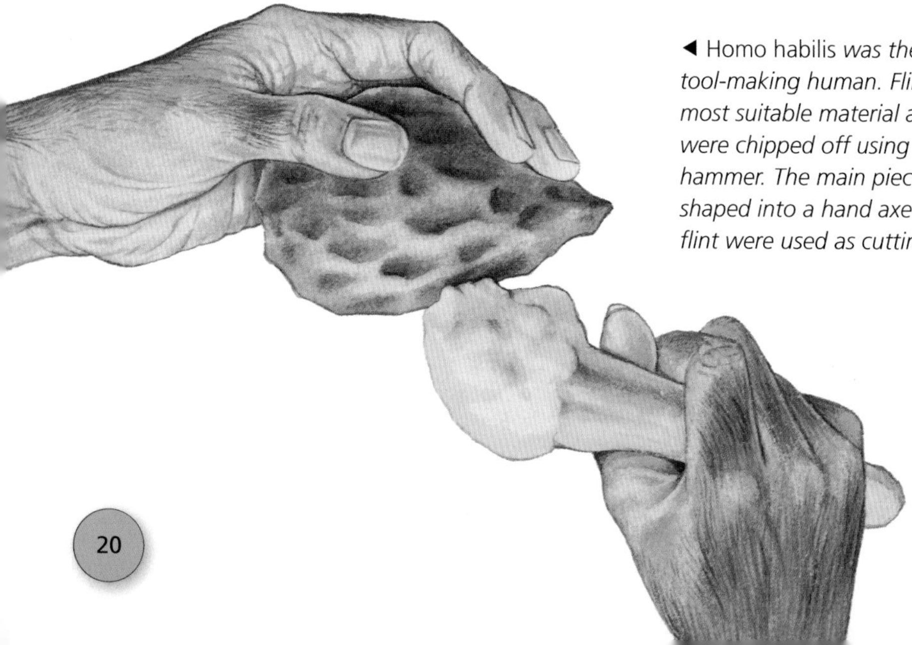

◀ Homo habilis *was the first tool-making human. Flint was the most suitable material and flakes were chipped off using a bone hammer. The main piece of flint was shaped into a hand axe. The flakes of flint were used as cutting tools.*

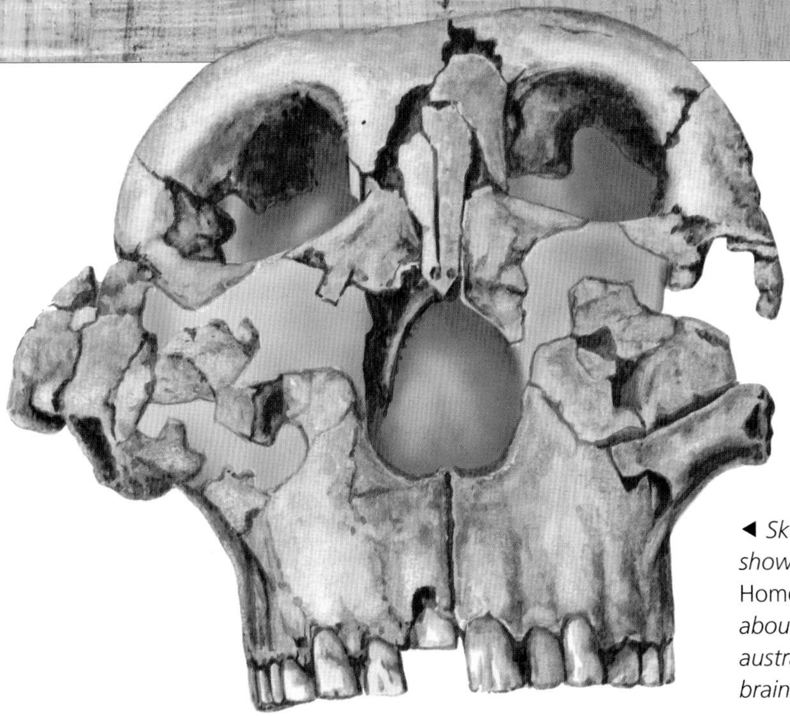

◄ *Skulls that have been found show that early species such as* Homo habilis *had brains of about 650 cc – twice as big as australopiths. Today's human brains measure about 1400 cc.*

- ***Homo habilis* is known** from pieces of hand bones, a jaw and a skull found in Tanzania's Olduvai Gorge in 1961.
- **The name means 'Handy Man'**. It was given because this species had a good grip for wielding tools – with a thumb that can be rotated to meet the tip of a finger. This is called an 'opposable thumb'.
- **Early *Homo* species** used stones to break open bones for the nourishing marrow inside. Later they sharpened stones to cut meat for eating and hides for making clothing. Experts believe that they may even have built simple shelters to live in.
- **Some experts think** that *Homo habilis* skulls suggest that these creatures could speak in a crude way, because of the shape of their brain. However many scientists disagree.

The first hunters

- **About two million years ago**, a much taller hominin appeared, with long legs and a straight back more like our own. Adults were 1.6 m tall, weighed 65 kg and had brains of about 850 cc, well over half as big as ours.
- **Scientists named this species** *Homo ergaster*, but are still arguing about how it should be classified in relation to very similar species such as *Homo erectus*.
- ***Homo ergaster* did not** just scavenge for meat like *Homo habilis*. It hunted large animals.
- **For hunting** and cutting up meat, *Homo ergaster* made double-edged blades or 'hand-axes' from pieces of stone, shaping them by chipping off flakes.

▼ *Experts call this method of making stone tools 'Acheulean', after a site in France.*

- **To hunt effectively**, *Homo ergaster* had to work as a team, so co-operation was the key to its success – and may have quickly led to the development of speech.
- ***Homo ergaster* may have painted** its body with red ochre (a mineral found in the ground).

DID YOU KNOW?
Longer legs and skills in co-operation helped Homo erectus to spread beyond Africa into Asia.

- ***Homo erectus*** ('Upright man') appeared shortly after *Homo ergaster*. Remains have been found as far from Africa as Java, in Southeast Asia. Stone tools 700,000 years old were found on the Indonesian island of Flores.
- ***Homo erectus* learned** to light fires, so it could live in colder places and make a wider range of food more edible by cooking.

◀ *By developing a greater variety of stone tools, early man was more successful at hunting and eating wild animals.*

New lands, new skills

- **Early human species** reached Europe much later than Asia. The oldest type found in Europe, called *Homo antecessor*, dates from 1.2 million–800,000 years ago. This may have been a kind of *Homo erectus*, or a separate species.
- **Later, around 800,000–600,000 years ago**, *Homo heidelbergensis* appeared in parts of Europe, Asia and Africa. It is named after a site in Germany.
- **Heidelberg Man** may be a single species that came from Africa or various species that evolved in different places.
- ***Homo heidelbergensis*** has many features in common with *Homo erectus*, but was a major step on the way to modern humans with, for the very first time, a brain as big as ours.
- **Heidelberg Man** made good stone tools, making the core first, then shaping the blade with a single blow.
- **This species** was probably the ancestor to Neanderthal Man, which lived in Europe from about 200,000–39,000 years ago.
- **Neanderthals were named** after the Neander valley in Germany, where remains were found in 1856.
- **Although slightly shorter** than modern humans, Neanderthals were much stronger and had bigger brains.
- **Neanderthals buried their dead**, often with tributes of flowers.
- **Around 28,000 years ago** Neanderthals were still living in Croatia – long after modern humans had appeared. No one knows why Neanderthal Man died out, leaving humans alone.

▼ *Most early hominin remains have been found in Africa. Many species – including modern humans – may have emerged first in Africa, then migrated elsewhere. These are sites where remains have been found.*

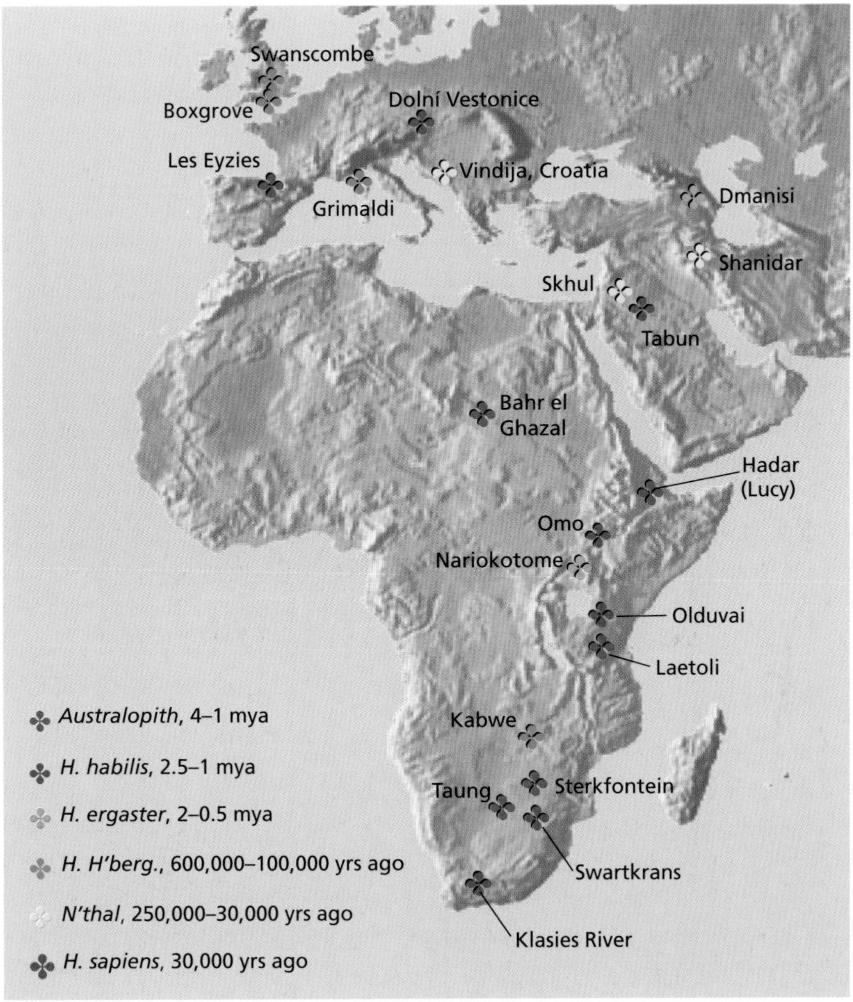

Modern humans

- **The scientific name** for modern humans is *Homo sapiens sapiens*. The word sapiens (meaning 'wise') is used twice to distinguish us from *Homo sapiens idaltu*, an extinct African subspecies dating from 160,000 years ago.
- **Some scientists think** that because we all share similar DNA, all humans are descended from a woman nicknamed 'Eve', whom they calculate lived in Africa about 200,000 years ago. DNA is the special molecule in every body cell that carries the body's instructions for life.
- **The earliest *Homo sapiens* skulls** were found in Africa, from the Omo Basin in Ethiopia to the Klasies River in South Africa.
- **About 125,000 years ago**, modern humans began to spread out into Asia and Europe from Africa.
- **About 50,000 years ago**, modern humans reached Australia by boat from Indonesia. They may have reached the Americas from Asia about the same time.
- **The earliest modern Europeans** are called Cro-Magnons, after the caves in France's Dordogne valley where skeletons from 35,000 years ago were found in 1868.

▶ *Both modern humans and Neanderthals used well-crafted spears for hunting.*

- **Modern humans lived alongside** Neanderthals for tens of thousands of years in the Middle East and Europe. Modern humans had a prominent chin and a flatter face, with a high forehead.
- **Modern humans were probably** the first creatures to use proper language. Some scientists think language was a sudden genetic 'accident' that remained and developed because it gave humans a huge advantage.
- **With modern humans** came rapid advances in stone tool technology, the building of wooden huts, population increase, and a growing interest in art.

▶ Homo sapiens *developed new skills, which over the ages would have a massive impact on the planet.*

Humans on the move

- **We have seen how** the genus *Homo* began to migrate from the African homelands about 750,000 years ago, long before modern humans.
- **Humans spread out of Africa** into the Near East around 125,000 years ago. Experts once thought that oceans had blocked migrations, but it now seems that boats have been used since the earliest days.
- **Around 50,000 years ago**, modern humans began the great expansion that took them to every continent except Antarctica within 20,000 years.
- **Humans spread across Asia** and Australasia 50,000–40,000 years ago. From 40,000–35,000 years ago, they moved across Europe.
- **The earliest dates** and routes by which humans reached the Americas are the subject of many different theories. By 13,000 years ago there had been a large-scale settlement from northeast Asia.
- **Early humans** were mainly nomadic hunters, always on the move, following animals into empty lands.

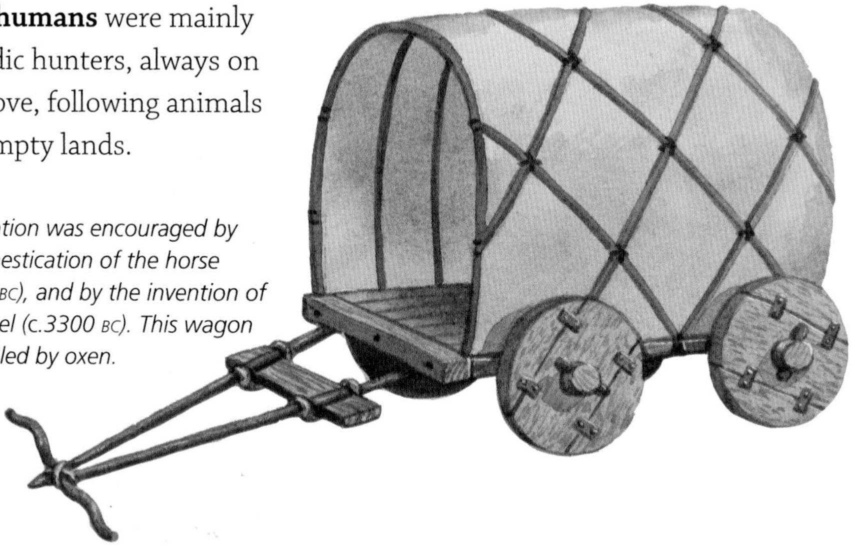

▶ *Migration was encouraged by the domestication of the horse (c.4000 BC), and by the invention of the wheel (c.3300 BC). This wagon was hauled by oxen.*

▲ *Changing climate and migrating herds meant that humans needed to move in order to survive.*

- **Changes in climate** triggered many migrations. People moved north in warm times and retreated during ice ages. When the last Ice Age ended, 10,000 years ago, hunters moved north through Europe as the weather warmed.
- **The rise of farming**, which took place at different times around the world, offered a permanent source of food. People no longer had to live as nomadic hunters.
- **The search for new farmland** or trading routes still led to migration however. Around 4000 years ago, peoples spread southward from their homeland in southern Russia into Europe and Asia.
- **About 3000 years ago**, the Sahara area began to dry up, and people living there moved to its fringes. People from the Niger and Congo river basins spread south and east through Africa.

Peopling of the Americas

- **The Americas** were the last of the continents that humans occupied.
- **The first Americans** may have been Australian aboriginals who arrived in South America by boat up to 50,000 years ago.
- **Ancestors of most** of today's indigenous peoples probably came to the Americas 20,000–35,000 years ago, from Asia, but these dates are disputed. The migrants are thought to have walked across the strip of land that once joined Asia and North America across the Bering Strait.
- **By 6000 BC**, they had spread south from Alaska and far down into South America.
- **There is evidence** that humans were living in Mexico over 20,000 years ago. At El Jobo in Colombia, South America, pendants that date back to 14,920 BC have been found.

▲ The name 'squash' comes from the native American word 'kutasquash', which means raw or uncooked. Squash is still a widely grown vegetable today.

▼ Carving wooden duck decoys for hunting is a North American tradition dating back thousands of years.

DID YOU KNOW?
A 50,000-year-old skull found in Colombia resembles the skulls of Australian aboriginals.

- **Ten thousand years ago**, groups of 'Paleo-Indians' on North America's Great Plains hunted now-extinct animals such as camels and mammoths. In the dry western mountains, desert peoples planted wild grass-seed.
- **In Mexico**, people began to grow squash, peppers and beans at least 8500 years ago. Corn (maize) was probably first grown in Mexico, about 7000 years ago.
- **About 5000 years ago**, a Siberian people (unrelated to today's Inuit) moved into the American Arctic.

▶ *Giant Colombian mammoths roamed South America during the last Ice Age. They were hunted for their hides and flesh.*

Peopling of Oceania

- **Australia was settled** as early as 50,000 years ago, when migrants crossed from Southeast Asia by boat. The oldest settlement in New Guinea is 40,000 years old.
- **Up until 5000 BC** the sea level was lower and Tasmania, Australia and New Guinea were all part of the same big landmass. Then a rise in sea levels made them into islands. Most early coastal sites are now lost offshore.
- **Today's Australian aborigines** are descendants of these original inhabitants.

▼ *The peoples of Oceania crossed the ocean in both small and large canoes thousands of years before the great European explorers.*

- **In about 4000 BC**, domesticated plants and animals reached New Guinea from Asia, and farmers drained fields around an area called Kuk Swamp. Many people, however, remained hunters.
- **From about 2000 BC**, people were sailing from Southeast Asia in canoes to colonize Melanesia and Micronesia – the islands of the western Pacific.
- **Early Pacific settlers** are known by their 'Lapita' pottery, which originated in the Molucca Islands of Indonesia.
- **The settlement** of the Pacific took thousands of years and was the greatest seaborne migration in history.
- **Canoes shown** in a 50,000-year-old cave painting in Australia match those that can still in use in the Pacific region.

The Stone Ages

- **The Stone Ages** were the periods of time before humans discovered how to work metals. Instead, they used stones to make tools and weapons, as well as wood, bone or ivory.
- **Stone Ages lasted** for different periods in different parts of the world.
- **Tools were made** by chipping away flakes to shape stones into hammers, spear heads and arrow heads, knives and scrapers.
- **People usually used local stone**, but sometimes good stones were imported from a great distance.
- **Early Europeans** used mainly flint for their stone tools. Africans used quartz, chert, basalt and obsidian.
- **In Europe**, there were three Stone Ages – Old (Palaeolithic), Middle (Mesolithic) and New (Neolithic).
- **The Palaeolithic** began two million years ago, when various human ancestors gathered plants and hunted with stone weapons.

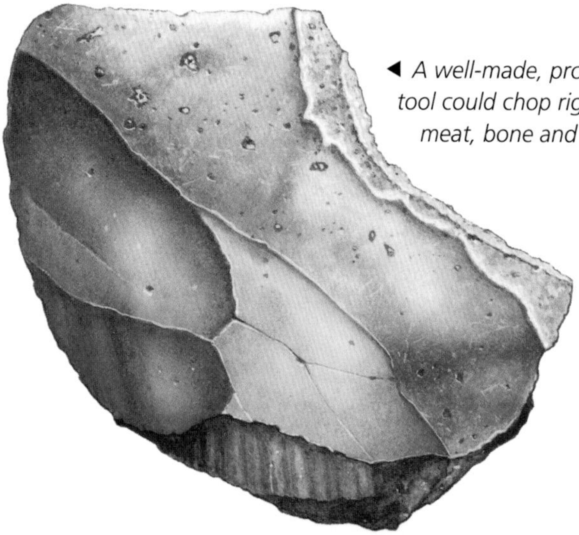

◀ *A well-made, properly shaped stone tool could chop right through wood, meat, bone and animal skin.*

◄ *During the Mesolithic period, hunters began to make much finer and more effective arrow heads and spear heads.*

- **The Mesolithic** was the transition from the Old to the New Stone Age – after the last Ice Age ended around 12,000 years ago.
- **The Neolithic** was the time when people began to settle down and farm. This occurred first in the Near East, about 10,000 years ago.
- **'Venus' figurines** are plump female figures shaped from stone. They date from about 38,000–11,000 years ago, and have been found from the Pyrenees to Siberia.

Cave painters

- **Prehistoric people** sometimes lived or took shelter in caves. Some of these were probably ritual centres, where people made paintings and drawings using ochre and soot as pigment.
- **The world's most famous** cave paintings, at Lascaux in France and Altamira in Spain, were accidentally discovered by children.
- **Carbon dating shows** that the paintings in Lascaux date back about 17,300 years, while those at Chauvet in France are nearly twice as old.
- **The pictures** at another French site, Cougnac, were painted over a period of 10,000 years.
- **Most paintings** in caves show large animals such as bison, deer, horses and mammoths. Many are beautiful works of art.
- **Cave artists** in Europe sometimes painted by spitting the pigment, a practice also followed by the Aborigines of Australia.
- **To reach** the 14,000-year-old paintings in France's Pergouset, you must crawl through 150 m of passages.

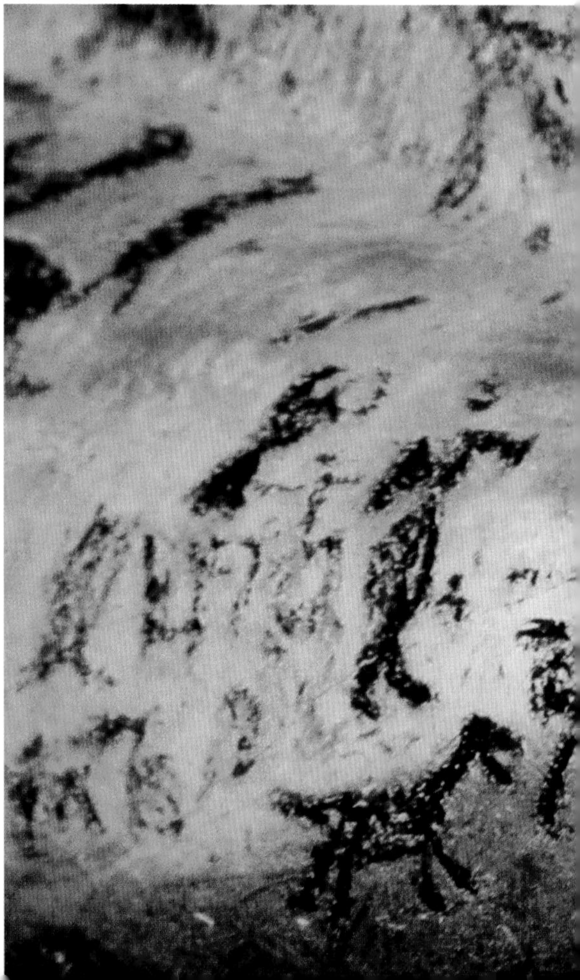

In the caves at Nerja in Spain there are rock formations that prehistoric people played like a xylophone.

DID YOU KNOW?

Aboriginal paintings on rocks in Arnhemland, Northern Territory, Australia, may be over 50,000 years old.

▼ *These paintings from Magura in Bulgaria are dated to between 8000 and 4000 years ago. They show hunting and dancing, and were painted with bat guano (droppings).*

The first farmers

- **Farming began** as people planted grasses for their seed (or grain) in the Near East, in Guangdong in China and in Latin America – and planted root vegetables in Peru and Indonesia, too.
- **Starch marks** on stone implements found in Papua New Guinea suggest yams may have been grown there at least 30,000 years ago.
- **Water chestnuts** and beans may have been farmed near Spirit Cave in north Vietnam from 11,000–7500 BC.
- **In about 9000 BC**, some communities in the Middle East abandoned the old way of life, hunting and gathering fruit, and settled down to farm. The rise of farming marks the start of the Neolithic or New Stone Age.
- **Emmer wheat and barley** were being grown in the Near East by about 8000 BC. Sheep and goats were tamed here soon after.
- **The ox-drawn plough** was used from *c.*5000 BC. The Chinese had used hand ploughs even earlier.
- **Crop irrigation canals** were dug at Choya Mami, near Mandali in Iraq, between 5500 and 4750 BC.
- **China, the Indus River valley**, Egypt and Babylonia all had extensive irrigation systems in place by 3000 BC.
- **The first farmers** reaped their grain with sickles of flint.
- **Farmers learned** to store food. Underground granaries at Ban-Po, Shaanxi, in China's Yellow River valley, date from about 4800 BC.

▲ *Farming in the Middle East began about 11,000 years ago, as people began saving grass seed to grow, so that they could produce flour to make bread.*

Megaliths

- **Megalith means 'great stone'**. They are found in many parts of the world and date from various periods.
- **Megaliths are monuments**, such as the tombs and henges built in western Europe in the Neolithic and Bronze Ages, between about 4000 and 1500 BC.
- **Menhirs are large standing stones**. Sometimes they stand by themselves, sometimes in avenues or circles.
- **The largest-known existing menhir** is the Grand Menhir Brisé at Locmariaquer, near Carnac in France. This single stone once stood 20 m tall and weighed 280 tonnes.
- **The largest stone circle** is at Avebury in Wiltshire, southern England.

▼ *The most famous avenues of stone are at Carnac in Brittany, France, where thousands of stones stand in long lines.*

▲ *It took about 1400 years to construct Stonehenge. The people of Neolithic Britain first built a ring of ditches, and giant stones from as far away as 350 km were slowly added. The biggest upright stones are 9 m high and weigh about 50 tonnes. Stonehenge may have been a temple or astronomical observatory.*

- **The most famous henge** is Stonehenge on Salisbury Plain, Wiltshire, England, built between 2950 and 1600 BC.
- **Some megaliths align** with amazing accuracy with astronomical events, such as sunrise at the summer solstice (midsummer day) and may have acted as calendars.
- **Erecting such stones** took huge teams of men working with enormous wooden rollers, levers and ropes.

DID YOU KNOW?

The Grand Menhir Brisé stone, near Carnac in France, is seven times as heavy as the biggest stones at Stonehenge, UK.

The first cities

- **The walls of the city of Jericho**, near the River Jordan in Palestine, are 11,000 years old. The city has probably been continuously occupied longer than anywhere else in the world.
- **People began to live in towns** when farming produced enough extra food for people to specialize in crafts such as basket-making and for people to begin to trade with each other.
- **Villages and small towns** probably first developed in Western Asia during the Neolithic period, from about 8000 BC. One of these was Aşıklı Höyük in Anatolia, Turkey.
- **One of the most remarkable** ancient towns was nearby at Catalhöyük in Anatolia, Turkey, which was occupied from 7000 to 5500 BC. Ten thousand people may have lived here.
- **The houses in Catalhöyük** were made from mud bricks covered with fine plaster. Some rooms were shrines, with bulls' heads and images of the Mother Goddess.
- **Tells are mounds** that have built up at ancient settlement sites in Western Asia, where mud-brick houses have crumbled away over the ages.

DID YOU KNOW?

Sumerian Ur was the first city to have a population of a quarter of a million, by about 2500 BC.

- **The first big city** was Eridu in Mesopotamia (modern Iraq's Abu Shahrain Tell), which has a temple dating from 4900 BC.
- **In 3500 BC**, about 50,000 people were living in Sumerian Uruk (modern Warka) on the banks of the Euphrates River in Iraq.

▲ *Houses in Catalhöyük were so tightly packed that people had to walk over flat roofs to get to their home, and then climb down a ladder to enter through an opening.*

The metal workers

- **The first metals** to be used by humans were probably lumps of pure gold and copper. They were beaten into shape to make ornaments in Turkey and Iran from about 6000 BC. Iron-nickel from meteorites was also used in Egypt about 3000 years later.
- **Metal ores** (metals mixed with other minerals) were probably discovered when certain stones were found to melt when heated.
- **Recent archaeological finds** have shown that copper was being smelted (extracted from ore) and worked as early as early as 7500 years ago. In Europe and Southwest Asia this marks the start of the Copper (or Chalcolithic) Age.
- **The Bronze Age** is the period when people first began to use the metal bronze. Bronze is an alloy (mixture) of copper with about ten percent tin. It is harder than copper and easier to make into a sharp blade.
- **The Bronze Age began** between 3500–3000 BC at various locations in southeastern Europe, and in Southwest and Southeast Asia.

▶ *Bronze axes were fitted on to wooden hafts.*

▶ *By 1000 BC, beautiful metal swords and other weapons with sharp blades were being made all over Europe and western Asia.*

- **Knowledge of bronze** spread slowly, but by 1500 BC it was in use all the way from Europe to India.
- **Bronze could be cast** – shaped by melting it at a temperature of over 900°C into a clay mould, which itself had been shaped using wax. For the first time people could make things in any shape they wanted. Skilled smiths across Eurasia began to cast bronze to make everything from weapons to cooking utensils.

DID YOU KNOW?

The Grand Menhir Brisé stone, near Carnac in France, is seven times as heavy as the biggest stones at Stonehenge, UK.

New cities and empires, new technologies, law-making and writing – human society was changing.

AFRICA

c.3400–1600 BC
Increasingly dry climate, the Sahara is now a vast desert.

c.3100 BC
Egypt united, with its capital at Memphis. Use of hieroglyphic script.

2686–2181 BC
The Old Kingdom in Egypt, the great age of pyramid-building.

2055–1650 BC
The Middle Kingdom in Egypt; improved architecture, temple-building and literature.

1550–1069 BC
The New Kingdom in Egypt, now at the height of its military power. Burials at Thebes, Valley of the Kings.

c.1200–750 BC
The North African coast is populated by ancestors of the Berber peoples and by Phoenician colonists.

c.1000 BC–AD 500
'Bantu expansion' – speakers of Niger-Congo languages migrate eastwards and southwards.

c.900 BC
Foundation of the kingdom of Kush in Sudan.

EUROPE

c.6000–3500 BC
Spread of farming across Europe.

c.4500 BC
Megalithic burial chambers.

c.3200 BC
Stone circles in northwestern France, Bronze Age metalworking skills.

c.3000–2000 BC
Stonehenge, a megalithic monument in southern Britain.

c.2800–1800 BC
The 'bell-beaker' culture spreads across Europe.

c.2700–1450 BC
The Minoan civilization on the island of Crete. Palaces, wall paintings, fine pottery.

c.1600–1100 BC
The Mycenaean culture of ancient Greece. Walled citadels and bronze weapons.

c.1100–800 BC
The Greek Dark Age, invasions, famine and depopulation.

ASIA

c.3500 BC
Sumerian city states in southern Mesopotamia, (modern Iraq).

c.3500–3000 BC
Innovation in Western Asia – the wheel, improved metalworking and pottery, the world's first writing systems.

c.2700 BC
Silk weaving invented in China.

c.2600–1900 BC
Peak of the Indus Valley civilizations, such as Mohenjo-Daro and Harappa.

2334 BC
The state of Akkad rules the world's first empire.

c.1800 BC
Shang civilization in northern China.

1792 BC
Hammurabi founds the first (Old) Babylonian empire.

c.1650 BC
Rise of the Hittite empire, based in Anatolia (modern Turkey).

c.950 BC
Rise of the Assyrian empire.

Civilization

NORTH AMERICA

c.4000 BC–AD 1800s
Head-Smashed-In-Buffalo Jump – a hunting and butchery site in Alberta, used for thousands of years.

c.3400–2900 BC
Watson Brake ritual mounds, Louisiana.

c.2500 BC
Arctic hunters making fine-bladed weapons settle in Alaska and the Bering Strait region.

c.1650–700 BC
Earthworks and mounds, Poverty Point, Louisiana.

c.1200 BC
Maize grown in the Mogollon highlands, New Mexico.

c.1000–800 BC
The Norton hunting tradition in the Arctic; clay vessels and oil lamps.

c.1070 BC
Great Serpent Mound, Ohio, an earthwork of the Fort Ancient culture.

c.1000 BC
The Adena culture in the woodlands of the east, rich burials.

CENTRAL AND SOUTH AMERICA

c.2600 BC
Large ritual site and settlement at Aspero, on the coast of Peru.

c.2500 BC
Loom-woven textiles and irrigation skills.

c.2300 BC
Ceramics produced in Central America.

c.1500 BC
Metalworking in Peru.

c.1200 BC
Urban civilizations in Central America, such as that of the Olmecs.

c.900 BC
Olmec symbols on the Cascajal Bock are the first writing in the Americas.

c.900 BC
Start of the Chavín civilization in the Peruvian Andes. Temple-building and metalworking skills.

c.500 BC
The Zapotecs of southern Mexico found the city of Monte Albán.

OCEANIA

c.2000 BC
Burials at the Roonka Flat dune in South Australia, an Aboriginal site occupied for many thousands of years.

c.2000 BC
Austronesians (migrants from the Indonesian archipelago) begin the settlement of Melanesia.

c.1600–500 BC
Spread of the Austronesian 'Lapita' culture across the Pacific, marked by a distinctive pottery.

c.1300 BC
Austronesian settlers sail eastwards to reach Fiji.

c.1100 BC
Austronesian settlers sail further, reaching Tonga and Samoa in Western Polynesia.

c.1000 BC
Permanent settlements with round stone houses in the more productive regions of Australia.

c.1000 BC
Long distance networks across Australia for exchanging goods and materials.

Mesopotamia

- **Mesopotamia is an ancient name** for the lands lying between the Tigris and Euphrates rivers, which flow through Turkey, Syria and Iraq. In Greek it means 'between rivers'.
- **Mesopotamia is often called** the 'cradle of civilization' because many ancient cultures arose here, including those of the Sumerians, Babylonians and Assyrians.
- **The first great civilization** was that of the Sumerians, who were farming irrigated land beside the Euphrates River in about 5000 BC. They lived in mud-brick houses.
- **By 4000 BC**, the Sumerian settlements of Eridu, Uruk and Ur had grown into towns with water supplies and drainage systems, as well as palaces and temple-mounds called ziggurats.

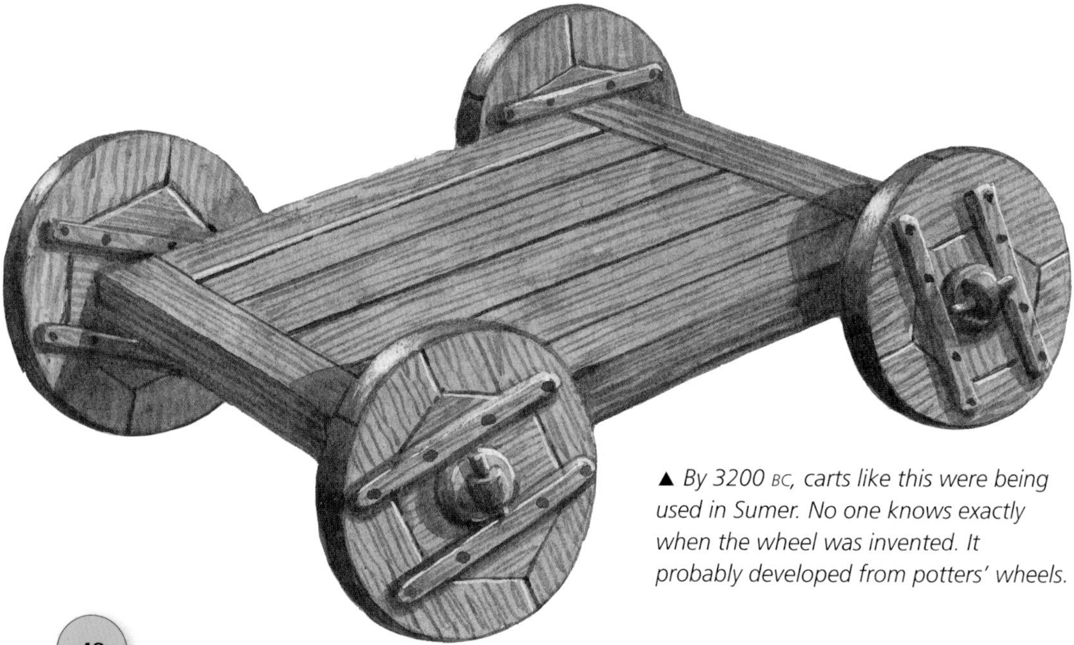

▲ *By 3200 BC, carts like this were being used in Sumer. No one knows exactly when the wheel was invented. It probably developed from potters' wheels.*

▶ *The Epic of Gilgamesh was composed around 2000* BC. *It tells the tale of Gilgamesh (right), a powerful king who had actually ruled Uruk in about 2700* BC. *When his people prayed for help, the gods created Enkidu, who met Gilgamesh in battle. But the two became friends and shared many adventures. The story remained popular in the region for many centuries.*

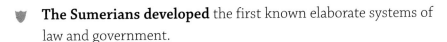

- **The first writing system** was devised by the Sumerians, with wedge-shaped ('cuneiform') marks on clay tablets.
- **The Sumerians cast** all kinds of beautiful objects – first in copper, then, from about 3500 BC, in bronze.
- **The Sumerian Epic of Gilgamesh** tells about a flood similar to that in the biblical story of Noah's Ark.
- **In 2350 BC**, Sumer was overrun by Sargon of Akkad, who created the world's first empire, however Sumerian power was re-established at Ur from 2112 BC.
- **The Sumerians developed** the first known elaborate systems of law and government.
- **At first**, each city or 'city-state' was run by a council of elders, but in wartime a lugal (leader) took charge. By 2900 BC, the lugals had become kings and ruled all the time.

Babylon

- **Babylon was one of the greatest cities** of the ancient world. It stood on the banks of the Euphrates River, near what is now Al Hillah in Iraq.

- **The city reached its peak** in two phases: the Old Babylonian Empire (1792–1234 BC) and the New Babylonian Empire (626–539 BC).

- **Babylon first grew** as a city from 2200 BC, but only when Hammurabi became king in 1792 BC did it become powerful. In his 42-year reign, Hammurabi's conquests gave Babylon a huge empire in Mesopotamia.

- **Hammurabi was a great law-maker**, and some of his laws were enscribed on a stone pillar, or stele, now in the Louvre in Paris. One of his main laws was that 'the strong shall not oppress the weak'. There were also laws to punish crimes and protect people from poor workmanship by builder.

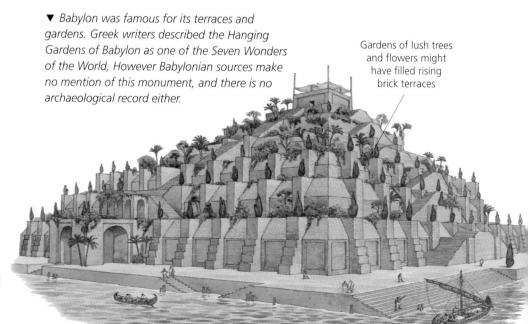

▼ *Babylon was famous for its terraces and gardens. Greek writers described the Hanging Gardens of Babylon as one of the Seven Wonders of the World, However Babylonian sources make no mention of this monument, and there is no archaeological record either.*

Gardens of lush trees and flowers might have filled rising brick terraces

▶ *Under Nebuchadnezzar II (630–562 BC), Babylon achieved its greatest fame. He is known for conquering Jerusalem and for his great building projects.*

- **After Hammurabi died**, Babylonian power declined and the Assyrians gained the upper hand. After long Babylonian resistance, the Assyrians destroyed the city in 689 BC only to rebuild it 11 years later.
- **Just 60 years later**, Babylonian king Nabopolassar and his son Nebuchadnezzar II crushed the Assyrians and built the new Babylonian Empire.
- **Under Nebuchadnezzar II**, Babylon became a vast, magnificent city of 250,000 people, with grand palaces, temples and houses.
- **The city was surrounded** by walls 26 m thick – glazed with blue bricks, decorated with dragons, lions and bulls, and entered by eight huge bronze gates. The grandest was the Ishtar Gate, which opened onto a paved avenue called the Processional Way.
- **The Babylonians were so sure** of their power that King Belshazzar was having a party when the Persians, led by Cyrus, attacked. Cyrus's men dug canals to divert the Euphrates River, then slipped into the city along the riverbed.

DID YOU KNOW?

The walls of Babylon were broad enough for a chariot to turn on its battlements.

Myths from Babylon

- **Myths from the Middle East** are the some of the oldest in the world, dating from about 2500 BC.
- **The Babylonian creation myth** grew from the Sumerian creation myth. It is called the Enuma Elish.
- **The Enuma Elish was found**, written on seven clay tablets in cuneiform script, by archaeologists excavating Nineveh in AD 1849.
- **The Enuma Elish** says that in the beginning the Universe was made of salt waters (Mother Tiamat), sweet waters (Father Apsu), and a mist (their son Mummu).
- **The waters gave birth** to new young rebellious gods who overthrew Apsu and Mummu.
- **Tiamat and her followers** (led by a god called Kingu) were conquered by a male Babylonian god, Marduk, in a battle of powerful magic.
- **The Babylonians pictured Marduk** with four eyes and four ears, so he could see and hear everything. Fire spurted from his mouth and haloes blazed from his head.
- **Marduk became** the new ruler. He made Tiamat's body into the Earth and sky. He appointed gods to rule the heavens, the Earth and the air in between.

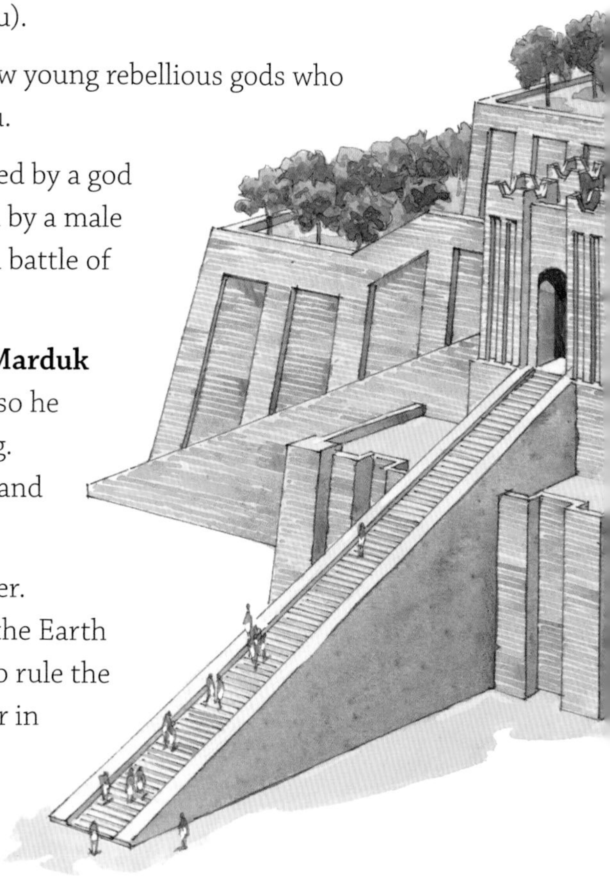

- **Humans were created** out of Kingu's blood. Marduk made them build a temple to himself and the other gods at Babylon.
- **Every spring**, Babylon was in danger of devastating flooding from the mighty rivers, Tigris and Euphrates. Historians believe that the Enuma Elish might have been acted out as a pantomime to please Marduk so he kept order and prevented the flooding.

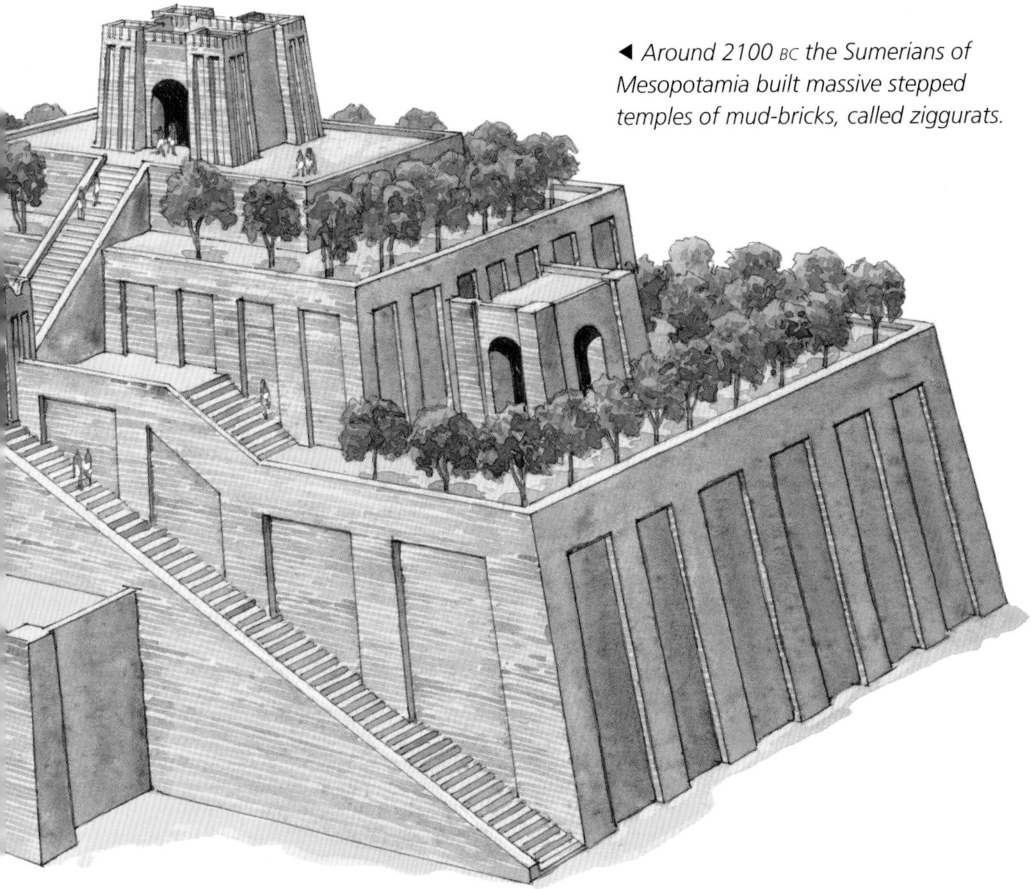

◀ *Around 2100 BC the Sumerians of Mesopotamia built massive stepped temples of mud-bricks, called ziggurats.*

Early China

- **In China**, farming communities belonging to the 'Yangshao culture' grew up beside the Yellow River between 5000–3000 BC.

- **By this time**, the region was ruled by emperors. The earliest Chinese emperors are known of only through myths and legends. Huangdi, 'the Yellow Emperor', was said to have come to the throne in 2697 BC.

- **In about 2690 BC** Huangdi's wife, Xi Lingshi, is said to have discovered how to use the cocoon of the silkworm (the caterpillar of the *Bombyx mori* moth) to make silk. Xi Lingshi was afterwards honoured as the 'Goddess of the Silkworm'.

- **By 2000 BC**, the Chinese were making beautiful jade carvings.

▶ *The Shang emperors were warriors. Their soldiers fought in padded bamboo armour.*

- **The Xia dynasty** is said to have ruled from about 2070–1600 BC. However their story has been mostly shaped by mythology.
- **The Xia** were followed by the Shang dynasty, which ruled in the Huang He valley until 1122 BC.
- **Shang emperors** had their fortunes told from cracks on heated animal bones. Marks on these 'oracle' bones are the oldest examples of Chinese writing.
- **Under the Shang**, the Chinese became skilled casters of bronze.
- **In the Shang cities** of Anyang and Zengzhou, palace temples were surrounded at a distance by villages of artisans.
- **Shang emperors** went to their tombs along with their sacrificed servants and captives, as well as entire chariots with their horses and drivers.

▶ *Silkworms (the larvae, or young, of the* Bombyx mori *moth) feed on mulberry leaves. Silk was invented in China, and for many years the method of making it was a closely guarded secret.*

The Indus River valley

- **From about 3300 BC**, a civilization developed from small farming communities in the Indus River valley in what is now Pakistan.
- **The remains** of over 100 towns of the Indus civilization have been found. The main sites are Mohenjo-Daro, Harappa, Kalibangan and Lothal.
- **Indus cities** were carefully planned, with straight streets, bath-houses and big granaries (grain stores).
- **At the centre** was a fortified citadel, built on a platform of bricks. The rulers probably lived here.
- **Indus houses** were built of brick around a central courtyard. They had several rooms, a toilet and a well.
- **Single-room huts** at all intersections are thought to be police posts.
- **The Indus civilization** had its own system of writing, which appears on objects such as carved seals – but no one has yet been able to decipher it.

▶ *Seals like this were used by Indus merchants to stamp bales of goods.*

▼ *The people of Mohenjo-Daro used ox-drawn carts. However, this form of transport would have been very slow and they probably relied on the river as their main source of transportation.*

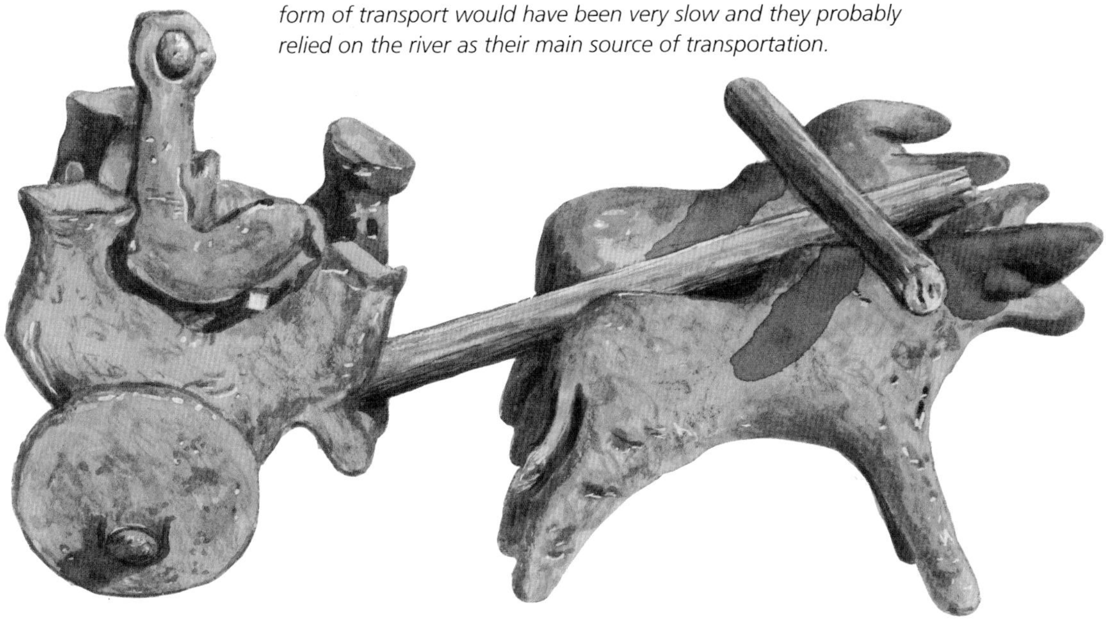

- **The settlments** of Mohenjo-Daro and Harappa had 35,000 inhabitants each by about 2500 BC.
- **By 1750 BC**, the Indus civilization had declined, perhaps because floods changed the course of the Indus River. War may also have played a part, with the arrival of northern invaders in the region in about 1500 BC.

DID YOU KNOW?
Soapstone trading seals from the Indus civilization have been found as far away as Bahrain and Ur.

Early India

- **To the east and southeast** of the Indus Valley, India was occupied by hunter-gatherers, farmers and cattle herders.
- **From about 2000–500 BC** there was a great period of change in Indian society and culture.
- **Close links exist** between the ancient Sanskrit language and Persian and European languages such as Latin, English, German and French. These connected languages are called 'Indo-European'. They are seen as evidence of major migration, trade or invasion into northern India during this period.
- **Traditionally**, historians talked of 'Aryan' invaders bringing new ideas to the 'Dravidian' inhabitants. This division of the Indian peoples into two 'races' is now questioned and the term, Aryan, is challenged by many historians.

▶ *India's ancient historical traditions still shape the lives of its peoples today. Here a Toda couple wear traditional native dress. The Toda are considered one of the earliest (Dravidian) tribes of India.*

- **The creation** of a strict 'caste' system with four social classes, dates from this period. People were split into four categories. Brahmins (priests) were at the top. Then came Kshatriya (warriors) and Vaisyas (merchants and farmers). At the bottom were Shudras (labourers and servants).
- **The caste system** has played a major part in Indian society into modern times.

▼ *Sanskrit is the oldest literary language of India, and simply translated it means 'refined' or 'polished'. It forms the basis of many modern Indian languages such as Hindi and Urdu. Urdu is also the national language of Pakistan.*

धेनुः ग्राम्यः पशुः ।

The Vedic Age

▲ *From the early beliefs of the 2nd millennium* BC *came the many rituals of Hinduism. One if the main deities is Shiva (shown above).*

- **The earliest Indian farmers** thought that Prithivi, the Earth, and Dyaus, the sky, were the parents of all gods and humans.
- **Northwestern cultural influences** from the Punjab region introduced a god called Varuna, who created the world by picturing everything in his eye, the Sun. The storm god Indra later took over as chief god, supported by human beings. He rearranged the Universe by organizing the heavens and the seasons.
- **The Hindu religion** grew out of such beliefs.

- **History and religious teachings** were passed on by word of mouth in spoken 'Books of Knowledge', or Veda. These make up the oldest Hindu scriptures and were composed over many centuries. They include the *Rig-Veda*, the *Sama-Veda* and *Yajur-Veda*.
- **The period during which Hindu** teachings developed into their classic form is called the Vedic Age. It begins in about 1750 BC.
- **From about 1100 BC** these beliefs gradually spread across the plain of the river Ganges, which was at that time being cleared of forest and turned into farmland.
- **A great centre** of the Vedic culture was a northern kingdom called Panchala, which thrived from about 850 BC. It was eventually absorbed into larger Indian empires.
- **The Vedic Age** lasted until about 500 BC.

▲ *The creator god Brahma is shown looking in all directions, to show that he has knowledge of all things.*

DID YOU KNOW?
Hindu mythology says the world is created, destroyed and re-created in cycles that go on forever.

The rise of Egypt

- **From about 5000–3300 BC**, farmers in Egypt banded together to dig canals to control the annual flooding of the river Nile and to water their crops.
- **By 3300 BC**, these farming villages had grown into towns. Rich and powerful kings were buried in big, box-like mud-brick tombs called mastabas.
- **In Egyptian towns**, craftsmen began to work copper and stone, paint vases, weave baskets and use potters' wheels.
- **Early Egypt was divided** into two kingdoms – Upper Egypt in the south, and Lower Egypt in the north, around the Nile delta.
- **In 3100 BC**, the legendary King Menes of Upper Egypt (possibly the same person as the historical Narmer) conquered Lower Egypt to unite the two kingdoms. Egyptian pharaohs (rulers) were always referred to as 'King of Upper and Lower Egypt'.

▶ *The ancient Egyptians built great cities and monuments along the Nile valley during the days of the Old Kingdom.*

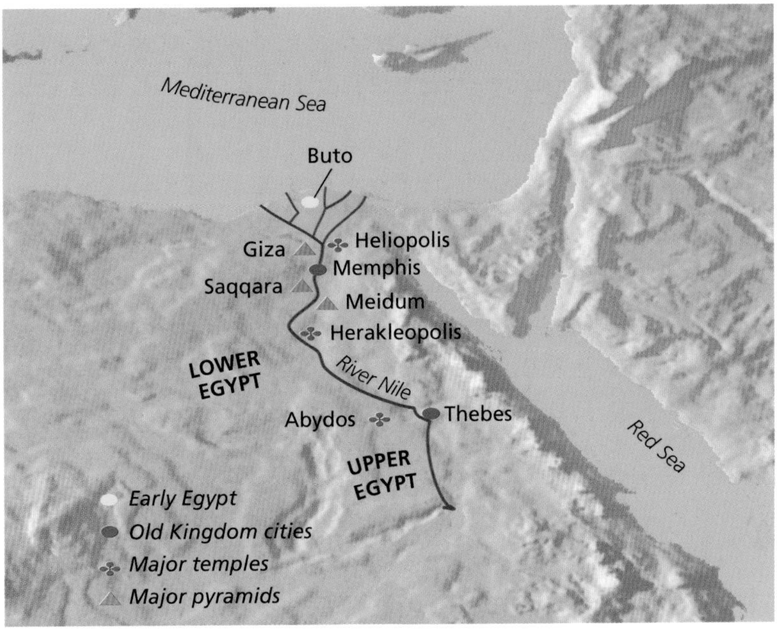

▲ *The principal sites and cities of ancient Egyptian civilization during the early period of its history.*

- **Menes founded a capital** for all Egypt at Memphis. Egypt's First Dynasty (family of rulers) – had begun.
- **After this Early Dynastic Period** came the Old Kingdom (2686–2181 BC), perhaps the greatest period of Egyptian culture.
- **Craftsmen made fine things**, scholars developed writing and the calendar and studied astronomy and maths.
- **The greatest scholar** and priest was Imhotep, minister to King Djoser (2667–2648 BC). Imhotep was architect of the first of the major pyramids, the Step Pyramid at Saqqara.

Egyptian pharaohs

- **Pharaohs were the kings** of ancient Egypt. They were also High Priest, head judge and commander of the army.
- **There were 31 dynasties** (families) of pharaohs between 3100 BC and 323 BC. Major historic periods included the Middle Kingdom (2055–1650 BC) and the New Kingdom (1550–1069 BC)
- **Egyptians thought of the pharaoh** as both the god Horus and the son of the sun god Re. When he died he was transformed into the god Osiris, father of Horus. Since he was a god, anyone approaching him had to crawl.
- **The pharaoh was thought** to be so holy that he could not be addressed directly. Instead, people referred to him indirectly by talking of the pharaoh, which is Egyptian for 'great house'. Only after about 945 BC was he addressed directly.
- **In official documents** the pharaoh had five titles: Horus, Two Ladies, Golden Horus, King of Upper and Lower Egypt and Lord of the Double Land (Upper and Lower Egypt), and Son of Re and Lord of the Diadems.
- **People believed** that the pharaoh's god-like status gave him magical powers. His uraeus (the snake on his crown) was supposed to spit flames at his enemies and the pharaoh was said to be able to trample thousands.
- **A pharaoh usually married** his eldest sister to keep the royal blood pure. She became queen and was known as the Royal Heiress, but the pharaoh had many other wives. If the pharaoh died while his eldest son was still a child, his queen became regent and ruled on his behalf.

DID YOU KNOW?
People thought the pharaoh had the power to control the weather and to make the land fertile.

- **To preserve their bodies** forever, pharaohs were buried inside massive tombs. The first pharaohs were buried in huge pyramids. Because these were often robbed, later pharaohs were buried in tombs cut deep into cliffs.

- **One of the greatest pharaohs** was Ramses II, who ruled from 1290–1224 BC. He left a legacy of many huge buildings, including the rock temple of Abu Simbel.

▼ *The pharaohs' prestigious officials were building great houses like this around 1200 BC.*

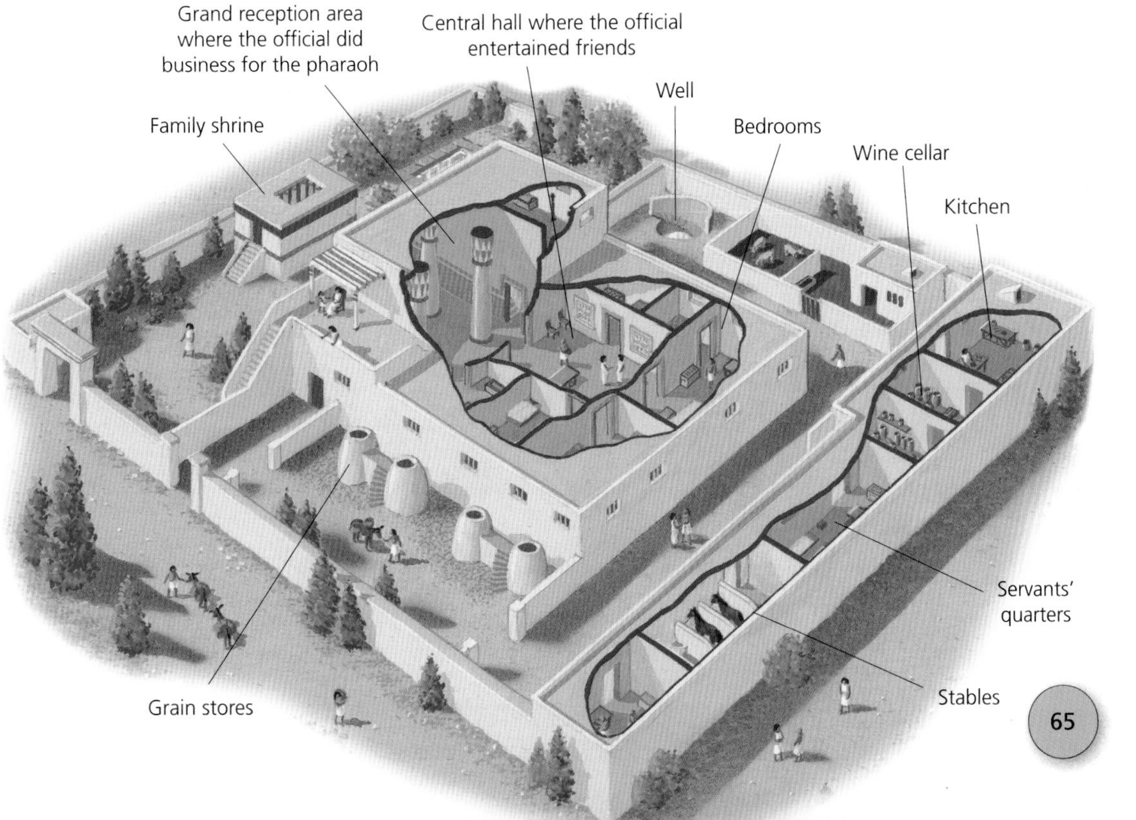

Life in Egypt

- **Egyptians washed every day** in the river or with a jug and basin. The rich were given showers by their servants.
- **Instead of soap** they used a cleansing cream made from oil, lime and perfume. They also rubbed themselves all over with moisturizing oil.
- **Egyptian women** painted their nails with henna and reddened their lips and cheeks with red ochre paste.
- **Egyptian fashions** changed little over thousands of years, and clothes were usually white linen.
- **Men wrapped linen** around themselves in a kilt. Women wore long, light dresses. Children ran around naked during the summer.

▼ *Egyptian women were highly conscious of their looks, wearing make-up and jewellery and dressing their hair with great care.*

▶ *In ancient Egypt, a man provided for his family, and his wife ran the home and was held in great respect. Some couples lived with the parents of the husband or wife.*

DID YOU KNOW?

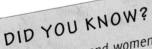

Egyptian men and women wore kohl eyeliner, made from the minerals malachite and galena.

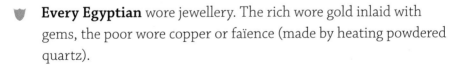

- **Every Egyptian** wore jewellery. The rich wore gold inlaid with gems, the poor wore copper or faïence (made by heating powdered quartz).
- **Egyptians loved to play** board games. Their favourites were 'senet' and 'hounds and jackals'.
- **Rich Egyptians held lavish parties** with food and drink, singers, musicians, acrobats and dancers.
- **The pastimes of rich Egyptians** included fishing or boating.

Tombs and mummies

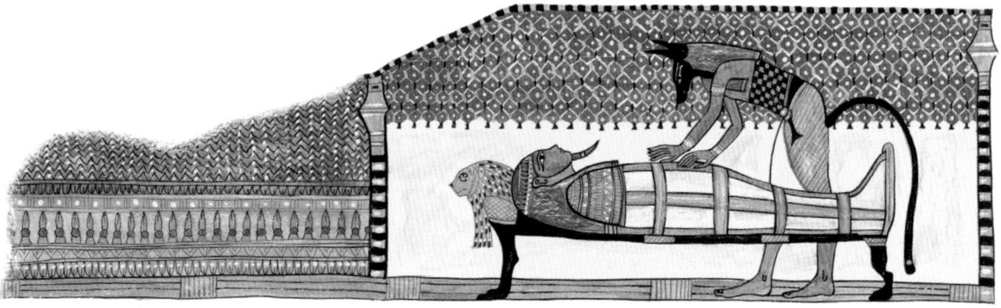

▲ *The ancient Egyptians believed that the jackal-headed god, Anubis, brought the souls of the dead into an underworld courtroom to be judged as good or bad.*

- **Egypt's huge pyramids** were tombs, designed to launch the dead person into the next world. The Great Pyramid of Giza was completed in about 2560 BC.
- **The ancient Egyptians** believed that people could enjoy life after death by preserving the body through mummification.
- **Part of mummification** involved removing the internal organs and placing them in pots called canopic jars. Each mummy had a mask, so every spirit could recognize its body.
- **People believed** that they would work in the afterlife, so models of their tools were buried with them. Pharaohs were buried with model servants called shabtis, to work for them.
- **The ancient Egyptians** copied their funeral rites from the funeral the god Horus gave to his father, Osiris. These were written down in a work called The Book of the Dead.
- **Egyptian myth** said that the dead person's soul, or ka, was brought to an underworld Hall of Judgement.

- **First, a jackal-headed god** called Anubis weighed the heart against a feather of truth and justice. If the heart was heavier than the feather, it was devoured by a crocodile-headed god called Ammit.
- **If the heart was lighter** than the feather, the god Horus led the ka to be welcomed into the Underworld by the god Osiris.
- **Tombs were filled** with precious items to be taken by the dead person's spirit into the next world. Robbers often broke into the tombs to steal the treasure.
- **From the 1500s BC** Egyptian royalty and nobles were buried in secret, guarded tombs hidden deep in rocky valleys near the city of Thebes.

▼ *For thousands of years the Great Pyramid remained the tallest building in the world. Experts still argue about how the stones were raised and fitted with such accuracy. Egyptians were expected to work for free on big public projects like these, as a kind of tax.*

Tutankhamun

▲ *A fabulous gold mask was found in Tutankhamun's innermost coffin, over the young king's mummified remains.*

- **Pharaoh of Egypt** from 1337–1327 BC was Tutankhamun. He was a boy when he became pharaoh and was only 18 when he died.
- **Tutankhamun lived** during the 18th dynasty, which ruled Egypt from 1150–1295 BC. It included the only female pharaoh, Queen Hatshepsut, and Thutmose III, who led Egypt to the peak of its power from 1479–1425 BC.
- **The father of Tutankhamun** was Akhenaten, who, with his queen Nefertiti, created a revolution in Egypt. Akhenaten replaced worship of the old Egyptian gods with worship of a single god, and moved the capital city to Amarna.
- **Tutankhamun's wife** was his half-sister Ankhesenamun. When he died Ankhesenamun was at the mercy of her husband's enemies, Ay and General Horemheb. She wrote to the Hittite king asking for his son to marry, but the Hittite prince was murdered on the way to Egypt.
- **The Valley of the Kings**, near Thebes on the river Nile, is the world's most famous archaeological site. It was the burial place of the 18th dynasty rulers and contains the tombs of 62 pharaohs and high officials.
- **Tutankhamun's tomb** was the only tomb in the Valley of the Kings not plundered over the centuries. When it was opened, it contained thousands of objects, including many fabulous carved and gold items.

DID YOU KNOW?
Tutankhamun's third, inner coffin was made of over a tonne of solid gold.

- **English archaeologist** Howard Carter discovered Tutankhamun's tomb in 1922.
- **Rumours of a curse** on those who disturb the tomb began when Carter's pet canary was eaten by a cobra – the symbol of the pharaoh – at the moment the tomb was first opened.
- **Experts worked out the dates** of Tutankhamun's reign from the date labels on wine-jars left in the tomb.

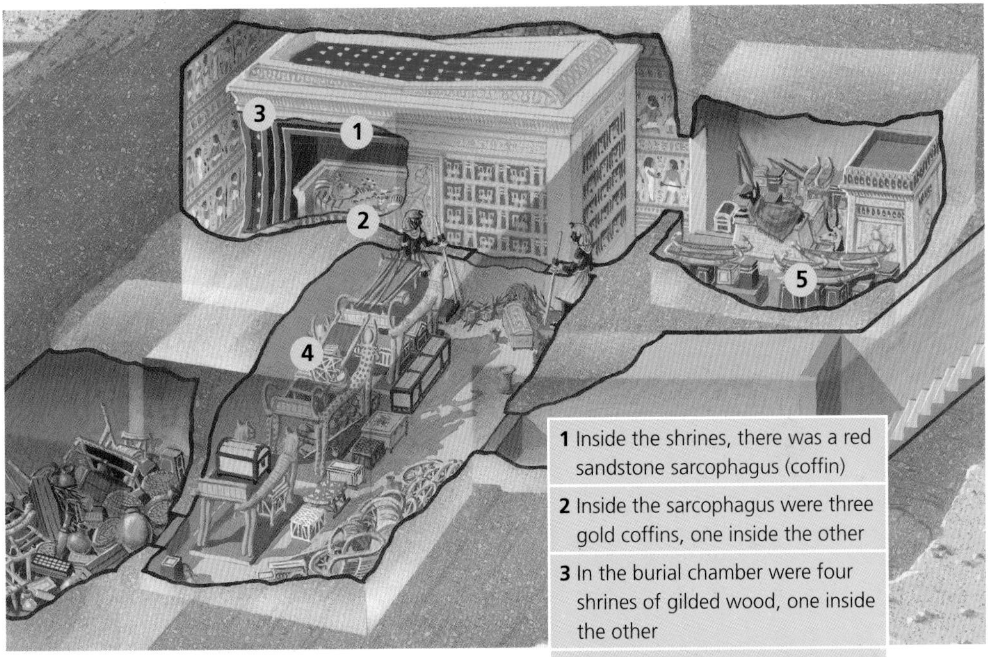

▲ *When Carter opened Tutankhamun's tomb, he came first to an anteroom. It took him three years to clear this room and enter the burial chamber, with its huge gold shrines containing the coffins.*

1 Inside the shrines, there was a red sandstone sarcophagus (coffin)

2 Inside the sarcophagus were three gold coffins, one inside the other

3 In the burial chamber were four shrines of gilded wood, one inside the other

4 Fabulous beds, chests, gold chariot wheels and carved animals in the anteroom were just a taste of the riches to come

5 Beyond the burial chamber was a treasury full of gold and other treasures

Egyptian writing

- **Ancient Egyptian writing** developed between 3300 and 3100 BC – perhaps inspired by Sumerian scripts.
- **The first Egyptian writing** is called hieroglyphic (Greek for 'holy writing'). The Egyptians called it the 'words of the gods', because they believed writing was a gift of the god Thoth.
- **There were over** 700 hieroglyphs in common use. Most are pictures or symbols and can be written from left to right, right to left or downwards. Each represented an object, an idea or a sound.

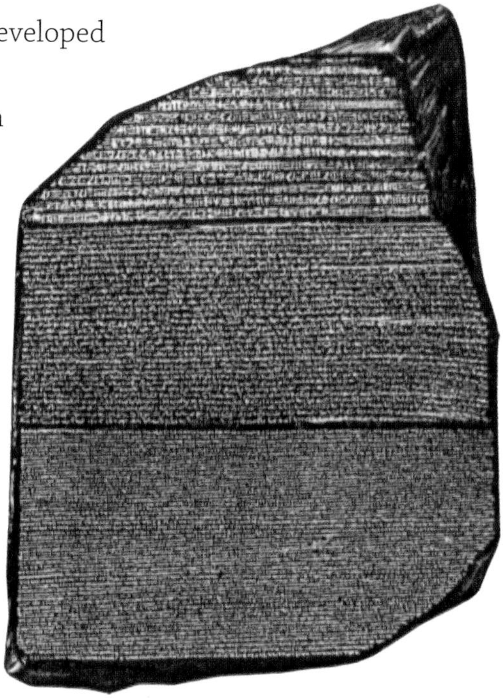

▲ *When Frenchman Jean-François Champollion translated the Greek text on the Rosetta Stone, he was able to crack the code of hieroglyphic script.*

- **Egyptians not only wrote** on tomb walls but wrote everyday things with ink and brushes on papyrus (paper made from papyrus reeds) or on ostraca (pottery fragments).
- **Words inside an oval shape** called a cartouche are the names of pharaohs.
- **Only highly trained scribes** could write. Scribes were very well paid and often exempt from taxes.

▲ *The walls of Egyptian tombs are covered in hieroglyphs.*

- **Other scripts were used** as well. Hieratic, from 1780 BC, was a shorthand version of hieroglyphs. In the later days of Egypt, an even quicker handwriting called 'demotic' was popular.
- **In AD 1799**, the French soldiers of Napoleon's army found a stone slab at Rosetta in Egypt. It was covered in three identical texts written in hieroglyphs, demotic and Greek.
- **In AD 1822**, Jean-François Champollion compared these and so deciphered the Rosetta Stone.

◀ *Papyrus was made by taking wet strips of the pithy stems of papyrus plants and pressing them side-by-side.*

The gods of Egypt

- **The mighty sun god**, Ra-Atum, was called many different names by ancient Egyptians.
- **The sun god** was sometimes pictured as a scarab beetle. This is because a scarab beetle rolls a ball of dung before it, as the ball of the sun rolls across the sky.
- **Myths say that the sun god** has a secret name, known only to himself, which was the key to all his power.
- **The ancient Egyptians** believed that part of the spirit of a god could live on Earth in the body of an animal. This is why their gods are pictured as humans with animal heads.
- **Hathor or Sekhmet** was the daughter and wife of Ra-Atum. She could take on the form of a terrifying lioness or cobra to attack and punish enemies of the sun god.
- **Osiris was the son** of Ra-Atum. He became king of Egypt and later, ruler of the underworld Kingdom of the Dead.

▶ *The blue scarab beetle Khephri is one of the many forms of the sun god. This amulet was made over 3000 years ago.*

◀ *This picture shows the god Osiris on his throne. He wears the crown of Egypt, as does his son, Horus, who faces him. The goddess Isis is standing behind Osiris.*

- **Osiris's brother**, Seth, represented evil in the Universe. He hatched a wicked plot to murder Osiris and take the crown of Egypt for himself.
- **Osiris's sister and wife** was called Isis. She was a powerful mother goddess of fertility.
- **Horus was Osiris's son**. He inherited the throne of Egypt. Ancient Egyptians believed that all pharaohs were descended from Horus, and therefore they were gods.
- **An amulet is a piece of jewellery** with magical powers. Many amulets were in the shape of an eye – either the sun god's or Horus's. The sacred eye was thought to have healing powers and to ward off evil.

Nubia, Kush and Axum

▼ *The ruins of over 200 pyramids of ancient Meroë have survived. They are steeply pointed monuments marking chambers that were used for cremated or buried bodies that had not been made into mummies.*

- **Civilization was developing rapidly** in Egypt, but the river Nile also supported new developments further south, in what is now Sudan and Ethiopia.
- **The far south of Egypt** and the north of Sudan were known as Nubia.
- **The first Nubian civilization**, called the A-group culture, appeared about 3200 BC in the north of Nubia, known as Wawat. It was taken over by the Egyptians in 2950 BC.
- **In about 2000 BC**, a new Nubian culture emerged in the then-fertile south, called Kush. The Kushites were black Africans.
- **Egypt conquered** the Kingdom of Kush in 1500 BC, but in 716 BC Kushites came to power in Egypt, with Shabaka reigning as pharaoh.
- **Kushite rule** in Egypt lasted 50 years. In 656 BC, the Assyrians drove the Kushites out of Egypt.
- **The Kushite home base** was the region of Napata in northern Sudan. The Kushites had learned iron-working skills. Napata had iron-ore, but little wood as fuel for smelting.
- **The Kushites** therefore moved their capital to Meroë – where they built great palaces, temples, baths and pyramids.
- **Meroë thrived** during the classical age. The Greeks called the whole of this region Ethiopia.
- **From AD 100**, the city of Axum – now in northern Ethiopia – grew rich and powerful, trading in ivory. In about AD 350, the Axumite king Aezanas invaded and overthrew Kush.

Southwest Asia

- **In ancient times** the lands of the Near and Middle East were centres of agriculture, city-building and civilization.
- **Many peoples** living in the region spoke related languages, belonging to a linguistic group known as Semitic. Modern Semitic languages include Arabic and Hebrew.
- **In about 2500 BC** Semitic speaking peoples of the region included the Akkadians, Canaanites and Amorites.
- **In 2371 BC**, an Akkadian called Sargon seized the throne of the Sumerian city of Kish. He conquered all Sumer and Akkad and created one of the world's first empires.
- **From 3000–1500 BC**, the Canaanite city of Byblos (in what is now Lebanon) was one of the world's great trading ports.
- **In about 2000 BC**, Amorites conquered Sumer, Akkad and Canaan.
- **The first Hebrews** were a Semitic-speaking tribe from southern Mesopotamia. Their name meant 'people of the other side' – of the Euphrates River.
- **According to Jewish**, Christian and Islamic scriptures, the first Hebrew leader was Abraham, who lived in the Sumerian city of Ur about 4000 years ago. He led his family to settle in Canaan.
- **Abraham's grandson Jacob** was also called Israel and the Hebrews were afterwards called Israelites.
- **About 1000 BC**, the Israelite people prospered under three kings – Saul, David and Solomon.

▶ *The Dead Sea Scrolls are ancient Hebrew manuscripts found by shepherds in 1947 in a cave near the Dead Sea. They include the oldest known texts of the Bible's Old Testament. Today the Scrolls are housed in a museum in Israel.*

Assyrian empires

- **The Assyrians** came originally from the upper Tigris valley around the cities of Ashur, Nineveh and Arbela.
- **In about 2000 BC**, Assyria was invaded by Amorites. Under a line of Amorite kings, Assyria built a huge empire. King Adadnirari I called himself 'King of Everything'.
- **The Old Assyrian Empire** lasted six centuries, until it was broken by attacks by Mitannian horsemen.
- **From 1114–1076 BC**, King Tiglath Pileser I rebuilt Assyrian power by conquest, creating the New Assyrian Empire.
- **Under Tiglath-Pileser III** (744–727 BC) the New Assyrian Empire reached its peak, and was finally overthrown by the Medes and Babylonians in 612 BC.

▶ *Assyrian palaces were decorated with fine stone carvings, showing gods, spirits and kings.*

▲ *This statue of winged lion, or lamassu, was intended to ward off evil spirits. It guarded the palace of the ruthless king Ashurnasirpal II at Nimrud. He ruled Assyria from 883–859 BC.*

- **Ruthless warriors**, the Assyrian soldiers grew beards and fought with bows, iron swords, spears and chariots.
- **The Assyrians built roads** all over their empire, so that the army could move fast to quell trouble.
- **They also built** magnificent palaces and cities such as Khorsabad and Nimrud.
- **Arab warriors** rode camels into battle for the Assyrians.

DID YOU KNOW?

The palace of King Assurbanipal (668–627 BC) was filled with books and plants from all over the known world.

The Phoenicians

▲ *Phoenicians were master seafarers. Broad merchant ships called gaulos carried cargoes. Many-oared rowing galleys defended the ports from attack.*

- **From about 3000 BC**, Semitic-speaking peoples such as the Canaanites lived on the coasts of the eastern Mediterranean Sea, around the great port of Byblos in what is now Lebanon.
- **From about 1100 BC**, their descendants became known as 'Phoenicians'.
- **This name comes from** comes from *phoinix*, the Greek word for a purple dye made famous by these people. It was made from the shells of Murex sea snails.
- **The Phoenicians** were great sea traders. Their ports at Tyre and Sidon bustled with ships carrying goods from all over the known world.

- **They made cloth** using wool from Mesopotamia and flax and linen from Egypt. They also made splendid jewellery from imported gems, metals and ivory.
- **The Phoenicians invented** the first alphabet. The Phoenician words *aleph* ('ox') and *beth* ('house') became the Greek letters alpha and beta. The word 'bible' and the prefix 'bibli-' (meaning 'books') come from the city of Byblos.
- **In about 600 BC**, Phoenician seafarers sailed from the Red Sea right around Africa and back into the Mediterranean.
- **As far west as Gades** (now Cadiz, in Spain), the Phoenicians set up colonies across the Mediterranean.
- **The greatest Phoenician colony** was the city of Carthage, in what is now Tunisia.

▼ *The Phoenicians were the greatest traders of the ancient world.*

The Minoans

▲ *The Minotaur of Greek myth was eventually slain by the hero Theseus.*

- **The Minoan culture** of Crete – a large island to the south of Greece – brought many civilized skills to Europe for the first time.
- **Minoan civilization began** in about 2700 BC, reaching its height from 2200–1450 BC. It then mysteriously vanished – perhaps after the volcano on the nearby island of Santorini erupted.
- **The name Minoan** comes from the myth of King Minos. Minos was the son of Europa, the princess seduced by the god Zeus in the shape of a bull.
- **Greek stories tell** how Minos built a labyrinth (maze) in which he kept the Minotaur, a monster with a man's body and a bull's head.
- **It is probable** that 'Minos' was a royal title, so every Cretan king was called Minos.

- **Catching a bull** by the horns and leaping over it (bull-leaping) was an important Minoan religious rite.
- **The Minoans were great seafarers** and traded all over the eastern Mediterranean.
- **At the centre** of each Minoan town was a palace, such as those found at Knossos, Zakro, Phaestos and Mallia.
- **The largest Minoan palace** is at Knossos. It covered 20,000 square metres and housed over 30,000 people.

▼ *The famous Minoan palace at Knossos. Its walls are decorated with frescoes (paintings) that reveal a great deal about the Minoans.*

The Mycenaeans

- **From 1600–1100 BC**, mainland Greece was dominated by a tough warrior people called the Mycenaeans.
- **The Mycenaeans** were Bronze Age warriors. They fought with long bronze swords, daggers, spears, ox-hide shields and bronze armour.
- **Mycenaeans lived** in small kingdoms, each with its own fortified hilltop citadel – called an acropolis.
- **At the centre** of a Mycenaean citadel there would be a great hall with a central fireplace, where warriors would sit, telling tales of heroic deeds.

▼ *The Mycenaeans are named after Mycenae, a citadel of stone in the Peloponnese region of Greece.*

◀ *Homer tells how Troy fell when the Greeks pretended to give up and go home, leaving behind a huge wooden horse. The jubilant Trojans dragged this into the city – only to discover Greek warriors hiding inside it.*

- **After about 1500 BC** Mycenaean kings were buried in a beehive-shaped tomb called a tholos, with a long, corridor-shaped entrance.
- **Centuries later**, a Greek poet known as Homer told how a city called Troy was destroyed by the Mycenaeans after a ten-year siege. Historians once thought this was just a story, but since Troy's remains were discovered in Turkey, some think a war may have really taken place, perhaps in the 1190s BC.
- **The Trojan War** in Homer's tale is caused by the beautiful Helen of Sparta. She married Menelaus, brother of King Agamemnon of Mycenae, but she fell in love with Prince Paris of Troy.
- **Helen and Paris eloped to Troy**, and Agamemnon and other Greeks laid siege to Troy to take her back.
- **The battle featured** many heroes – such as Hector, Achilles and Odysseus.
- **The Greeks finally captured Troy** when Greek soldiers hid inside a wooden horse the Trojans brought into their city.

Homer's heroes

- **Homer is a Greek poet** said to have written the ancient world's two greatest poems: *The Iliad* and *The Odyssey*.
- **Homer** probably lived in the 9th century BC in Ionia, on what is now the Aegean coast of Turkey, or on the island of Chios.
- **No one is certain** if Homer actually existed, or if he composed all of both poems. Most current experts think that he did.
- **In Homer's time** there was a great tradition of bards. These were poets who recited aloud great tales of heroic deeds. They knew the poems by heart and so never wrote them down.
- **The Iliad and the Odyssey** are the only poems from the times of the bards that were written down and so survive. They may have been written down at the time, or later.
- **After Homer's time**, the two great poems were used in religious festivals in Greece.
- **For centuries** after Homer's time, Greek children learned to read, and learned about the legends of the past, by studying Homer's work.

◀ *Nothing is known for certain about Homer, but legend says that he was blind.*

- **In the 2nd century BC**, scholars at the Alexandrian Library in Egypt studied the poems. A few scholars came to the conclusion that they were so different in style they must have been written by two different poets.
- ***The Iliad* is a long poem** in lofty language about the Trojan War, in which the Greeks besiege the city of Troy to take back the kidnapped Helen.
- ***The Odyssey* tells of a great journey** made by hero Odysseus, and his adventures along the way.

▼ *Odysseus and his crew escape the fury of the blinded, one-eyed, man-eating giant Polyphemus.*

The Odyssey – an epic tale

- **Homer's *The Odyssey*** is an adventure story that follows the Greek hero, Odysseus, after the Trojan War, on his long and difficult sea voyage home.
- **Odysseus and his men** have to face many magical dangers on their journey, including ferocious monsters and terrifying giants.
- **On one occasion**, some of Odysseus' sailors eat lotus fruit, which makes them forget all about returning to their families and homes.
- **Odysseus has to sail** safely past the Sirens. These are half-woman, half-bird creatures who live on a craggy seashore. They sing a magical song that lures sailors to steer their ships onto the rocks to their deaths.
- **The goddess of war**, Athena, acts as Odysseus's patron, giving him special help and guidance.
- **The sea god Poseidon** hates Odysseus and seeks to shipwreck him.
- **By the time Odysseus** finally reaches his palace in Ithaca, he has been away for 20 years. Disguised as a beggar, only his faithful old dog recognizes him.

DID YOU KNOW?

Unlike its companion poem, The Iliad, The Odyssey has a happy ending.

▲ *One Greek legend says that the Sirens were so furious when Odysseus escaped their clutches that they drowned themselves.*

- **Once home**, Odysseus's troubles are not over. Powerful suitors are pressurizing his faithful wife, Penelope, for her hand in marriage, so they can seize Odysseus's crown.
- **Women often hold** positions of great power in the poem. For instance, Circe is a very powerful sorceress who turns some of Odysseus's sailors into pigs. The goddess Calypso keeps Odysseus captive on her island for seven years.

Where was Troy?

- **Troy is the city** in the ancient Greek poet Homer's famous epic, *The Iliad*. It was once thought to be purely mythical.
- **In 1822**, British scholar Charles McClaren suggested that Homer's Troy might be in Turkey. He pinpointed a mound called Hisarlik near the Dardanelles – a narrow sea linking the Black Sea and the Aegean.
- **German archaeologist** Heinrich Schliemann began digging at Hisarlik mound in 1871.
- **In 1873**, Schliemann uncovered fortifications and remains of a very ancient city, which he believed to be Troy.
- **Schliemann also found** a treasure of gold and silver, which he called Priam's treasure after the Trojan king Priam, mentioned in *The Iliad*. He smuggled this out of Turkey to take to Europe.
- **In 1876**, Schliemann was digging at Mycenae in Greece. He came across what he thought was the tomb of Agamemnon – king of the Trojans' enemies in Homer's Iliad.
- **In the 1890s**, Wilhelm Dörpfeld showed that Hisarlik mound is made of nine layers of city remains. This is because the city was destroyed by fire or earthquake nine times. Each time the survivors built on the rubble.
- **Schliemann thought Homer's Troy** was Troy II, second layer from the bottom. Dörpfeld thought it was Troy VI.
- **Troy I to V** are now thought to date from the early Bronze Age (*c*.3000–1900 BC).

Experts now think Homer's Troy may be Troy VIIa, a layer of the seventh city, dating from about 1250 BC.

▼ *When Schliemann found this gold mask at Mycenae in 1876, he thought it must be Agamemnon's. In fact, it dates from 300 years earlier.*

Australia's 'Dreamtime'

- **Far beyond Europe**, Asia and Africa, other cultures and civilizations were living in very different landscapes, making new inventions and discoveries and telling tales based upon myths and legends.
- **By 1000 BC** Australia's Aboriginal peoples had perfected the art of survival in bush and desert terrain. They controlled and made use of fire to aid their hunting and cultivation.
- **Some places were suitable** for making more permanent settlements.
- **Aboriginal tribes** were led by elders. They traded precious stones, flints, shells, weapons and food over long distances.

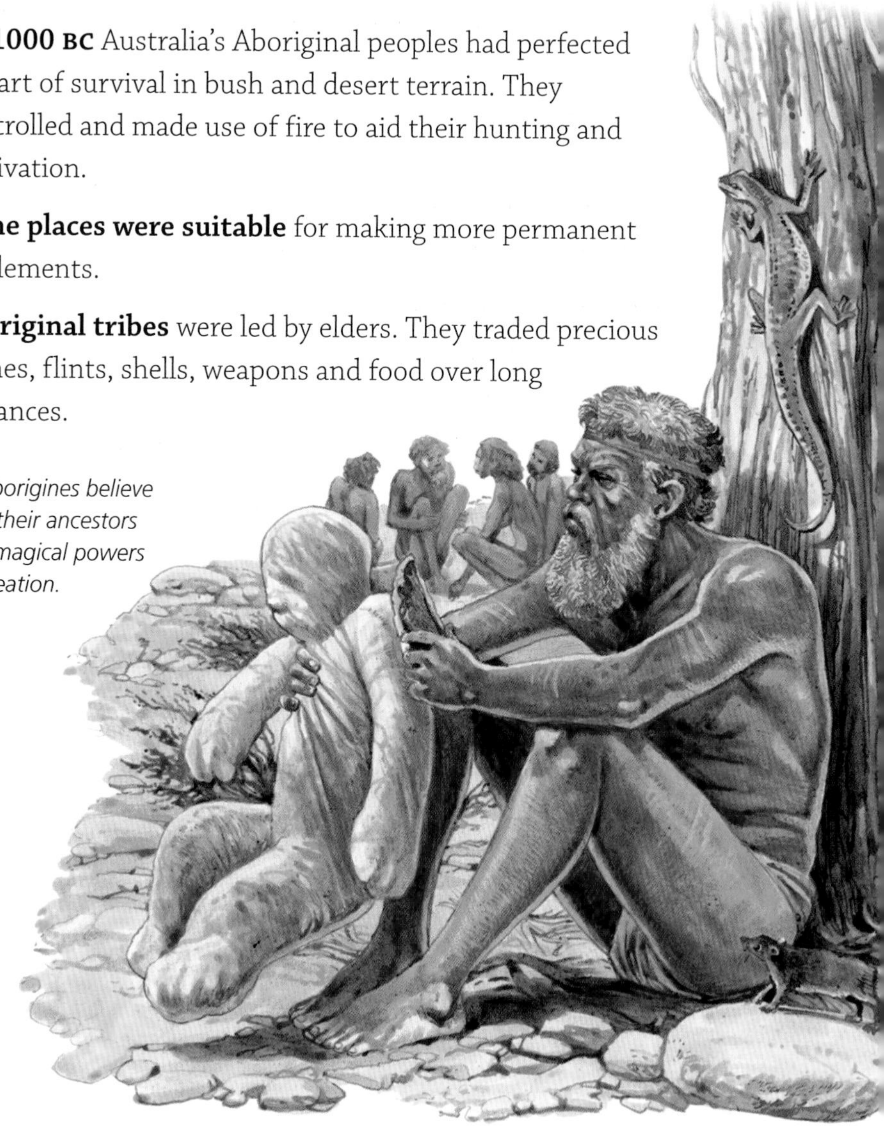

▶ *Aborigines believe that their ancestors had magical powers of creation.*

▶ *This Aboriginal artwork shows a monster called a Bunyip, much feared by children.*

- **The landscape they walked through** was sacred to the spirits of their ancestors, as were the animals and plants.
- **The creation mythology** of the Aborigines is called the Dreamtime.
- **There are various** Dreamtime stories, which came from different tribes. Most Dreamtime mythology says that in the beginning, the Earth was just a dark plain.
- **Aborigines** from southeastern Australia believed heroes from the sky shaped the world and created people.
- **Myths from central Australia** say that people were carved out of animals and plants by their ancestors who then went back to sleep in rocks, trees or underground – where they are to this day.
- **Tribes from the northeast** believed that everything was created by two female ancestors who came across the sea from the Land of the Dead.
- **A wise rainbow snake** plays an important part in many Dreamtime myths.

Across the Pacific

▲ *Outriggers are traditional boats of Polynesia, and are named after rigging that sticks out to the sides to aid stability. Easy to pull ashore, and perfect for shallow waters, they are ideal for island life.*

- **There are about 20,000 to 30,000 islands** scattered across the Pacific Ocean. They are divided into three main groups, known as Melanesia ('black islands'), Micronesia ('small islands') and Polynesia ('many islands').
- **The 'Lapita' culture** of the Austronesians who settled these islands, spread westwards from about 1600 BC. It had reached Fiji by about 1300 BC, and Tonga and Samoa by about 1100 BC.
- **A second wave of migrants** moved east from Fiji, Samoa and Tonga to the Marquesas Islands about 2000 years ago.
- **Hawaii was not reached** until about AD 300, Rapa Nui (Easter Island) until about AD 400, and Aotearoa (New Zealand) until about AD 1250.

- **The settlers crossed** the ocean in large double canoes and smaller outriggers.
- **In their canoes** the settlers took crops such as coconuts, yams, taro and breadfruit, and livestock such as pigs and chickens.
- **Hundreds of different cultures**, languages and styles of woodcarving developed across the region.

▼ *There are about 600 huge stone moai statues on Easter Island, on platforms called ahus. No one knows what they were used for.*

DID YOU KNOW?

The biggest moai statues on Easter Island are up to 12 m tall and weigh 90 tonnes.

Oceania myths and rituals

- **Myths from western Polynesia** say that in the beginning, the creator god Tangaroa lived in a dark emptiness known as Po.
- **Some stories tell** how Tangaroa formed the world by throwing down rocks into the watery wastes.

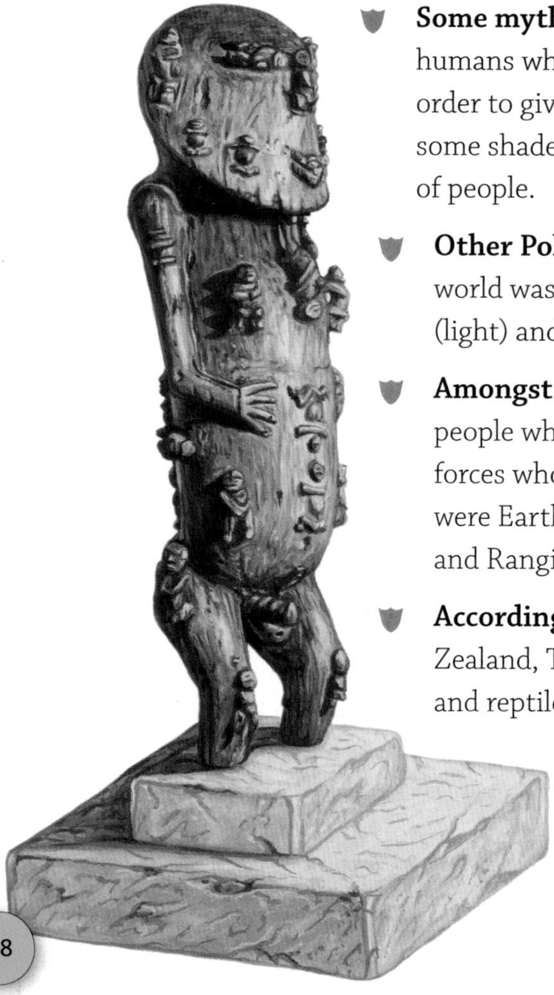

- **Some myths say** that Tangaroa created humans when he made a leafy vine in order to give his messenger bird, Tuli, some shade – the leaves were made up of people.
- **Other Polynesian myths** say that the world was created by the joining of Ao (light) and Po (darkness).
- **Amongst the Maoris**, the Polynesian people who settled New Zealand, the two forces who joined together in creation were Earth Mother and Sky Father – Papa and Rangi.
- **According to Maori stories** from New Zealand, Tangaroa was the father of fish and reptiles.

◀ The powerful god Tangaroa is an important figure in the mythologies of many South Pacific islands.

▲ *The beautiful island of Tahiti, today in French Polynesia, was an important staging post in the settlement of the Pacific.*

- **Other gods in myths** from New Zealand include Haumia father of plants, Rongo father of crops, Tane father of forests, Tawhiri god of storms, and Tu father of humans.
- **Myths say that certain gods** were more important than others. These 'chief gods' vary from island to island, according to who the islanders believe they were descended from.
- **Tattooing was a common ritual** amongst the Maoris and the Samoans. The word comes from the Polynesian, *tatu*.
- **Another word**, *tabu*, meant an action that was forbidden because it was too sacred or too terrible. We still use the word 'taboo'.

Civilization in the Americas

▲ *The Olmec heads were carved from huge blocks of volcanic rock weighing up to 14 tonnes. No one knows how they were moved.*

- **By about 2000 BC** there were permanent villages and extensive farms in Mexico and Central America, growing corn, beans, squash and other crops.
- **Between 1200–400 BC**, a remarkable culture was developed by the Olmec people of western Mexico.
- **The Olmecs** had a counting system and a calendar. Symbols on a stone, dating to before 900 BC, probably represent the first writing in the Americas.
- **The ruins** of a huge Olmec pyramid have been discovered at La Venta in Tabasco, Mexico.
- **The Olmecs carved** huge 'baby-face' heads from basalt with enormous skill – apparently only with stone chisels, since they had no metal.
- **The Zapotec civilization** of Mexico founded a city called Monte Albán in about 500 BC.

- **In South America**, huge religious sites were being built in what is now Peru as early as 2600 BC.
- **From 900 BC** the Chavín civilization spread from the religious centre of Chavín de Huantar in the Peruvian mountains.
- **From AD 100–700**, America's first big city developed at Teotihuacán, with vast pyramids and palaces.
- **Teotihuacán may have been** the world's biggest city by AD 300, with a population of over 250,000.

▼ *The main street at Teotihuacán, near Mexico City, is known as The Avenue of the Dead. It was originally 2.5 km long.*

New ideas, technologies, crafts and inventions – and new classical empires.

AFRICA

c.600 BC
The first circumnavigation of Africa, by Phoenician seafarers in the service of Egypt.

c.550 BC–AD 300
The Nok culture of Nigeria; iron-working and fine terracotta statues.

c.400 BC
The Phoenician city state of Carthage (in modern Tunisia) at the height of its power.

332 BC
Alexander the Great conquers Egypt, founding the Greek city of Alexandria.

264–146 BC
The three Punic Wars, fought between Carthage and Rome, ending in the destruction of Carthage.

30 BC
Egypt becomes part of the Roman empire.

c.AD 100
Rise of the kingdom of Axum in Ethiopia, trading with the Roman empire and Asia.

c.AD 350
Speakers of Niger-Congo languages reach southern Africa, part of the great expansion of 'Bantu' peoples.

EUROPE

c.800–650 BC
The Hallstatt culture of Central Europe develops advanced iron-working skills.

c.800 BC
Rise of the Etruscan city states in Italy.

509 BC
In Italy, Rome ends rule by kings to become a republic.

c.500–300 BC
The golden age of Greek culture – philosophy, architecture, drama, politics.

c.400 BC
La Tène artistic style spreads through northwestern Europe. The spread of Iron Age cultures later termed 'Celtic'.

AD 117
The Roman empire (founded in 27 BC) reaches its greatest extent, taking in much of Europe, Southwest Asia and North Africa.

AD 330
Constantinople (later Istanbul) founded by the emperor Constantine as Rome's eastern capital.

AD 410
Rome is sacked by Visigoths, end of the western Roman empire

ASIA

550–330 BC
The first Persian (Achaemenid) empire, from Egypt to the Indus River.

334–329 BC
Alexander the Great of Macedon leads the Greek conquest of the Persian empire.

322 BC
The Maurya empire in India, ruled by Chandragupta.

221 BC
All China is united as an empire under the Qin dynasty.

206 BC–220 AD
The Han dynasty rules China, a period of wealth and inventiveness.

c.100 BC
The great age of Petra, a Nabataean trading city cut from rock faces in the desert of Jordan.

AD 300
The Yamato period in Japan, spread of wet rice farming to all islands.

AD 320–550
The Gupta empire rules India, advances in art, mathematics and philosophy.

The Ancient World

NORTH AMERICA

c.800 BC
Decline of the Saqqaq culture in Greenland, tent-dwelling hunters of marine animals.

c.500 BC
Rise of the Early Dorset (Tuniit) tradition across the Arctic. Masks, carved wood, bone and soapstone.

c.500 BC–AD 1500
First Nation cultures develop across Canada.

c.500 BC
During the Early Basketmaker II culture in the American southwest, hunting and gathering gives way to maize cultivation.

c.400 BC–AD 400
Norton Mounds archaeological site, Michigan; ritual burials with artefacts made of bone, antler, shell and copper.

c.300 BC–AD 500
Spread of the Hopewell tradition in the chiefdoms of the northeast and midwest, long distance trade networks, impressive burials.

c.AD 1
North Pacific coastal cultures, craft skills using wood and bark.

c.AD 50–500
Late Basketmaker II culture in the American southwest; permanent settlements, fired pottery, increased maize cultivation, basket-making.

CENTRAL AND SOUTH AMERICA

c.800 BC–AD100
Important pre-Classic Mayan sites in Central America.

c.250 BC
Mayan hieroglyphic inscriptions.

c.200 BC–AD 800
The Nazca culture of southern Peru – pottery, textiles and ritual patterns and pictures scraped on the desert soil.

c.100 BC–AD 250
Construction of Teotihuacan, a large Mexican city with pyramid temples, avenues, housing and wall paintings.

c.AD 100–600
Rise of the Moche culture in northern Peru; painted pottery, gold-working, stepped pyramids, irrigation.

c.AD 250
Spectacular treasure-filled tomb of the Lord of Sipán, Peru.

c.AD 250
Start of the Classic period of Mayan civilization; major urban centres and monuments.

c.AD 400
Rise of the Marajaora Island culture in the mouth of the Amazon River.

OCEANIA

c.500 BC
Settlement of Australia's Torres Strait islands by Melanesians.

c.200 BC
Settlement of the Marquesas Islands (now in French Polynesia).

c.AD 1
Increase in the number of shell middens (tips) on the Australian coast. Perhaps more seafood was needed due to a rise in population.

c.AD 100
A new wave of seafaring across the Pacific. Migrations from Fiji, Samoa and Tonga.

c.AD 200
End of the Lapita pottery tradition in the western Pacific.

c.AD 300
Polynesian settlers reach the Hawaiian islands.

c.AD 400
Polynesian settlers reach Rapa Nui (Easter Island).

c.500 AD
Polynesian settlers from Tahiti reach the Cook Islands.

Iron Ages

- **Discovering how to smelt** and work iron changed the course of human history. Iron and steel were far harder than bronze, and were ideal for making tough weapons, farming tools and utensils.
- **At first** iron was used for making small objects and ornaments. Peoples of Mesopotamia and the Hittites, from Anatolia (in what is now the Asian part of Turkey) mastered the art of smithing between 1500–1200 BC.
- **New iron weapons** such as long swords turned armies into deadly killing machines.
- **The use of iron** spread into Greece and southeastern Europe. In northern Italy the Villanovan culture marks the start of the Iron Age there, from about 900–700 BC, and the rise of the Etruscan city states.
- **In Central Europe** later phases of the Hallstatt culture are marked by highly skilled iron-working, after about 800 BC. From about 500 BC the Celtic cultures of western Europe were also typified by fine iron work.
- **At this time** an Iron Age was also racing ahead across Asia, in India and China. By the fourth century BC the Chinese were using large bellows and coal-fired furnaces to produce cast iron, hundreds of years before the Europeans mastered this technology.

▲ *Iron, durable and sharp, transformed warfare in the ancient world.*

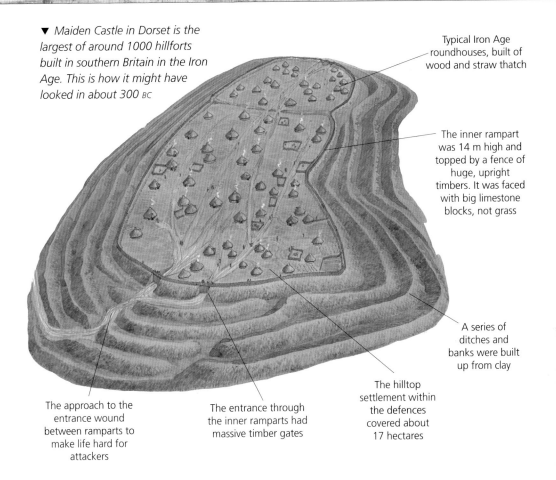

▼ *Maiden Castle in Dorset is the largest of around 1000 hillforts built in southern Britain in the Iron Age. This is how it might have looked in about 300* BC

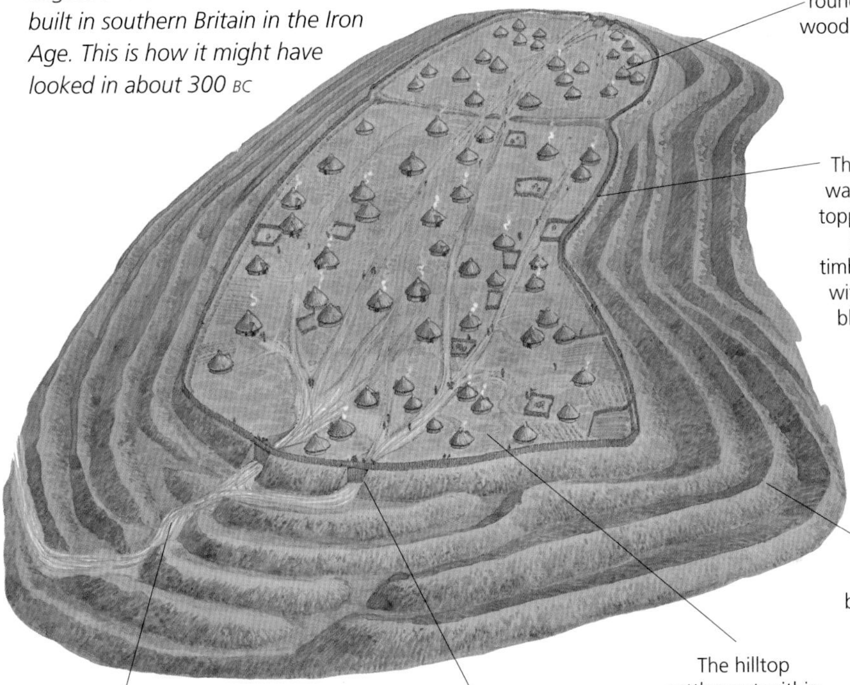
Typical Iron Age roundhouses, built of wood and straw thatch
The inner rampart was 14 m high and topped by a fence of huge, upright timbers. It was faced with big limestone blocks, not grass
A series of ditches and banks were built up from clay
The hilltop settlement within the defences covered about 17 hectares
The entrance through the inner ramparts had massive timber gates
The approach to the entrance wound between ramparts to make life hard for attackers

- **Chinese iron-working** brought about great changes in ploughing, cooking, mining and building.
- **In Africa**, the Iron Age began about 3000 years ago in ancient Egypt and Nubia. The city of Meroë was one centre of production, as was the Nigerian plateau during the Nok culture, from about 550 BC.
- **Iron-working** was so important to communities that some even believed it had magical qualities. Greeks, Romans, Celts and Germanic peoples all worshipped smith gods.

China behind the Wall

▼ *The Great Wall of China was first built of earth bricks in 220–206 BC, under Qin Shi Huangdi. Much of the brick and stone wall seen today dates from the AD 1400s.*

- **China's ruling Shang dynasty** was replaced in about 1046 BC by the Zhou.
- **The Zhou extended territory** far across China, but the kingdom was divided into feudal states, each with its own ruler. After 770 BC this resulted in fragmentation and rivalry.
- **Even so**, this was a time of new technologies, such as iron-working. There were the first Chinese poets, and great thinkers such as Laozi and Kong Fuzi (known in Europe as Confucius) whose ideas have shaped Chinese civilizations ever since.
- **One of the western** Zhou states was called Qin. In 256 BC it overthrew the Zhou, and by 221 BC it was in control of all China.
- **The victorious Qin ruler**, Zheng, expanded the empire and styled himself Qin Shi Huangdi, the First Emperor of Qin.
- **He had the various northern defences** of China joined with a single 4000-km-long Great Wall, built to protect the empire from invading nomads.
- **Shi Huangdi's rule** was centralized and very strict. He banned books that were of no practical use and he is said to have buried 460 dissident scholars alive. When his eldest son Fusu objected, he was banished.

- **There were three attempts** to assassinate the first emperor. He became very fearful of death and longed for immortality.
- **Qin Shi Huangdi** died in 210 BC. His body was taken secretly to the capital by minister Lisi with a fish cart, in order to hide the smell of rotting flesh. Lisi sent a letter to Fusu, pretending it was from his father, telling him to commit suicide. Fusu did so, and Lisi came to power, although civil war followed.
- **Qin Shi Huangdi was buried** in a vast mausoleum near Xi'an, with an army of 8000 life-sized individual clay soldiers and horses. Discovered in 1974, it was named the Terracotta Army.

▼ *The great tomb of the Terracotta Army (or Warriors) is located near Xi'an, central China. In their underground chambers, the life-size figures are arranged in precise military formation.*

Chinese faith and philosophy

▶ *Confucius believed that court officials should not plot for power, but study music, poetry and the history of their ancestors.*

- **China's rich mythology** dates back to its earliest days, with beliefs in demons, spirits, gods and goddesses. The first ruler of the Shang dynasty became revered as the divine 'Jade Emperor'.
- **Many legends** explained that it was the duty of China's rulers to keep order and balance in the Universe. During the Zhou dynasty, rulers became revered as the 'Sons of Heaven'.
- **Many Chinese traditions**, such as ancestor worship, were at the core of the teachings of a philosopher called Kong Fuzi (known in the West as Confucius). He believed in an ordered society based upon morality and respect within both family and government.
- **Confucius was born** in the state of Lu (Shandong province) in 551 BC and lived until 479 BC. After mastering the six Chinese arts – ritual, music, archery, charioteering, calligraphy (writing) and arithmetic – Confucius went on to become a brilliant teacher.

DID YOU KNOW?
Confucianism, Daoism and Buddhism form the three pillars of traditional Chinese beliefs.

- **Confucius argued** that all men should be educated in order to make the world a better place, and that teaching could become a way of life.
- **He told statesmen** this golden rule: 'Do not do to others what you would not have them do to you.'
- **Traditional Chinese views** about the harmony of spirit and nature formed the basis of a philosophy, and later a religion, known as Daoism. Dao means 'the Way'.
- **The founder** of Daoism was a teacher called Laozi, who may have lived in the sixth century BC, or perhaps later.

◀ *Little is known about Laozi, the founder of Daoism. Legend has it that while travelling on an ox one day, he was stopped at a border post. There he wrote down his teachings. He then vanished and was never seen again.*

Han China

- **In 210 BC**, the small Han kingdom in China was ruled over by Liu Bang. Liu Bang was a poor villager who had come to power as the Qin empire broke down.
- **In 206 BC** Liu Bang led an army on the Qin capital, Xiangyang. He looted Shi Huangdi's tomb, and burned the city and the library containing the books Shi Huangdi had banned – the only existing copies.
- **In 202 BC**, Liu Bang proclaimed himself to be the first Han emperor and took the name Gaozu.
- **During the long reign** of Emperor Wu (Han Wudi, 141–87 BC), Han China reached its peak. China became as large as the Roman Empire. Art and science thrived.

▼ *Western China is ringed by high mountains. This ancient silk trading route winds between China and Sikkim in northern India.*

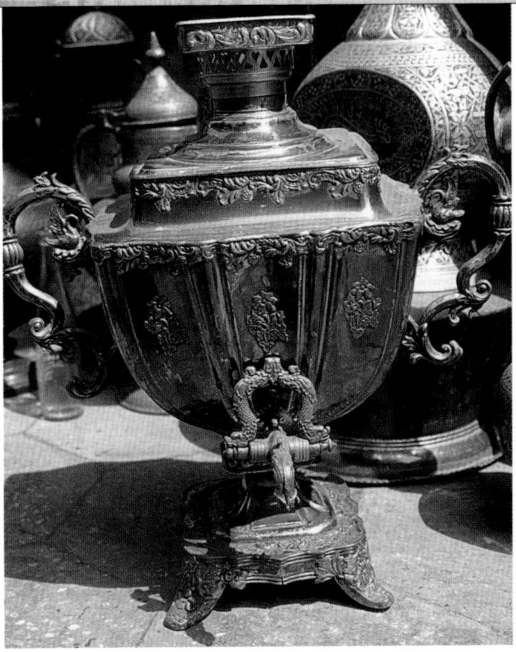

▶ *Beautiful objects such as this bronze urn were traded between China and Europe along the famous Silk Road for thousands of years.*

- **Beautiful cities** grew large and craftsmen made many exquisite things from wood, paint and silk. Sadly, many of these lovely objects were destroyed when Han rule ended.
- **Silk, jade and horses** were traded along the Silk Route, a network of routes which wound westwards through Central Asia as far as the Roman Empire.
- **Han emperors** tried to recover the lost writings and revive the teachings of Confucius, which had been suppressed during Qin rule. In 165 BC the first exams for entry into the civil (public) service were held. In about AD 50, Buddhist missionaries reached China for the first time.
- **By AD 200**, the Han emperors were weakened by ambitious wives and their guards. Rebellions by a group called the Yellow Turbans, combined with attacks from the north, ended Han rule.

Chinese inventions

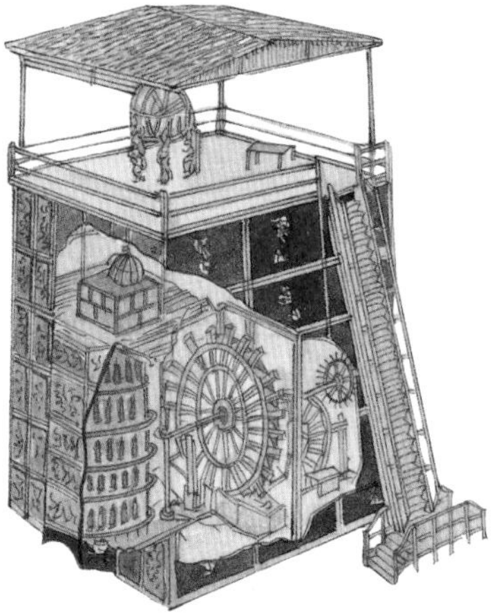

▲ *In AD 723 the Chinese invented mechanical clocks, about 600 years earlier than Europe. This is Su Sung's 'Cosmic Engine', an amazing 10-m high clock built in AD 1090.*

- **For many centuries** the Chinese led the world in new technologies and ingenious inventions. Some of these only reached Europe many centuries later.
- **The stirrup** was probably invented in China in the 3rd century BC. This gave warriors stability and leverage when fighting on horseback.
- **The Chinese** made huge advances in boat building. The ship's rudder was used from the 1st century AD, and 100 years later ships' safety was improved with watertight compartments (bulkheads). Multiple masts and fore-and-aft rigging also appeared in the 2nd century AD.

▲ *A compass called a sinan was made by the Chinese over 2000 years ago. A ladle made of magnetic lodestone spins on a bronze plate to point south.*

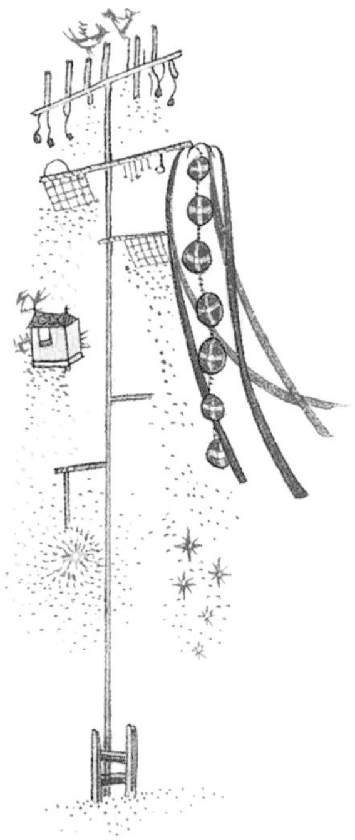

▶ *The Chinese discovered gunpowder and made the first guns about 1100 years ago. They also became famous for their fireworks.*

- **Kites have been** a Chinese passion ever since the 5th century BC, and were soon being made large enough to carry a man. Practical parachutes may date back to the 2nd century BC.
- **The Chinese were mining** surface coal about 5500 years ago, and using petroleum and natural gas as a fuel in the 4th century BC.
- **Porcelain**, a fine ceramic fired at very high temperatures, was produced during the Han period and would become China's most famous export. Another classic Han invention was paper.
- **Cast-iron ploughs** were made for China's farmers in China in about 200 BC, as was a rotary fan used for winnowing (separating grain from the husks).
- **One of the oldest** surviving printed books is the Diamond Sutra, printed in 868. However, printing in China goes back even earlier, to the 7th century AD.

▲ *Acupuncture involves sticking needles in certain points on the body to treat illness. The Chinese used acupuncture at least 1800 years ago – but probably much earlier.*

▲ *The 'Heaven-Rumbling Thunderclap Fierce Fire Erupter'. This was a gunpowder-fired device that shot out shells of poisonous gas.*

Ancient Japan

- **The earliest people** to live in Japan were called the Ainu. A small number of their descendants still live on Hokkaido island today.
- **Archaeologists have found** pottery made by prehistoric hunter-gatherers. They refer to this as the Jomon culture.
- **In about 350 BC** new migrants from China arrived in Japan. They brought with them knowledge of rice growing, working in bronze and iron, and making pottery on the wheel. This is called the Yayoi culture.

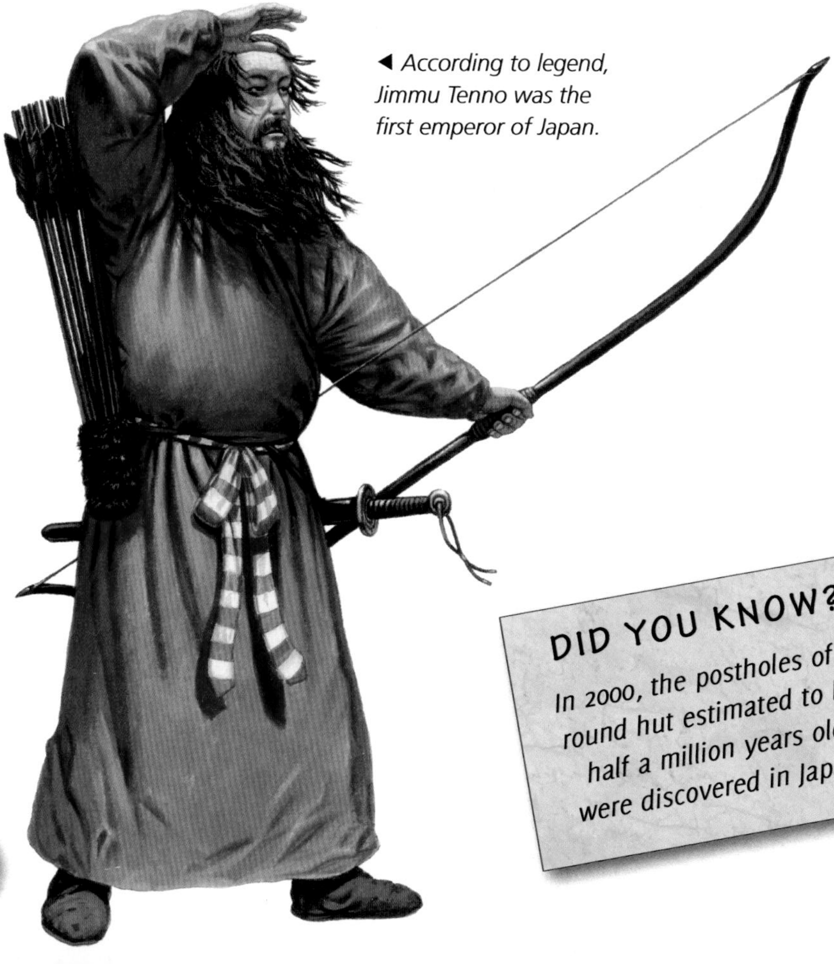

◀ *According to legend, Jimmu Tenno was the first emperor of Japan.*

DID YOU KNOW?

In 2000, the postholes of a round hut estimated to be half a million years old were discovered in Japan.

◀ *Shinto priests believe that all things that inspire awe – from twisted trees to dead warriors – can have* kami *(spirits).*

- **The Yayoi also brought** a nature religion with them, which later became known as Shinto, the 'Way of the Gods'.
- **The period** from about AD 300 is known as the Tomb (or Kofun) culture, marked by the impressive burials of Japanese leaders.
- **In the AD 400s** a clan called Yamato became powerful on Honshu, around Kyoto. Their leaders claimed descent from a legendary emperor of 660 BC called Jimmu Tenno. They claimed that his line stretched back to the Sun goddess herself.
- **The Yamato line** of emperors has ruled Japan ever since.
- **The Buddhist religion** arrived in Japan in the year AD 552.

Japan's ancient myths

- **The myths** of the early Japanese do not tell of a supreme spirit. Instead, they suggest that a divine force flows through all nature in the form of millions of gods.
- **The storm god Raiden** got his name from two Japanese words: *rai* for thunder and *den* for lightning.
- **Susano was the god** of seas and oceans. He was banished from heaven and sent to live in the Underworld.
- **Inari was the god of crops**. He is pictured as a bearded man holding sheaves of rice and riding on a fox – his servant and messenger.

▼ *Masks of spirits, demons and gods are used in a form of Japanese theatre called Noh. It is developed from ancient dance dramas and religious festivals.*

▶ *The religion of Buddhism spread to Japan from India. Worshippers follow the teachings of the Buddha, or 'enlightened one'.*

- **Over the centuries**, the number of nature gods increased as warrior heroes, religious leaders and emperors became gods, too.
- **In the 6th century**, Buddhism was introduced into Japan and a pantheon of Japanese Buddhist gods and goddesses developed.
- **In Japanese Buddhism**, Amida is the god of a paradise for the dead. He has two helpers, Kwannon, the goddess of mercy, and Shishi, the lord of might.
- **Japanese myth says** that there are about 500 immortal men and women called Sennin who live in the mountains. They can fly and work powerful magic.
- **A Shishi is a spirit** pictured as a cross between a dog and a lion (a character that came originally from Chinese mythology). It is believed to ward off evil demons, and Shishi statues are sometimes found at the entrances to temples and houses.
- **There are seven Japanese gods** of luck, called Shichi Fukujin, which means 'seven happiness beings'.

The rise of Hinduism

- **Hindus believe** that one great spirit, Brahman, is in everything. They worship this spirit as thousands of different gods.
- **The god who creates** the world is Brahma. He emerges from a lotus flower, floating on the floodwaters of chaos and thinks everything into being
- **The god Vishnu preserves** the balance of good and evil in the Universe by being born on earth as a human from time to time, to help men and women.

- **The god Shiva** is the destroyer god. He combats demons and keeps the Universe moving by dancing.
- **After each** 1000 Great Ages, Shiva destroys the world by fire and flood. He preserves the seeds of all life in a golden egg, which Brahma breaks open to begin the rebirth of creation.

◀ *Hindu temples are ornately decorated with statues and carvings of the gods.*

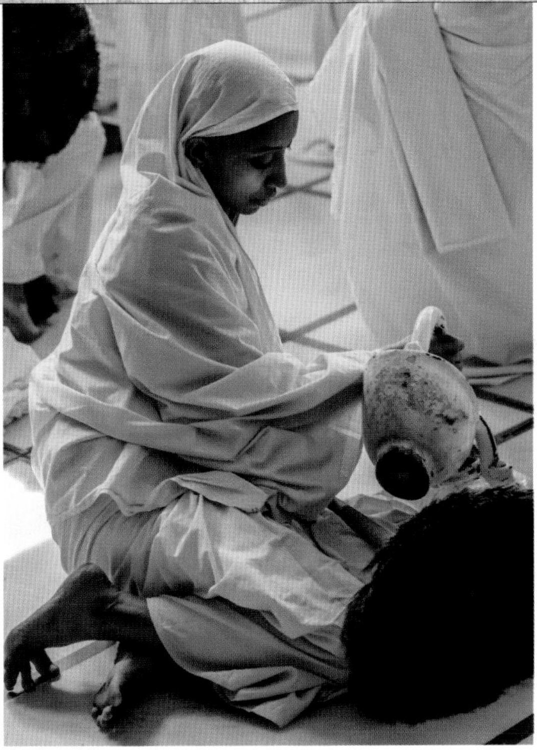

◄ *A Jain nun attends a religious festival in India. The Jain religion is part of the Sramana movement that challenged traditional Vedic teachings.*

- **By the end** of the Vedic age, in about 500 BC, large towns were developing in Hindu India. Society was changing, and new forms of worship appeared.
- **The mainstream Hindu beliefs** which had developed over the centuries were now challenged by a movement called Sramana, which was also rooted in ancient Indian custom and tradition.
- **It also influenced** the teachings of Buddhism and Jainism, a religion that preaches non-violence and the sanctity of all forms of life.

DID YOU KNOW?

Sramana gave rise to the practice of yoga, a system of spiritual and physical discipline.

The Ramayana

◀ *Hindus believe that the hero Rama was one of the ten human forms of the god Vishnu.*

- **Two great epic poems** were composed in ancient India – the *Mahabharata* and the *Ramayana*.
- **The *Ramayana* focuses** on the battle between the forces of good and evil in the Universe.
- **The *Ramayana* was written** in the Sanskrit language. Its date is uncertain. Some scholars believe it was written down in the 7th century BC, but others place it in the 4th century.
- **The poem was written** by a revered Hindu poet called Valmiki.
- **Like the Greek epic** *The Iliad*, the *Ramayana* involves the rescue of a stolen queen (called Sita). Like the Greek epic *The Odyssey*, the *Ramayana* follows a hero (Prince Rama) on a long and difficult journey.

- **Prince Rama's enemy** is the mighty demon, Ravana. He can work powerful magic, but is not immortal and can be killed.
- **The demon Ravana's** followers are known as Rakshasas. They can shape-shift and disguise themselves so they do not appear evil. This way, they can tempt good people to do the wrong thing.
- **The poem demonstrates** that it is important to respect animals. Rama needs the help of the hero Hanuman and his army of monkeys to rescue Sita.
- **The story says** that Rama and Sita are earthly forms of the great god Vishnu and his wife, Lakshmi.
- **The legend ends** when Rama has ruled as king for 10,000 years and is taken up to heaven with his brothers.

▶ *The monkey god Hanuman was the son of the wind and a great hero who helped Prince Rama.*

Gautama Buddha

- **Siddhartha Gautama** was born at Lumbini, Nepal about 563 BC, or according to some, in about 480 BC. He lived until the age of 80.
- **He became known** as the Buddha, a title meaning 'enlightened one'. He was founder of the Buddhist religion, which in the centuries that followed spread across India, Central Asia, Tibet, Mongolia and China, Japan, Burma and Southeast Asia.
- **Siddhartha grew up** as a young prince, living a life of luxury. When he was 16 years old, he married his cousin the Princess Yasodhara, who was the same age as him.
- **Siddhartha had powerful visions**. The first three told him that life involved ageing, sickness and death. The fourth told him he must leave his wife and become a holy man.

▼ *Young Buddhist monks in traditional saffron-coloured robes. They are taught to follow eight steps towards truth and wisdom.*

DID YOU KNOW?

Nirvana means enlightenment, the peace of mind achieved after all material desires have been abandoned.

▲ *Many statues of the Buddha show him sitting cross-legged, in deep meditation.*

- **After six years** of self-denial, Siddhartha sat down under a shady bo tree to think – and after several hours, great wisdom came to him.
- **The Buddha** spent the rest of his life preaching his message around India. He taught that life brings suffering. Only by rejecting materialism and individualism can one find peace, awareness and eventually enlightenment.

Mauryan India

- **In 321 BC**, the first great Indian empire was created by Chandragupta Maurya (*c*.325–297 BC). Its capital was Pataliputra.
- **The Mauryan Empire** at its peak included most of modern Pakistan, Bangladesh and all but the far south of India.
- **The most famous** of the Mauryan emperors was Chandragupta's grandson, Asoka (*c*.265–238 BC).
- **After witnessing** an horrific battle, Asoka was so appalled by the suffering that he resolved never to go to war. Instead, Asoka devoted himself to improving the lot of his people.
- **Asoka became** a Buddhist and his government promoted the Dharma, the 'Universal Law' of Buddhism.

▶ *Banyan trees have many trunks, each originating from its branches. They were planted to provide shade for travellers along newly built roads.*

▶ *During and after Asoka's reign, dome shrines called stupas were built all over India and Nepal.*

- **The Universal Law** preached religious tolerance, non-violence and respect for the dignity of every single person.
- **Asoka's men** dug wells and built reservoirs all over India to help the poor. They also provided comfortable rest-houses and planted shady banyan trees for travellers along the new roads.
- **Asoka said** 'all men are my children', and sent out officials to deal with local problems.
- **A vast secret police force** and an army of 700,000 helped Asoka to run his empire.

DID YOU KNOW?
Asoka's Sarnath lion insignia is now the national emblem of India.

Gupta India

- **The Guptas** were a family of rulers who reigned in northern India from AD 320 to about 550. This was one of India's golden ages, when literature, sculpture and other arts were at their peak.
- **The Guptas were originally** a family of rich landowners, who took over control of the small kingdom of Magadha in the Ganges valley.
- **Chandragupta I** came to the throne in AD 320. He extended his lands by making advantageous marriages.
- **Chandragupta's son**, Samudragupta, and his grandson, Chandragupta II, gained control over much of northern India by military conquests.
- **The Hindu** and Buddhist religions both began to develop and flourish during the Gupta period.
- **Beautiful temples** and religious sculptures were created across northern India.
- **In about AD 450**, Kalidása, India's greatest poet and dramatist, wrote his famous play *Sákuntala*, filled with romance and adventure.
- **Music and dance** developed their highest classical form.
- **Hindu mathematicians** developed the decimal system (counting in tens) that we still use today.
- **The Guptas' power** declined during the 500s, under repeated attacks by a people from the north, called the Huns.

▲ *Hindu and Buddhist sculptures and paintings of the Gupta period have been the model for Indian art down the centuries*

Medes and Persians

- **Connections between** the 'Indo-European' languages of Europe and Asia suggest that waves of migrants from the north settled in Persia (modern-day Iran) between about 1500–1000 BC.
- **Descendants of these peoples** included groups known as Medes and Persians.
- **In 612 BC** the Medes, allied with Babylon, sacked the Assyrian city of Nineveh. A new Median empire now straddled Asia.

◀ *Rich carvings adorned the walls at Persepolis – the great city and palace of Darius' reign.*

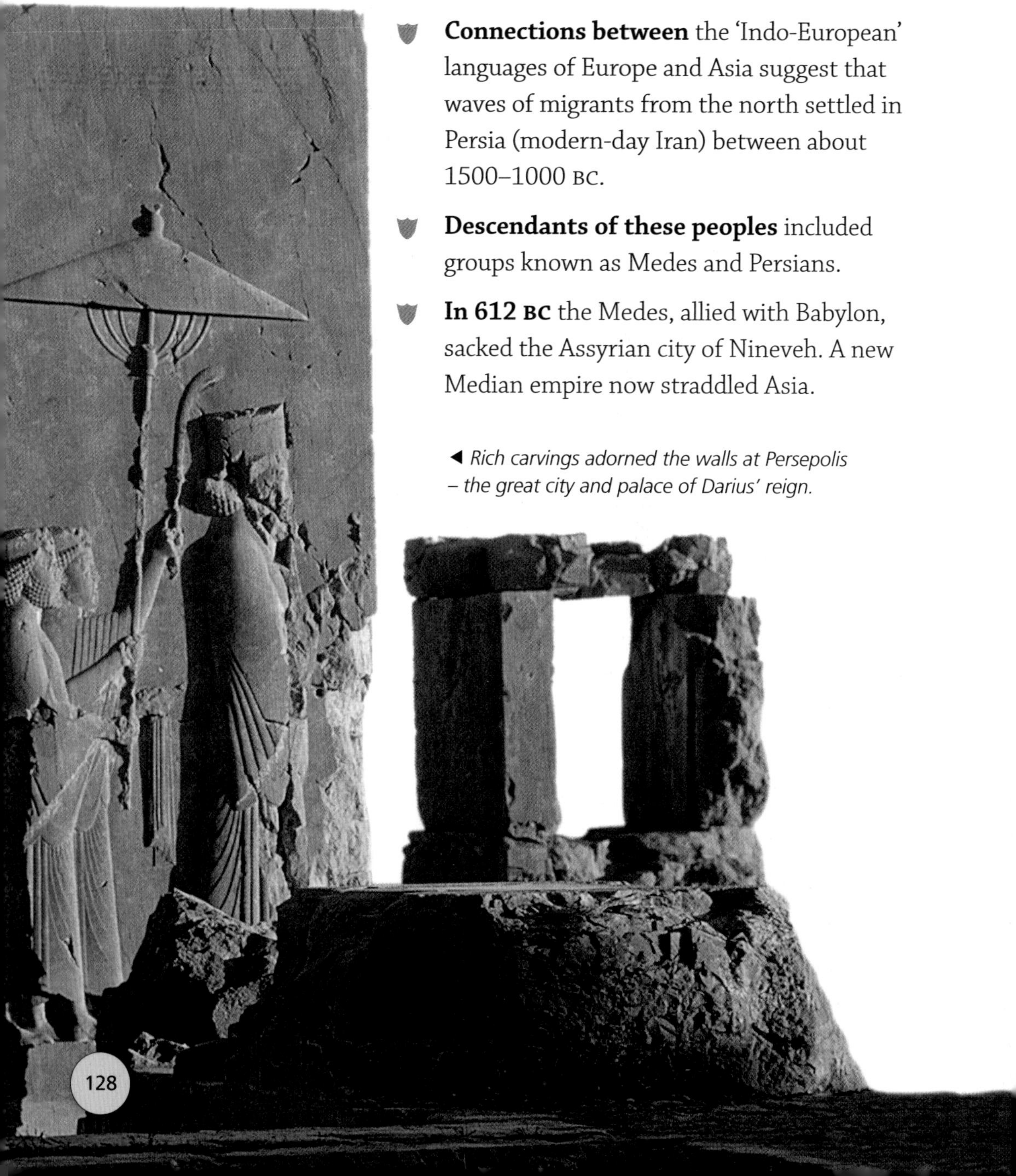

▶ *Darius the Great ruled Persia from 521–486 BC.*

- **In 550 BC**, the Medes themselves were overthrown by the Persians. The Persian king, Cyrus II, was the grandson of a Median king called Astyages.
- **Cyrus II** had an army of horsemen and very skilled archers. He went on to establish a great Persian empire.
- **The Persian Empire** was ruled by the Achaemenid family until it was destroyed by Alexander the Great of Macedon in 330 BC.
- **Under the rule of Darius I**, the Persian Empire reached its greatest extent. Darius who called himself Shahanshah ('King of kings') introduced gold and silver coins, and also brought chickens to the Middle East.
- **Darius built** a famous road system and divided his empire into 20 satrapies (provinces), each ruled by a satrap (governor).
- **Officials who travelled** around the empire and reported any trouble back to the king were known as the 'King's Ears'.
- **The Persians built** luxurious cities and palaces – first at Susa, then in Darius's reign, at Parsa (Persepolis).

Gods of Persia

- **The earliest Persians** worshipped nature deities such as Tishtrya, god of fertility, and Anahita, goddess of the lakes and oceans.
- **In ancient times**, the god of victory, Verethragna, was worshipped widely through the Persian empire by soldiers. Like the Hindu god Vishnu, he was born ten times on Earth to fight demons. He took different animal and human forms.
- **The human heroes** of Persian myths and legends were also worshipped as god-like rulers. One was the hero Faridun, who battled a monster of evil and imprisoned him at the ends of the Earth.
- **From the 6th century BC**, the beliefs of a prophet called Zarathustra (or Zoroaster) spread through Persia. In this religion, Zoroastrianism, the ancient gods feature as angels called Yazatas.
- **The chief god** of Zoroastrianism is called Ahura Mazda, later known as Ohrmazd. Ahura Mazda was said to be Zoroaster's father. Zoroaster's mother was believed to be a virgin, like Jesus' mother, Mary, in the Christian scriptures.

◀ The tomb of Cyrus the Great, the founder of the Persian Empire, who ruled from 549–529 BC.

▶ *A thousand years ago a Persian god called Mithra was adopted by many Roman worshippers. He is shown here slaying a bull to make the world fertile with its blood.*

- **According to Zoroaster**, creation is protected by seven spirit guardians known as Amesha Spentas.
- **Zoroastrians believe** that everyone is looked after by a guardian spirit, or Fravashi. These spirits represent the good in people and help those who ask.
- **People from** the ancient Zoroastrian religious class or caste became known in Europe as the Magi.
- **The Romans founded** a secretive religious cult named after the Persian god Mithra. Mithraism became popular across the Roman empire from the 1st–4th century AD. Historians now believe Mithraism owed more to Roman than Persian beliefs.

The Iron Age Celts

- **The Greeks** referred to people living beyond their northern border as Keltoi.
- **Many centuries later** historians adopted this term as 'Celts', when describing the Iron Age peoples of temperate Europe.
- **These Celts** were made up of many different tribes and cultures. Some of them shared iron-working skills and other technologies, as well as religious beliefs and customs.
- **The Gauls** (in France, Belgium, the Alps and northern Italy), the Gaels (in Ireland) and the Britons (in Great Britain) are often described as Celts. They were divided into tribes, but they did not see themselves as a single people and were rarely united.
- **After about 800 BC** Iron Age cultures were transferred across the Celtic world, mostly by contact, travel or migration rather than by invasions. They followed trading routes, along the Danube and the Rhône rivers or up the Atlantic coasts.

◀ *In Britain the Iron Age can be dated from about 800 BC to the Roman occupation in AD 43. Smiths (metal workers) were very important people in Celtic communities.*

- **Hillforts may have served** as tribal gathering places, or as administrative or trading centres.
- **After about 450 BC** many Celtic cultures are associated with a decorative style of arts and crafts, named 'La Tène' after an archaeological site in Switzerland. Beautiful whirls and spirals appear on ornaments, jewellery, and military equipment.
- **In the 4th and 3rd centuries BC** Gauls sacked Rome and invaded the Balkans and Greece, even settling in Galatia (in modern Turkey).
- **The Celts were fierce fighters**, but both Gauls and Britons came under increasing attack as the Roman empire expanded from the 2nd century BC to the 1st century AD.

▶ *This warrior of the Celtic Iron Age carries a long sword into battle, and an oval shield. His body is tattooed and his hair is spiked with lime.*

Celtic beliefs

- **Iron Age peoples** across Europe worshipped earth goddesses, gods of the sky and sun, as well as gods and spirits associated with particular tribes and places.
- **Celtic gods included** the skilful Lugus (Lugh or Lleu), Taranis god of thunder, Cernunnos the horned god, the Morrígan (crow goddess of the battlefield), Epona or Rhiannon the goddess of horses.
- **Springs and wells** were holy places, as were lakes and islands. Sometimes precious objects or weapons were thrown into lakes as offerings.
- **There was a close interest** in animals such as stags, wild boars and fish, which are often featured in art.
- **In Britain, Ireland and Gaul** the priests were called Druids. They came from aristocratic families and had great power. Druids also served as teachers, lawmakers and envoys.

▼ *This beautiful gold neckband is called a torc. It was a symbol of wealth and high status, and also of spiritual power.*

- **Shrines could be groves** of oak trees, or in some places enclosures and structures where sacrifices were made.
- **Several great festivals** happened throughout the Celtic. Samhain was a fire festival at the end of October, when spirits walked the land. Imbolc took place at the end of January, celebrating the goddess Brigid. At May Day, Beltain celebrated fertility, while Lughnasa at the end of July was a summer festival.

▲ *This horned figure is from a famous silver cauldron found at Gundestrup in Denmark. It probably represents the god Cernunnos. He holds up a torc and a serpent.*

DID YOU KNOW?

Trees and plants too were held to be sacred by Celtic peoples, especially the oak and the mistletoe.

Ancient Britons

- **Historians used to think** that the Celtic culture of Iron Age Britain was introduced by a series of invasions from mainland Europe.
- **They now believe** that new ideas and technologies were mostly adopted as a result of contact through trade and travel. In the late Iron Age there may have been some settlement of the southeast by Belgic Gauls.

▼ *People of Iron Age Britain lived in roundhouses like this, with a steeply pitched, thatched roof.*

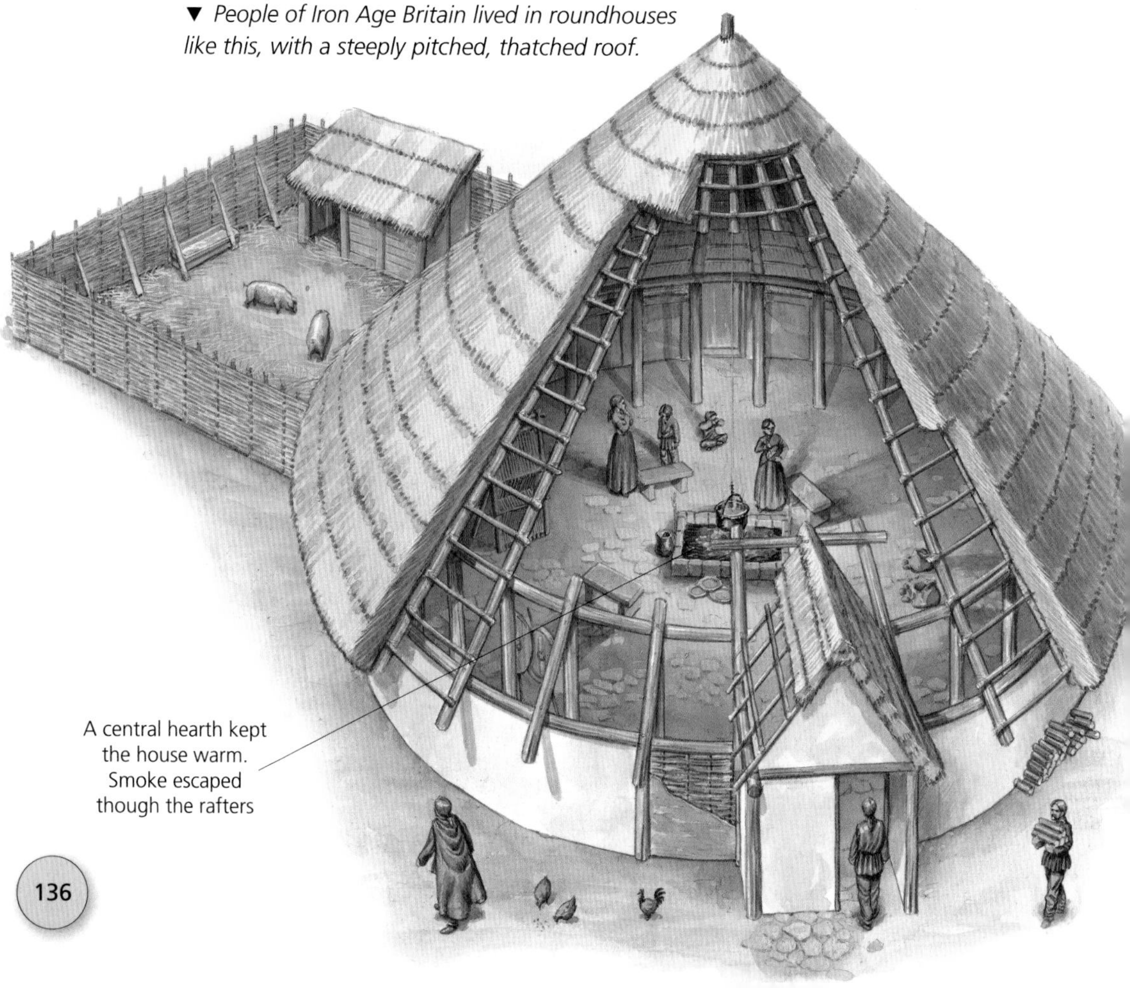

A central hearth kept the house warm. Smoke escaped though the rafters

- **The Iron Age** way of life had been adopted across the island of Great Britain by about 800 BC. The high point of the Celtic period coincided with the early period of La Tène art, from about 450–200 BC.
- **During the Iron Age** small communities living around hillforts developed into larger tribes, led by chieftains, nobles and druids.
- **By the 1st century BC** the rulers of the biggest tribes had become kings and queens. Women held considerable power in Celtic society.
- **The Britons lived** in thatched roundhouses, built of timber and clay or stone.
- **They cleared forests** and farmed the land, growing barley and wheat and raising cattle, pigs, goats and sheep. They ate apples, honey and hazelnuts.
- **They hunted wild boar** and deer in the woods. Like all Celts, they were fond of feasting, drinking and telling stories.
- **The Britons were skilled** with horses and chariots. Fighting might involve skirmishes with other tribes, but it was chiefly after Julius Caesar led the Roman army attacks on southern British tribes in 55–54 BC that full-scale warfare broke out.

Ancient Irish

- **Prehistoric Ireland** had first been settled from northern Britain in the Mesolithic period, about 8000 years ago. Farming began in the Neolithic period, about 5000 years ago. The Irish Bronze Age lasted from about 2500–500 BC.
- **Ireland's early history** is evidenced by impressive megalithic monuments and burial chambers, by bronze weapons and fine working in Irish gold.
- **Ireland's later mythology** describes various peoples such as the Fir Bolg and the Tuatha Dé Danann. It is possible that these stories reflect waves of settlement or invasions in ancient times.
- **The Irish Iron Age** begins in about 500 BC and unlike in Britain it remained uninterrupted by invading Romans. New settlers may have come westwards from Britain or northwards up the Atlantic coasts of western Europe.

▶ *The Iron Age Irish wore clothes of wool or linen, warm cloaks and jewellery.*

▲ *The Hill of Tara was an important site in Ireland from the Neolithic period, through the Iron Age to the early Middle Ages, when Ireland's High Kings were crowned by this ritual stone.*

- **With them** from about 400 BC came the culture of the Iron Age Celts, including in a few places examples of art in the La Tène style.
- **Irish Celts** were both warriors and herdsmen who valued cattle highly. Cattle raids were a common feature of everyday life.
- **The Irish revered Druids** and honoured the Celtic gods and festivals.
- **When Great Britain** was occupied by the Romans, the Irish traded and raided across the Irish Sea.

DID YOU KNOW?

Irish society was divided into tuatha (clans or tribal groupings), which later evolved into kingdoms.

The rise of Greece

- **As the Bronze Age** gave way to the Iron Age, Greece began to emerge from years of invasion, depopulation and famine. The period from about 800–500 BC is known as the Archaic period.
- **The Greek population** grew rapidly. City states (*poleis*, singular *polis*) were founded on islands and on the Greek mainland. From the word *polis* come modern words in English such as politics, police and polite.
- **A typical Greek city** had a hilltop citadel or acropolis with a temple, and a busy market place or agora.

- **Greek adventurers** founded colonies on the coasts of the Aegean and Anatolia, around the Black Sea and the Mediterranean, as far away as Italy and France.
- **Some city states** were ruled by kings, others by dictators known as tyrants. Some were governed by councils of wealthy aristocrats.

◀ *Greek cargo ships carried oil, wheat and wine for trading. The sailors painted eyes on either side of the prow in the hope they would scare away evil spirits.*

▲ *A Greek house may have looked like this 2600 years ago, with first-floor bedrooms overlooking a central courtyard.*

- **In 508 BC** a man called Cleisthenes brought in a new system of government in Athens. It was called democracy, meaning 'rule by the people'.
- **Women, slaves or foreign-born citizens** could not vote in the Athenian Assembly, but this marked the start of a political process that continues today.
- **Pottery**, writing and sculpture flourished.
- **The early Greeks** loved athletics, which formed part of religious rituals. The four Panhellenic (all-Greece) events were the Olympic, Pythian, Isthmian and Nemean Games.
- **The Olympic Games** started in 776 BC and became the most important. They were held every four years at Olympia.

Greece's golden age

- **The Greek city states** formed alliances or fought each other, but they did not unify as a single kingdom or empire.
- **There were several hundred** *poleis* in ancient Greece during the Classical period (500–336 BC).
- **Athens became a great centre** of culture, wealthy from its silver mines and protected by a powerful navy.
- **Sparta was a military state**, ruled by two kings. Its soldiers were trained to be tough and self-disciplined.
- **Greek soldiers** were called hoplites. They fought on foot with round shields, bronze, crested helmets and spears. The Spartans invented a packed wedge formation called a phalanx, which was hard to break up in battle.

- **Greek warships** with three banks of oars were called triremes. They had a narrow fighting deck and aimed to ram and sink the enemy fleet. Triremes were crewed by working people of the *polis*, not by slaves or professional sailors.
- **Between 499–449 BC** the Greek states repeatedly clashed with the might of the Persian empire. The Persians invaded twice, but were defeated in great battles at Marathon and Plataea.
- **Greece's Classical Age** laid the foundations for almost all European civilizations that followed, especially those of the Romans and the Byzantines.

◀ *The ancient Acropolis and the magnificent temple of the Parthenon still overlook the modern city of Athens*

Greek thinkers

- **The great thinkers** of ancient Greece were called philosophers. Philosophy is Greek for 'love of wisdom'.
- **The key philosophers** were Socrates, Plato and Aristotle.
- **Socrates (466–399 BC)** believed people would behave well if they knew what good behaviour was and challenged people to think about truth, good and evil.
- **Plato (427–348 BC)** argued that behind the messy chaos of everyday experience there is a perfect and beautiful Idea or Form. He also tried to find the ideal way of governing a state.
- **Aristotle (384–322 BC)** argued that for true knowledge you must find the 'final cause' – why something happens.
- **Aristotle was the first** great scientist, stressing the need to collect data, sort the results and interpret them.

▼ *Aristotle, the brilliant tutor to Alexander the Great, was thought of as the ultimate authority on almost every subject for over 2000 years.*

DID YOU KNOW?
Archimedes showed how the effect of a lever could be worked out by maths.

- **Many of the basic ideas** in philosophy, even today, come from Socrates, Plato and Aristotle, and other Greek philosophers such as Epicurus and Diogenes.
- **Greek mathematicians** such as Euclid, Apollonius, Pythagoras and Archimedes worked out many of our basic rules of maths. Most school geometry still depends on the system devised by Euclid.
- **Greek astronomers** like Aristarchus and Anaxagoras made many brilliant deductions – but many of these were forgotten. Aristarchus realized that the Earth turned on its axis and circled the Sun. Yet it was almost 2000 years before this idea was generally accepted.

▶ *Euclid, the great Greek mathematician and author of the 13-volume work* Elements, *was teaching in Alexandria around 300 BC.*

Greek arts

- **In the heyday of ancient Greece**, thousands of sculptors, architects, painters, dramatists and poets were creating a wealth of beautiful works of art.

- **The Greeks made graceful statues** and friezes to decorate temples and homes. They were carved mostly from marble and limestone and then painted, although in surviving statues the paint has worn away.

- **The most famous sculptors** were Phidias (*c.*490–420 BC), Praxiteles (*c.*330 BC), Lysippus (*c.*380–306 BC) and Myron (*c.*500–440 BC). Phidias' huge gold and ivory statue of the god Zeus was famed throughout the ancient world.

- **Greek architects** such as Ictinus and Callicrates created beautiful marble and limestone temples fronted by graceful columns and elegant friezes. The most famous is the Parthenon in Athens.

- **The Greeks had three styles** for columns: the simple Doric, the slender Ionic, topped by scrolls, and the ornate Corinthian, topped by sculpted acanthus leaves.

- **The style created** by the Greek temples of the Classical Period has inspired architects ever since.

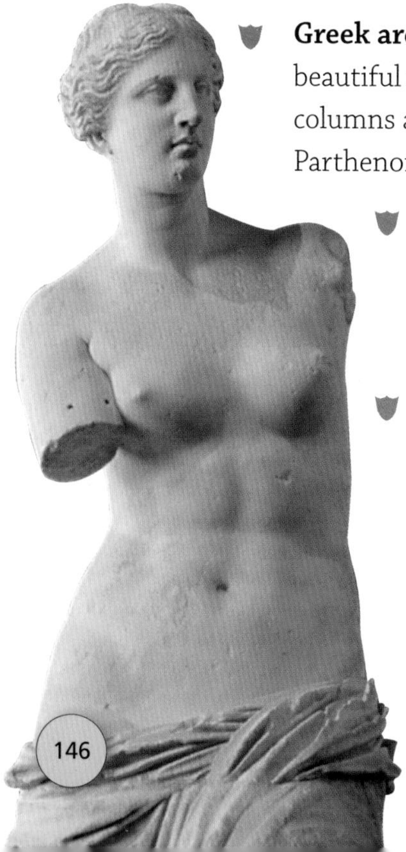

◀ The famous Venus de Milo was found on the Aegean island of Milos in 1820. It was carved in Greek Antioch (now in Turkey) around 150 BC and shows Aphrodite, the Greek goddess of love (known to the Romans as Venus).

1 Audiences took cushions to sit on and picnics to sustain them through very long plays.

2 A typical theatre, like the Theatre of Dionysus in Athens, seated 14,000 in stadium-like rows.

3 A 'chorus' of actors linked the scenes with verse and songs.

4 The circular acting area was called the orchestra.

5 Scenes were played by just two or three actors, each wearing a mask.

6 Behind the orchestra was a house or skene where the actors changed. Later, this became a backdrop.

7 In later Greek theatre, the skene developed side wings, called paraskinia.

▲ *Formal drama was developed in ancient Greece in the Archaic and Classical periods. Huge audiences watched plays in open-air arenas.*

- **The Greeks believed** that different arts (such as dance or poetry) were inspired by one of nine goddesses, who were known as the Muses.

- **Lyric poetry** (capable of being accompanied by a lyre) was typical of the Greek *polis*. Instead of telling an epic, heroic tale as Homer had done, lyric poets such as Sappho and Pindar expressed personal thoughts and feelings.

- **Greek drama** had its roots in religious festivals. It included both tragedy and, in the Classical Period, comedy. Great dramatists included Aeschylus, Euripides and Sophocles, who wrote the tragedy of King Oedipus.

DID YOU KNOW?

The Colossus of Rhodes was a huge 37-m-high statue cast in bronze by Chares of Lindos in 280 BC. It stood by the harbour on the Greek island of Rhodes.

Classical mythology

- **The Greeks believed** that Mount Olympus in northern Greece was the home of the gods.
- **Greek gods and goddesses** have human qualities. They act because of love, hate and jealousy.
- **Myths say** that giants called the Cyclopes gave Zeus the gift of thunder and lightning, and Poseidon the gift of a fishing spear called a trident, with which he could stir up sea storms, tidal waves and earthquakes.
- **The gods were believed** to have taught humans life skills: Zeus – justice, Poseidon – ship-building, Hestia – home-making, and Demeter – farming.
- **The gods** (except for Artemis, the hunter goddess) opposed human sacrifice and cannibalism. Zeus once punished King Lycaon for eating human flesh by turning him into a wolf.

▶ *The Greek sea god Poseidon, whose Roman name is Neptune, held a trident with which he could stir up waves into terrible sea storms.*

- **The Greek gods and goddesses** sometimes fell in love with humans. Their children were heroes, such as Heracles and Perseus.
- **The gods and goddesses** of ancient Greece were adopted by the Romans, under new names. Hence Zeus became Jove, Hera became Juno, Poseidon became Neptune, and so on.
- **The stories** about Greek and Roman gods, spirits and heroes are known as Classical mythology.
- **The ancient Greeks and Romans** believed that spirits called dryads lived inside trees.
- **In Latin**, the language of the Romans, *templum* means the space where a shrine to a god was erected. This is where the word 'temple' comes from.

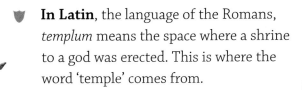

DID YOU KNOW?

Greeks and Romans would sometimes leave small offerings at the shrine of a god. These could be food, flowers, money or sweet-smelling incense.

Tales of the Titans

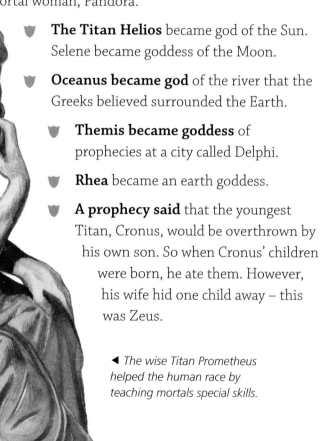

- **The Titans** were 12 immortals in Greek and Roman mythology. They were giants, and we still describe gigantic things as 'titanic'.
- **The strongest of the Titans** was Atlas – he held up the sky. The cleverest was Prometheus.
- **A Titan called Epimetheus** is said to have married the first mortal woman, Pandora.
- **The Titan Helios** became god of the Sun. Selene became goddess of the Moon.
- **Oceanus became god** of the river that the Greeks believed surrounded the Earth.
- **Themis became goddess** of prophecies at a city called Delphi.
- **Rhea** became an earth goddess.
- **A prophecy said** that the youngest Titan, Cronus, would be overthrown by his own son. So when Cronus' children were born, he ate them. However, his wife hid one child away – this was Zeus.

◀ *The wise Titan Prometheus helped the human race by teaching mortals special skills.*

- **When Zeus was older**, he fed Cronus a cup of poison that caused him to vomit up all the other children he had swallowed. These emerged as the fully grown gods and goddesses: Poseidon, Hades, Hera, Demeter and Hestia.
- **Zeus and his brothers and sisters** fought against the Titans for ten years. The Titans were finally overthrown when the gods and goddesses secured the help of the Hundred-handed Giants and the Cyclopes.
- **The Titans were hurled** into an underworld realm of punishment called Tartarus. There, they were bound in chains forever.

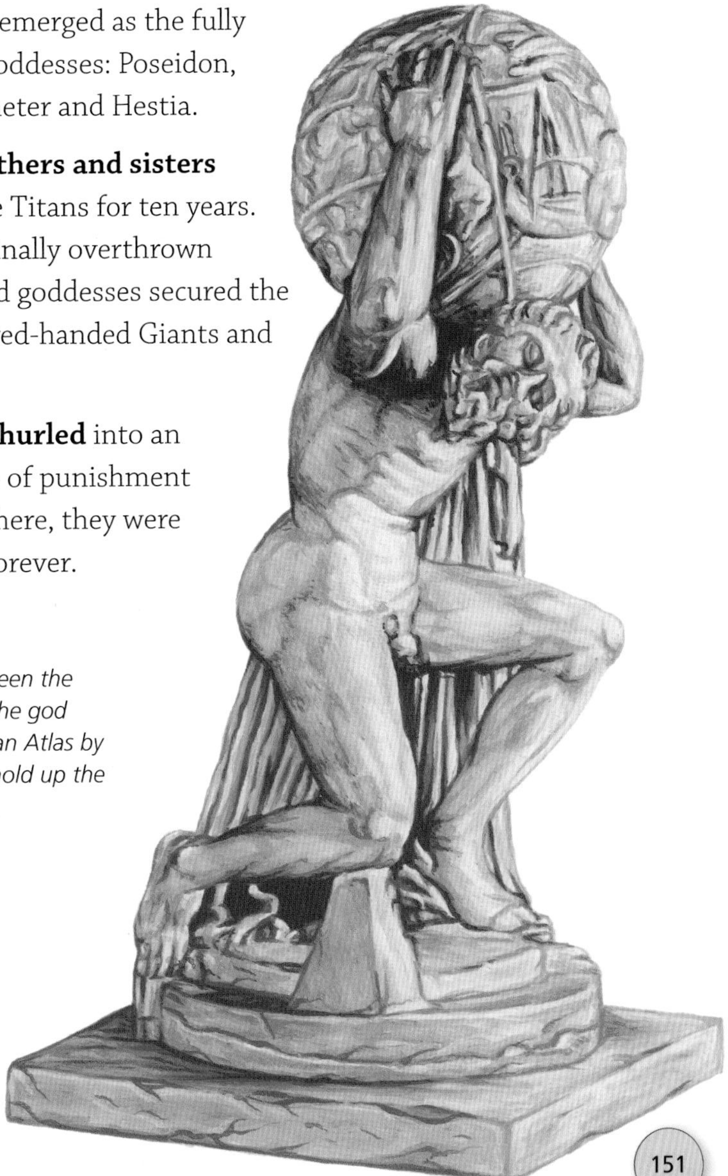

▶ *After the war between the gods and the Titans, the god Zeus punished the Titan Atlas by commanding him to hold up the skies on his shoulders.*

Alexander the Great

- **Alexander the Great** was a young Macedonian king who became one of the greatest generals in history. He built an empire stretching from Greece to India.
- **Alexander was born** in 356 BC in Pella, capital of Macedonia. His father, King Phillip II, was a tough fighter who conquered neighbouring Greece. His mother was the fiery Olympias.
- **As a boy**, Alexander was tutored by the famous philosopher Aristotle. A story tells how he tamed the unrideable horse Bucephalus, which afterwards carried him as far as India.
- **When Alexander was 20**, his father Philip II was murdered by a bodyguard and he became king. Alexander quickly stamped out rebellion.
- **In 334 BC**, Alexander crossed the narrow neck of sea separating Europe from Asia with his army. Within a year, he had conquered the Persian Empire.

▶ A modern statue of Alexander and his horse Bucephalus towers over the seafront at Thessaloniki in northern Greece.

- **In 331 BC**, Alexander led his army into Egypt, where he was made pharaoh and founded the city of Alexandria.
- **In 327 BC**, he married a Bactrian princess called Roxana.
- **After capturing** the city of Babylon and finishing off the Persian king, Darius III, Alexander led his conquering army into India.
- **Here his homesick troops** finally asked to go home. In 325 BC, Alexander had ships built and carried his army down the Indus River and returned to Babylon. Within a year, he fell ill and died.
- **On his death**, Alexander's vast empire was divided between his generals, who ruled in their own right. Greek ('Hellenistic') culture thrived in Asia and Egypt for several centuries.

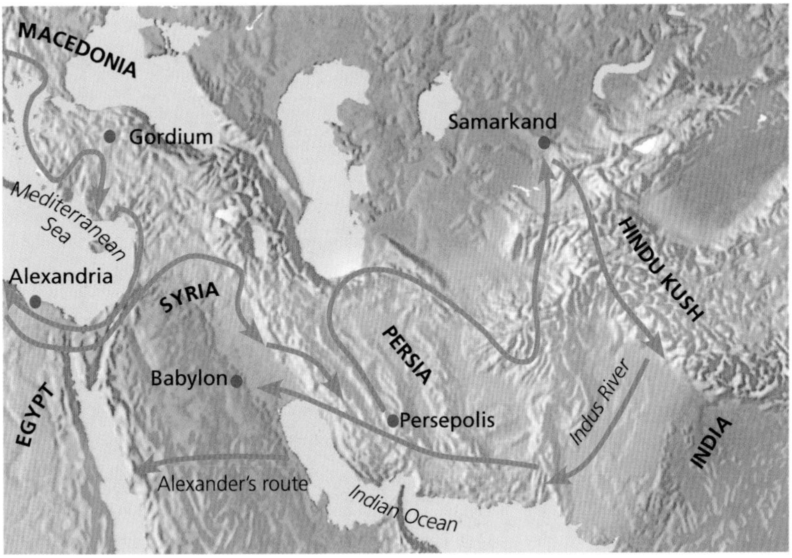

▲ *In just nine years and a series of brilliant campaigns, Alexander created a vast empire. No one knows exactly what his plans were. However, the teachings of his tutor Aristotle were important to him, and he had his own vision of different peoples living together in friendship.*

The Etruscans

- **After the Bronze Age**, the Iron Age Villanova culture dominated northern and central Italy from about 900–700 BC. Greek traders also began to influence the culture of the region.
- **From about 700 BC**, Etruria (the region of Italy now known as Tuscany) saw a new 'Etruscan' culture develop and then spread. The Etruscans founded 12 city states, including Rome itself.
- **Tradition suggested** that the Etruscans originally came to Italy from the Aegean region, but the latest DNA evidence makes it likely that they were from northern Italy.
- **Etruscan rulers suffered** from an uprising by the Romans in 509 BC. Soon they were also clashing with Greeks and Gauls. Divided amongst themselves, the Etruscans were eclipsed by the Romans in the centuries that followed.
- **The Etruscans** were skilled potters and brilliant metal workers, especially in gold. They were engineers and architects, mastering the building of arches, vaults and domes.

▶ *The Etruscans had a strong belief in the afterlife. They buried bodies or ashes in elaborate tombs, which reveal to us all kinds of details of their everyday lives.*

▼ *The spirit of ancient warfare is shown in this model of an Etruscan charioteer. The Etruscans had been defeated by about 280 BC.*

- **Like the Greeks**, the Etruscans were great seafarers, traders, colonisers and pirates.
- **The Etrucans produced** splendid tombs, with memorial figures in stone, clay or bronze. The statues show great humanity and an easy equality of status between men and women.
- **All aspects of life** in ancient Rome were greatly influenced by the Etruscans.

The Aeneid

- **Where did the Romans** come from originally? A Roman poet called Virgil, writing in 29 BC, provided an imaginative answer.
- **He was commissioned** by the emperor Augustus to write an explanation in the form of a grand poem, very like Homer's *Iliad* or *Odyssey*.
- ***The Aeneid*** was the result. This long epic poem follows the adventures of a Trojan prince called Aeneas, after the end of the Trojan War.
- **Aeneas was already a minor character** in *The Iliad*, fighting many times against the Greeks.
- **In the 6th century BC** it was popular to illustrate part of the legend of Aeneas on Greek vases – how Aeneas carried his father to safety out of the smoking ruins of Troy.
- **Virgil designed *The Aeneid*** to give Augustus and the Roman empire a glorious history. He explains that the gods themselves instructed Aeneas to travel to Italy, to be the ancestor of a great race – the Romans.
- **The poet shows** how Augustus Caesar was directly descended from the mighty hero.
- **In *The Aeneid***, Aeneas falls in love with Queen Dido of Carthage and then abandons her, sailing for Italy. Virgil probably made up this myth to explain the hatred that existed between Rome and Carthage in the 3rd century BC.

Virgil worked on the tale for the last ten years of his life. As he lay dying of a fever, he asked for the poem to be burnt. However, Augustus Caesar overruled his wishes.

DID YOU KNOW?

A great Italian poet called Dante Alighieri (1265–1321) used Virgil's style and legends of the Aeneid as the basis for his poem, 'The Divine Comedy'.

▼ *According to one ancient source, the poet Virgil was tall and dark with the appearance of a countryman.*

The birth of Rome

- **According to legend**, Rome was founded in 753 BC by the twins Romulus and Remus, who were said to have been brought up by a she-wolf.
- **By 550 BC**, Rome was a big city ruled by Etruscan kings.
- **In 509 BC**, the Roman people drove out the kings and formed themselves into an independent republic.
- **Republican Rome** was ruled by the Senate, an assembly made up of 100 patricians (men from leading families).
- **In theory**, Rome was governed by the people. However, real power was in the hands of patricians. Plebeians (ordinary citizens) had little say in matters of state. Slaves had no power or rights at all.

▼ Senators were men from leading families who had served the Roman republic as judges or state officials. They made new laws and discussed government plans.

- **Plebeians fought** for power and, by 287 BC, gained the right to stand as consuls, the highest official posts.
- **In the 400s and 300s BC**, Rome extended its power all over Italy, by both brute force and alliances.
- **By 264 BC**, Rome rivalled Carthage, the North African city that dominated the western Mediterranean. In 164 BC Rome destroyed Carthage totally after the three Punic Wars.
- **By 130 BC**, Rome had built a mighty empire stretching from Spain to Turkey and along the North African coast.

▼ *The first rules of the Roman legal system were recorded in 450 BC in a document called the Twelve Tables. The Roman system forms the basis of many legal systems today.*

The Romulus myth

- **The myth of Romulus and Remus** tells how twin boys grew up to build the foundations of the mighty city of Rome.
- **Versions of the myth** were written by many of the greatest Roman writers, such as Livy, Plutarch and Virgil.
- **According to the legend**, Romulus and Remus were descendants of the hero Aeneas. They were the sons of a princess and the war god, Mars.
- **As babies**, the twin boys were cast out by their evil great uncle, who had stolen the king's crown from their grandfather. They survived because a she-wolf found them and let them drink her milk. A bird also fed them by placing crumbs in their mouths.

▶ *The wolf's cave in Rome was known as the Lupercal, and in 2007 archaeologists located a shrine from the age of Augustus, which may have been honoured as this legendary site.*

- **When the twins** grew up they overthrew their wicked uncle, restoring their father to his rightful throne.
- **The twins built a new city** on the spot where they had been rescued by the she-wolf. However, they quarrelled about who should be ruler of the city, and Romulus killed Remus.

- **Romulus became king** of the new city and named it Rome, after himself.
- **The new city had too many men** and not enough women. Romulus hatched a plot whereby he held a great celebration and invited neighbouring communities – then captured all their women.
- **Romulus built a strong army** to defend Rome from attacks by local tribes. He brought about a 40-year period of peace.
- **One day**, Romulus was surrounded by a storm cloud and taken up to heaven, where he became a god.

▼ *You can still see the ruins of the mighty ancient city of Rome in the modern-day Italian capital. The huge round amphitheatre called the Colosseum overshadows the impressive central square, or Forum.*

Rome on the rise

- **By 290 BC** Rome had conquered all of Italy. By 146 BC it was in control of Greece.
- **As Rome's power spread**, the creation of plantations worked by slaves put small farmers out of work. The gap between rich and poor widened.
- **Many joined the army** to escape poverty and became more loyal to their generals than to the Senate (the government's ruling body).
- **Two popular generals**, Pompey and Julius Caesar, used their armies to take over Rome and suspend the Republic.
- **Julius Caesar** and Pompey argued, and after battles right across the empire, Caesar gained the upper hand.
- **Once in power**, Julius Caesar restored order and passed laws to reduce people's debts.

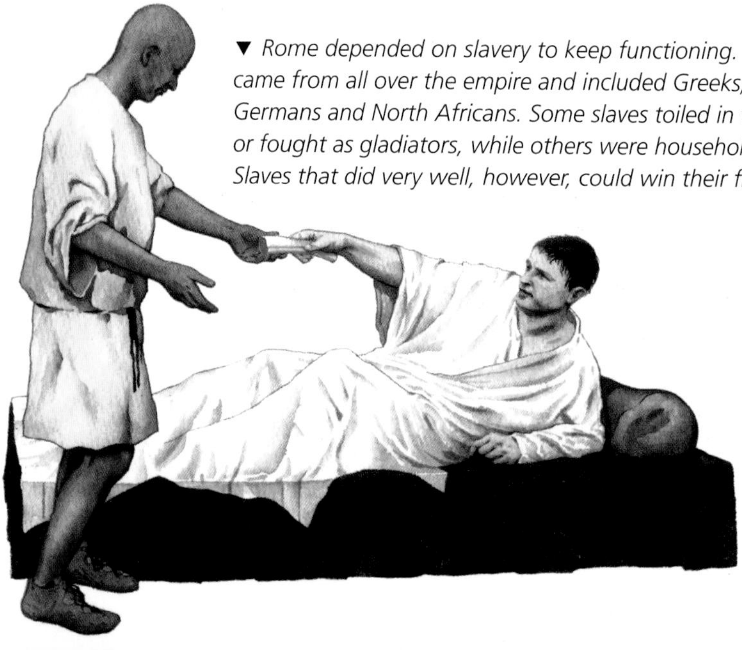

▼ *Rome depended on slavery to keep functioning. Slaves came from all over the empire and included Greeks, Britons, Germans and North Africans. Some slaves toiled in the mines or fought as gladiators, while others were household servants. Slaves that did very well, however, could win their freedom.*

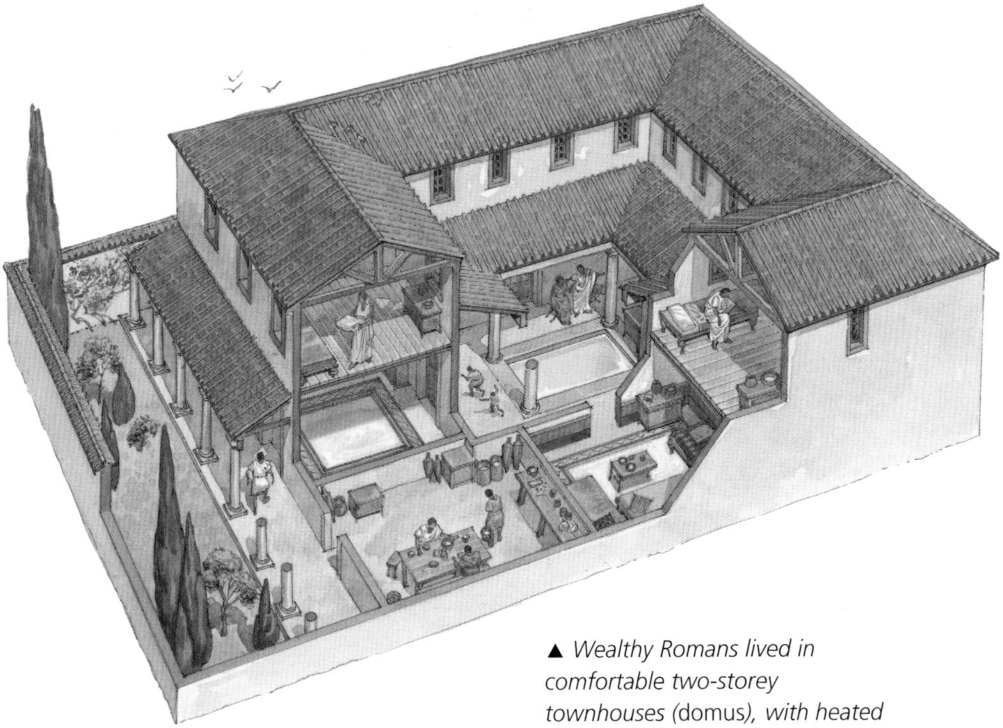

▲ *Wealthy Romans lived in comfortable two-storey townhouses (*domus*), with heated pools and underfloor heating.*

- **Caesar was made dictator** and ruled Rome without the Senate.
- **In 44 BC** a senator called Brutus killed Caesar to restore the Republic – but after many years of fighting, Caesar's place was taken by another general, Octavian, Caesar's great nephew and adopted son and heir.
- **By 27 BC** Octavian was so powerful that he took on the powers of an emperor under the name of Augustus.
- **During Augustus' reign**, rebellious parts of Spain and the Alps were brought under control and the empire was expanded along the Rhine and Danube Rivers.

Julius Caesar

- **Gaius Julius Caesar** (100–44 BC) was Rome's most famous general and leader. He was also a great speaker who had the power to excite huge crowds.
- **Caesar's individuality** was clear from the start. At 17, he defied Sulla, the dictator of Rome, and married Cornelia, the daughter of the rebel leader Cinna. Cornelia died when Caesar was about 30.
- **Caesar began as a politician** and made himself popular by spending his own money on public entertainments.
- **In 60 BC**, he formed a powerful but informal *triumvirate* (group of three people) with Crassus and Pompey, which dominated Rome.
- **In 58 BC**, Caesar led a brilliantly organized campaign to conquer Gaul (France), and in 55–54 BC he invaded southern Britain.
- **Pompey was alarmed** by the fame that Caesar's conquests brought him. The two began a war that lasted five years, ending in Egypt in 48 BC, where Caesar met and fell in love with Cleopatra.

◀ *A statue of Caesar in Rome, Italy. Caesar was not only a brilliant general, but a great statesman who brought in many reforms and tried to stamp out corruption.*

▲ *Caesar planned all kinds of bold economic, social and government reforms – but had been unable to carry many of them out by the time he was assassinated.*

- **By 45 BC**, Caesar had become the undisputed master of the Roman Empire. He was proclaimed dictator for life. Caesar was asked to become king, but he refused.
- **On 15 March, 44 BC** – a date known as 'the Ides of March' – Caesar was stabbed to death as he entered the Senate. His assassins were a group led by Brutus and Cassius, who thought that Caesar's ambitions posed a threat to Rome.

DID YOU KNOW?

Caesar wrote an account of his campaigns in Gaul that is a classic of historical writing.

Cleopatra and Rome

- **Cleopatra (69–30 BC)** was the last Macedonian Greek ruler of Egypt. She was descended from Ptolemy, a general of Alexander the Great who made himself king of Egypt after Alexander died.

▲ *Octavian described Cleopatra as a wicked temptress – and the idea has stuck. Her people in Egypt, however, thought of her as a great, just and much-loved queen.*

- **Cleopatra may have been beautiful**. She was certainly intelligent, charming and highly determined.
- **In 51 BC**, Cleopatra became queen when her father died. Her ten-year-old brother Ptolemy became king.
- **Ptolemy's guardians** seized power and drove Cleopatra out. She was restored to the throne by the Roman armies of Julius Caesar.
- **Legend has it** that Cleopatra had herself delivered to Caesar rolled up in a carpet. Whatever the truth, Caesar fell in love with her, and she had a son, Caesarion, by him.
- **Caesar invited Cleopatra** and Caesarion to Rome, where she stayed until 44 BC, when Caesar was brutally assassinated.
- **The Roman general** Mark Antony went to Cleopatra for her support in his bid for power in Rome. He too fell in love with her. They later married and had three children.

- **Mark Antony** returned to Rome to make a political marriage to Octavia, sister of Octavian. However, he soon returned to Cleopatra.
- **Mark Antony and Cleopatra** were ambitious and strove to take over the eastern part of the Roman Empire. However their armies were defeated at the Battle of Actium, off Greece, in 31 BC by the forces of Octavian (later known as the emperor Augustus).
- **As Octavian pursued them both** to Alexandria, Cleopatra spread rumours that she was dead. In despair, Mark Antony stabbed himself. He died in her arms. Cleopatra tried to make peace with Octavian but failed. She took her own life by placing an asp, a poisonous snake, on her breast.

▲ *Much has been made of Mark Antony and Cleopatra's romantic relationship, but theirs was also a strong political alliance.*

Roman power

- **For 200 years** after Augustus became emperor in 27 BC, Roman emperors ruled over an empire so large and secure that citizens could talk of the *Pax Romana* (Roman Peace).
- **The Romans built** straight roads to move their troops about quickly. On the whole, they governed peacefully and also built hundreds of towns in the Roman manner.
- **After Augustus died** in AD 14, his stepson Tiberius succeeded him. Then came a succession of Augustus' descendants, including Gaius, Claudius and Nero.
- **Gaius (AD 37–41)** was nicknamed Caligula ('little boots') because of the soldiers' boots he wore as a child.
- **Soon after Caligula** became emperor, an illness left him mad. He spent wildly, had people whipped and killed, married and murdered his sister and elected his horse as a minister. His enemies may have exaggerated stories about him, but he was eventually murdered by soldiers of the guard.
- **Claudius (AD 41–54)** replaced Caligula. People thought he was stupid because he stuttered and was physically disabled. However, he proved to be one of the wisest and most humane of all emperors.

▶ *Gladiators fought, often to the death, in big arenas called amphitheatres to entertain people.*

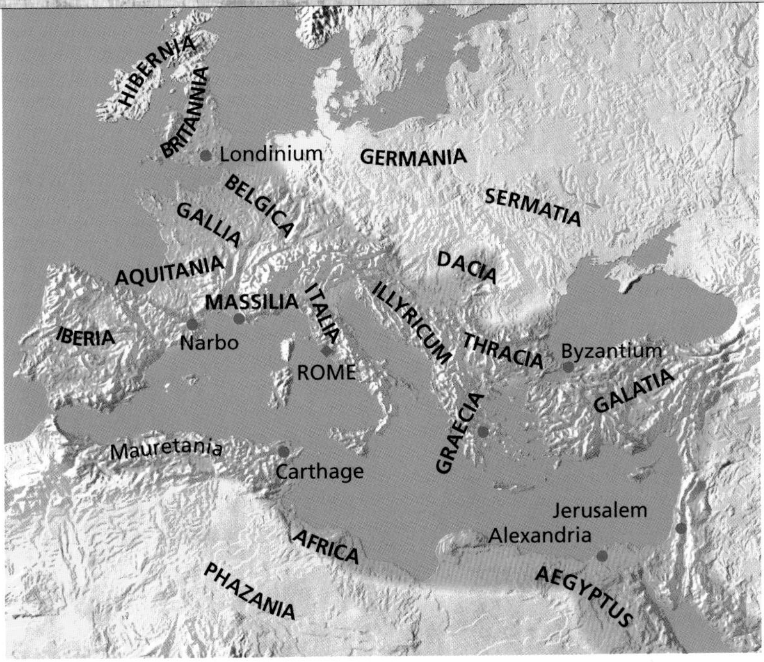

▲ *The orange area of this map shows the empire at its peak under the Emperor Trajan (AD 98–117). It was divided into areas called provinces, such as Britannia (England and Wales) and Gallia (France). Each had its own Roman governor.*

- **Claudius was probably poisoned** by his fourth wife Agrippina, who wanted power for her son Nero.
- **The power of Roman emperors** reached a peak under the 'Antonines' – Nerva, Trajan, Hadrian, Antoninus and Marcus Aurelius. They ruled from AD 96–180.

DID YOU KNOW?

Roman historian Suetonius claimed that Nero sang and played the lyre during Rome's great fire in AD 64.

- **The Roman Empire** grew only a little after Augustus's death. Britain was conquered from AD 43, and Emperor Trajan took Dacia (now Hungary and Romania).

Roman towns

▲ *The remains of the Forum in Rome give a glimpse of just how magnificent Roman cities must have been.*

- **Roman towns** were the biggest and most sophisticated the world had ever seen. They were not built on rigid grids like later Hellenistic cities, but they all had certain features in common.
- **A Roman town** had two main streets and many side streets with spaces in between called insulae (islands).
- **The insulae were tightly packed** with private houses – houses of the wealthy, called *domus* and tenement blocks (also called *insulae*). The bigger Roman houses had courtyards.
- **Traffic jams** were so common that many towns banned carts from the streets during daylight.
- **Most towns** had numerous shops, inns (*tabernae*), cafés (*thermopolia*) and bakeries (*pistrina*).

- **The forum** was a large open market and meeting place that was surrounded on three sides by a covered walkway. On the fourth side were the law courts and the town hall (basilica).
- **Most towns** had many grand temples to Roman gods.
- **There was a large open-air theatre** in most towns. There was also a games arena, or stadium, where warriors called gladiators fought and chariot races were held.
- **The bath houses** (*thermae*) were places where people came to sit around and dip into hot and cold baths in magnificent surroundings.
- **Towns had highly advanced** water supplies and sewage systems.

▼ *The town of Pompeii was buried by the eruption of Mount Vesuvius, in* AD *79. Today, tourists can walk the streets of the excavated site.*

The Roman legions

- **Rome owed its power** to its highly efficient and disciplined armies.
- **In a crisis**, Rome could raise an army of 800,000 men.
- **Under the Republic**, the army was divided into legions of 5000 soldiers. Legions were made up of ten cohorts. Cohorts, in turn, consisted of centuries containing 80–100 soldiers.
- **Each legion** was led by a *legatus*. A cohort was led by a *tribunus militum*. A century was led by a *centurion*.
- **Roman infantry** carried a short sword or *gladius* (60 cm long) and two throwing spears. They also wore armour – at first, vests of chainmail and a leather helmet; later, metal strips on a leather tunic and an iron helmet.

▼ *The tight testudo ('tortoise') formation protected troops from missiles as they advanced.*

- **The Roman army** also included foreign auxiliary (support) troops, cavalry and other specialist units.
- **After 100 BC**, most Roman soldiers were professionals, who joined the army for a 20 year term, but often served far longer before retiring. Food accounted for about a third of their wages.
- **In training**, soldiers went on forced 30-km marches three times a month. They moved at 3 km per hour, carrying very heavy packs.
- **Soldiers were flogged** for misbehaviour. Mutiny was punished by executing one in ten suspects. This was called decimation.
- **Roman armies** built huge siege engines and catapults when they had to capture a town.

▶ *Roman soldiers had to be tough – while on the march they carried all their weapons and armour, plus a pack filled with clothes, food and tools for digging and building.*

How Romans lived

- **In the big cities**, or in luxurious country villas, rich Romans had a comfortable way of life.
- **For breakfast**, Romans typically ate bread or wheat biscuits with honey, dates or olives, and water or wine.
- **A Roman lunch** (*prandium*) consisted of much the same items as breakfast.
- **Romans had the main meal** (*cena*) in the afternoon, typically after a visit to the baths. This became a very lavish affair with three main courses, and each course had many dishes.
- **Rich Romans** had a lot of free time, since slaves did all the work. Leisure activities included gambling by tossing coins (*capita et navia*) and knucklebones (*tali*).
- **Public entertainments** were called *ludi* (games). They included theatre, chariot races, and fights with gladiators and animals.
- **The Emperor Trajan** held a gladiator contest that lasted 117 days and involved 10,000 gladiators.
- **Romans had more slaves** than any empire in history. Some were treated cruelly, but others lived quite well.
- **Between 73–71 BC**, a Thracian gladiator called Spartacus led a revolt of slaves that lasted two years, until it was crushed by Roman armies.

DID YOU KNOW?

The Circus Maximus chariot racetrack in Rome held up to 250,000 spectators.

▼ *These are the Roman baths at Bath, in England. Public baths were places to relax, talk, do business, clean and oil one's body, have a massage or take exercise.*

Roman Britain

- **The European frontier** of the Roman empire ran along the rivers Danube and Rhine, along coastlines and cliffs. It was guarded by forts and fortified towns, by naval bases, watchtowers and beacons.
- **The northwestern frontier** ran through northern Britain. The Roman conquest of Britain began in AD 43, when general Aulus Plautius landed his army in Kent.
- **There was a major uprising** led by Queen Boudicca of the Iceni tribe in AD 60, but by AD 78 the Romans had most of what is now England and Wales under control.

▼ *Hadrian's Wall ran from the River Tyne to the Solway Firth. It was an expression of Roman power, and may have served as a series of checkpoints and economic controls as well as a defence.*

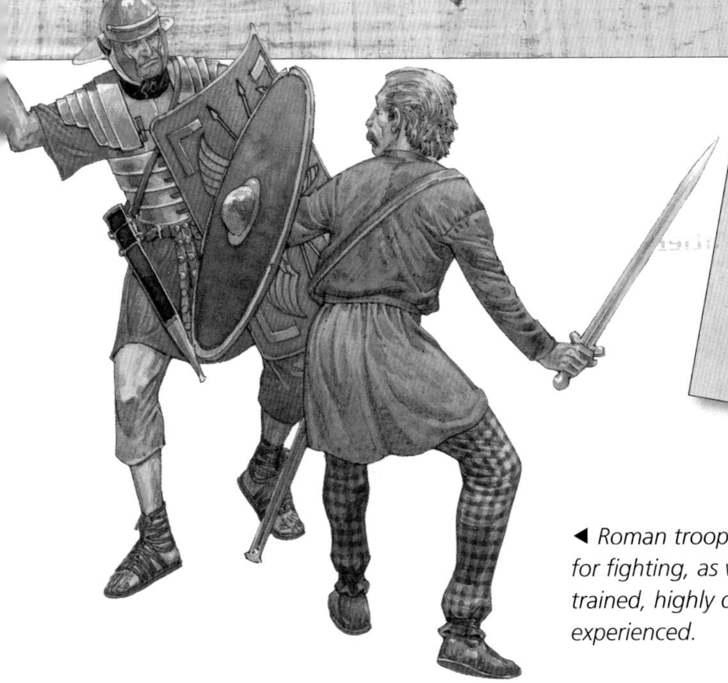

DID YOU KNOW?
The Romans built the first proper towns in Britain, with typical Roman features such as baths and theatres.

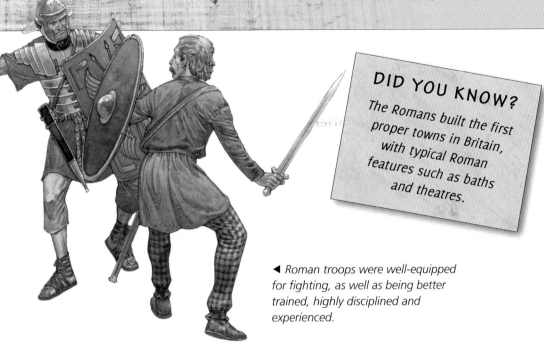

◀ *Roman troops were well-equipped for fighting, as well as being better trained, highly disciplined and experienced.*

- **They advanced** into the lands of the Caledonii (modern Scotland) but could not hold the far north permanently. Built in AD 122–130, the 118-km-long stone wall that is now called Hadrian's Wall became Rome's final frontier.
- **The Roman army** in Britain was powerful. There were three legions (5000 men each) at York, Chester and Caerleon, plus 40,000 auxiliaries.
- **Roman Britain** was ruled by a Roman governor, but the Romans co-opted local chiefs to help. Contact between rulers and ruled created a culture known as Romano-British.
- **During the 3rd and 4th centuries AD**, Roman power seemed less secure. There were mutinies and power struggles. Irish raiders attacked in the west. Picts from beyond the Wall raided the north and Germanic Saxon warriors attacked southeastern coasts.
- **By AD 410** the Romans had withdrawn their legions from Britain.

Jesus Christ

- **Jesus Christ** was ~~one of~~ the world's great religious leaders. The religion of Christianity is based on his teachings.
- **The dating system** based on Jesus' birth is slightly inaccurate. He was a Jew, probably born between 4–1 BC at Bethlehem, in Palestine. At this time Rome controlled most of the region.
- **Our knowledge** of Jesus' life comes from four books in the Bible's New Testament: the gospels of Matthew, Mark, Luke and John. He is also mentioned by ancient historians such as Tacitus and Josephus.
- **The Bible tells** how his young virgin mother, Mary, became miraculously pregnant after a visit by the archangel Gabriel, and that Jesus is the only Son of God.

▼ *Many Christian pilgrims come to see the Church of the Nativity in Bethlehem, the supposed site of Jesus' birth.*

DID YOU KNOW?

After his death, Jesus was said to have been resurrected – brought to life again.

▶ *The word 'Christ' is actually a title. It comes from the Greek word* Christos, *which means 'anointed one'.*

- **Little is known** of Jesus' childhood. His teaching began after he was baptized by John the Baptist at the age of 30.
- **Jesus' mission** was to announce that the Kingdom of God was coming. From his many followers, he chose 12 apostles to help him spread the word.
- **Jesus is said** to have performed many miracles.
- **Many Jews felt** that Jesus was a troublemaker. They had the Roman governor, Pontius Pilate, put him to death by crucifixion (nailing to a cross).

Early Christians

- **The first Christians** were Jews in Palestine, but followers like Paul soon spread the faith to gentiles (non-Jews) and countries beyond Palestine.
- **At this time**, new religions and cults were becoming popular in the Roman Empire. At first, Roman rulers tolerated Christians, but after AD 64, they saw Christians as a threat and persecuted them.
- **Persecution strengthened Christianity** by creating martyrs such as St Alban, a Romano-British citizen who was beheaded between AD 209–305.
- **In AD 313**, the Roman emperor Constantine gave Christians freedom of worship and called the first great ecumenical (general) Church council in AD 325.
- **By AD 392**, Christianity was the official religion of the Roman Empire.
- **The Roman Empire split** into East and West, and eventually the Church did too. The West focused on Rome, and the East on Constantinople. The head of the Western church was the Pope, and the head of the Eastern church was called the Patriarch.
- **The first Pope** was Jesus' apostle St Peter, and there has been an unbroken line of popes ever since. The power of the popes really began with St Gregory, in AD 590.
- **Many early Christians** began to live apart as monks in religious communities called monasteries. These became centres of learning. From about AD 400 monks began to spread the Christian faith across northwest Europe.

▼ *Constantine was a successful and well-regarded soldier. When he became emperor he became known as Constantine the Great. He made Christianity legal, so that it could become the official religion of the empire.*

The fall of Rome

- **After the death** of the emperor Marcus Aurelius in AD 180, Rome was plagued by serious political struggles.
- **The Praetorian Guard** (the emperor's personal soldiers) chose or deposed emperors at will – there were 60 emperors between AD 235 and 284 alone.
- **The empire fell into anarchy** and was beset by famine, plague and invasions.
- **Diocletian** (emperor from AD 284) tried to make the empire easier to govern by splitting it in two – East and West.

▼ *After the emperor Constantine moved his capital there in AD 330, Byzantium (now Istanbul in Turkey) became the main defender of Roman civilization.*

▶ *This coin was minted during the reign of Constantine. The inscription translates as 'Constantine, dutiful and wise ruler'.*

- **Constantine**, commander of the Roman armies in Britain, defeated his rivals to become emperor. It is said that before the main battle, he saw a Christian cross in the sky. After his victory, he became Christian.
- **In AD 330**, Constantine made Byzantium (modern-day Istanbul) his capital and called it Constantinople.
- **After Constantine's death**, the empire fell into chaos again. It became split permanently into East and West.
- **The Western empire** increasingly suffered attacks from peoples outside the empire. Vandals invaded Spain and North Africa. Goths attacked from the North.
- **In AD 410**, Western Goths (Visigoths) led by Alaric invaded Italy and sacked Rome, burning and looting. In AD 455, Vandals sacked Rome again. In AD 476, the Western empire finally collapsed.
- **The Eastern empire** continued in various forms through the Middle Ages, but Europe's Classical age was now ended.

The invaders

- **Who were the invaders** who closed in on Rome's empire in the west in these years? The peoples of the empire called them 'barbarians'. They regarded them as uncivilized and outlandish.
- **The word 'barbarians'** was first used by the ancient Greeks, to describe peoples from outside their classical, urban world.
- **To the Romans**, the barbarians seemed ill-disciplined in battle. They rode horses and appeared in vast, wild, terrifying hordes.
- **It was true** that these peoples rarely lived in large towns. They often lived in forts or farming settlements, or were on the move in search of new territory.
- **Many were brave warriors**, but many were also skilled craftsmen and poets.
- **The Goths were Germanic peoples** who overran the western Roman Empire in the 4th and 5th centuries AD. They were divided into Ostrogoths in the east, near the Black Sea, and Visigoths on the River Danube. It was the Visigoths who, under their king Alaric, finally broke Rome in AD 476.
- **The Vandals were a German tribe** who arrived in Europe from the east in the 1st century BC. When driven west by the Huns in about AD 380, they took over Spain and North Africa. Vandals swept through Italy in AD 455 to sack Rome.
- **The Huns were nomads**, possibly from the steppes of Mongolia, who arrived in Europe in about AD 370, driving out everyone before them, until they were finally defeated in AD 455.

- **Western Europe** saw invasions by Germanic peoples – Franks, Angles, Saxons, Jutes and many more.
- **The 'barbarians' soon mixed** with the peoples of the empire and adopted Roman traditions and the Christian faith. These were the makers of medieval Europe.

▼ *Alaric was the great Gothic leader who took Rome in AD 410. He looted the city but spared the churches. Alaric planned to settle in Africa, but a storm forced him to stop at Cozenza in southern Italy, where he died.*

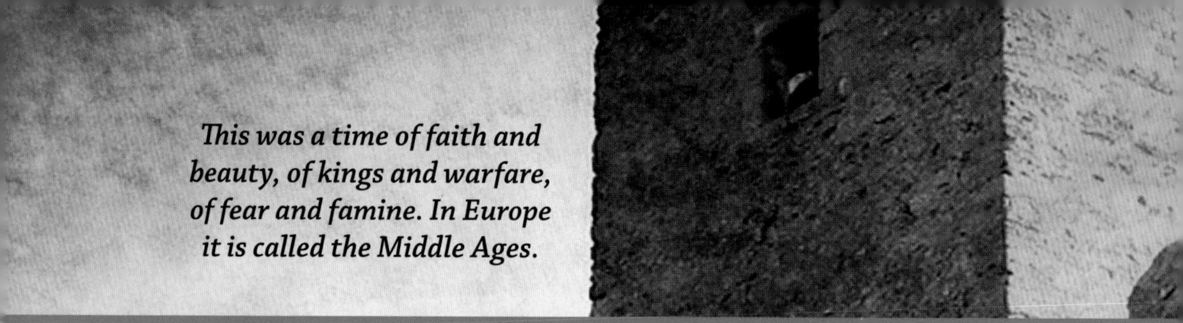

This was a time of faith and beauty, of kings and warfare, of fear and famine. In Europe it is called the Middle Ages.

AFRICA

641
Arabs conquer Egypt and advance across North Africa.

c.830–c.1235
Empire of Ghana, West Africa.

c.900
Rise of the Swahili culture on the East African coast.

c.1000s–1300s
The stone-walled stronghold of Great Zimbabwe.

c.1200
Rock-hewn Christian churches in Ethiopia.

c.1230
Rise of the Mali empire in West Africa.

c.1390
Rise of the kingdom of Kongo, Central Africa.

c.1430
Rise of the Songhai empire in West Africa. University at Timbuktu.

EUROPE

539
The great church of Hagia Sophia, Constantinople (capital of the Byzantine empire).

711
Moorish Muslims invade Spain.

787
Earliest recorded raid by Viking warriors.

800
The Frankish king Charlemagne is crowned emperor in Rome, a predecessor of the Holy Roman Emperors.

882–1240
Kievan Rus, a federation of Eastern Slavs.

1030
Normans expand into southern Europe. They conquer England in 1066.

1096
Christian Europe embarks upon the First Crusade, aiming to recapture Jerusalem.

1453
Constantinople falls to the Ottoman Turks, end of the Byzantine empire.

ASIA

618–907
The Tang dynasty rules China. Prosperity, due to trade along the Silk Road.

661
The Umayyad Caliphate rules from Damascus, replaced by Abbasid rule from Baghdad in 750.

710
Rise of the centralized Nara state in Japan.

802–1351
The Khmer empire of Cambodia, 12th century temple of Angkor Wat.

848–1279
Height of the Chola kingdom in southern India. Temple-building and influence across Southeast Asia.

960–1279
Song dynasty in China. Inventions, advanced technology and culture.

1096
Start of the Crusades, a series of wars between Christians and Muslims in southwest Asia.

1206
The Mongol leader Genghis Khan begins his conquest of Asia.

The Medieval World

NORTH AMERICA

c.600–1400
Cahokia, a Native American city beside the Mississippi River.

c.900–1100s
Thule culture, based on whaling, spreads from Alaska to Greenland.

c.900–1200
Irrigation canals being dug in the Southwest.

980s
Vikings from Norway and Iceland settle along the coasts of Greenland.

1000
Vikings attempt to settle on the coasts of Labrador and Newfoundland.

c.1050–1125
Height of the ancient Pueblo cultures around Chaco Canyon, in the Southwest.

c.1200
Maize farming and chiefdoms known as the Southeastern Ceremonial Complex.

c.1400–1500
Ozette, a maritime hunting village in Washington State (later preserved under a mudslide).

CENTRAL AND SOUTH AMERICA

c.600–950
The Tiwanaku empire is at its height in Bolivia.

c.600–800
The Late Classic period of the Maya. The city of Tikal in Guatemala is rebuilt.

c.600–1200
The Maya city of Chichen Itza in Yucatán, Mexico.

c.600–1100
The Wari empire thrives in Peru.

c.800–1000
Toltec rule in central Mexico, with its capital at Tula.

c.900–1000
The great city of Chan Chan established as capital of the Chimú empire in northern Peru.

1428
In the Valley of Mexico, the Aztecs form a powerful Triple Alliance with Texcoco and Tlacopan.

1438
Founding of the Inca empire, with its capital at Cuzco in Peru.

OCEANIA

c.900
Aborigines mining rock at Mount Isa, Queensland, Australia.

1100
Increased agriculture and irrigation on the Hawaiian islands.

c.1250
Powerful chiefdoms grow up across the Pacific.

c.1250
Giant stone statues called moai erected on Rapa Nui (Easter Island).

c.1250
Funeral of the great Melanesian chief Roy Mata, on Vanuatu.

c.1285
Polynesians settle in Aotearoa (New Zealand) establishing the Maori culture.

c.1350
The hill fort or *pa* is built during New Zealand's Maori Classic period.

c.1400
Moas (giant birds) are hunted to extinction on New Zealand.

Byzantine empire

- **In AD 476**, when the Roman Empire finally collapsed in the west, Rome's eastern capital, Constantinople, continued as a great centre of civilization. Its rise and fall mark the limits of the Middle Ages.
- **In the six years** after Constantine made this city his capital, builders, architects and artists created one of the world's most magnificent cities.
- **Constantinople was at the focus** of trade routes between Asia and Europe. Silks, gems and ivories were traded for gold, grain, olives and wine. By charging 10 percent on all goods coming in and out, the city became rich.
- **When the great emperor** Justinian I came to the throne in AD 527, he tried to rebuild the Roman Empire. His general, Belisarius, reconquered Italy, and by AD 565 this 'Byzantine' Empire (named after the ancient city of Byzantium) stretched right around the Mediterranean.
- **Justinian built** hundreds of churches, including the famous Hagia Sophia. He also modernized Roman law, to create what is still the basis of many Western legal systems. This is called the Code of Justinian.

▶ *Justinian I was the greatest Byzantine emperor, although his general's secretary, Procopius, described him as 'a demon incarnate'. He ruled with his beautiful former actress wife, Theodora. Justinian relied on her for support and advice, and it was she who changed laws to improve the lives of women and the poor.*

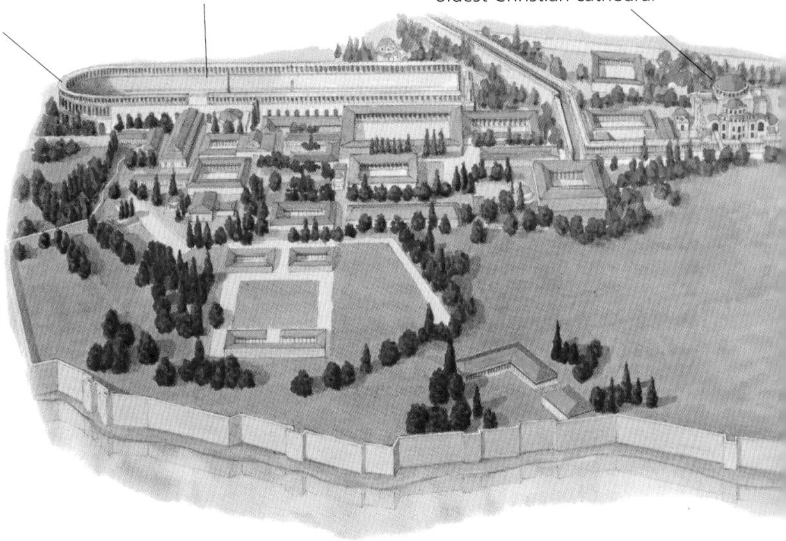
The Hippodrome was based on the Circus Maximus in Rome
60,000 spectators watched chariot races here
The Hagia Sophia, now a museum, is the world's oldest Christian cathedral

▶ *At its height, Constantinople was graced by some of the ancient world's most magnificent buildings. This picture shows the tranquil palace quarter. The rest of the city was noisy and crowded.*

- **The Byzantine Empire** was under constant attack – from Goths, Huns, Persians, Avars, Bulgars, Slavs, Vikings, Arabs, Berbers, Turks, even Christian Crusaders.
- **It repelled attackers**, often with its secret weapon, 'Greek fire', invented in AD 650. This was a mixture of quicklime, petroleum and sulphur, which burst into flames when it hit water.
- **In 1204**, Constantinople was ransacked by Crusader knights who were short of money. Almost every treasure in the city was stolen and it never recovered from this devastating blow. The city's population dwindled from one million to just 60,000 over the next 200 years.
- **Constantinople** was finally conquered by the Turkish sultan Mehmed II in 1453.

DID YOU KNOW?

Of the 88 Byzantine emperors, 29 died violent deaths. Endless conspiracies at court have given us the word 'Byzantine' for dark intrigues.

Monks and nuns

IN NATALE SCI
VENZEZLAVVI
DVCIS ET MARTI
SCDM LVCAM
IN ILLO TEMP
DIXIT
IHC DIS
CIPVLIS SVIS
SIQVIS VENIT
AD ME·ET NON ODIT PATRE
SVV ET MATREM ET VXOREM ET
FILIOS ET FRATRES ET SORORES·
ADHVC AVT ET ANIMA SVA·N POTE
MEVS ESSE DISCPLS·ETQ NON BAIO
LAT CRVCE SVA ET VENIT POST ME·
NON POTEST MEVS ESSE DISCPLS·
QS ENI EXVOLENS TVRRIM EDIFI
CARE N PRIVS SEDENS COPVTAT

▲ *Irish and Anglo-Saxon monks laboured to create beautiful illustrated books by hand. This is the Lindisfarne Gospel.*

- **In both** Christianity and Buddhism, some devout people step out of ordinary life and live in a monastery, a community devoted to religion.
- **The earliest Christian monastery** was that of St Anthony of Thebes, who went to live in the Egyptian desert in about AD 271, and attracted loyal followers. St Basil the Great (*c.*AD 329–379) and his sister Macrina the Younger founded monasteries for men and women on their estate in Cappadocia (now in Turkey).
- **The founding** of religious communities is called monasticism. It spread rapidly throughout the Byzantine Empire between the 4th and 7th centuries AD.
- **In the West**, monasticism grew more slowly, so St Martin of Tours (AD 316–397) sent out monks to start new communities.
- **They were very successful** in Britain and Ireland. Monasteries such as Lindisfarne and Malmesbury were centres of learning in the early Middle Ages. The great scholar-monk St Bede (*c.*672–735) was known for his *Ecclesiastical History of the English People.*

- **One inspirational monastic settlement** in the British Isles was on the Scottish Isle of Iona, founded by the Irish abbot Colm Cille (St Columba) in 563.
- **St Benedict** (*c.*480–547) developed a particular way of living for monks at Monte Cassino, Italy. By the year 1000, many monasteries followed Benedictine rules.
- **Monasteries in northern Europe** were very vulnerable to raids by the Vikings, who were not Christian. Monks were often killed and many treasures looted or destroyed.

▶ *Before the days of mass-printing, monks hand-copied texts because they needed books for their studies.*

The Frankish kingdoms

- **When Gaul was part** of the Roman empire, some of its Celtic population were enslaved or driven away, but over the years other Gauls adopted a 'Gallo-Roman' way of life, speaking Latin.
- **In the later days** of Roman rule, Germanic tribes began to attack the empire. The Romans used other Germanic tribes to help them defend their borders, rewarding them with land. In AD 357 one of these groups, the Franks, was even allowed to set up a kingdom in Gaul.
- **In AD 486**, Clovis, a king of the Salian Franks, invaded and created a new 'Merovingian' kingdom covering modern France and Belgium.
- **The name 'France'** comes from the Franks. Both Gauls and Franks were ancestors of the French. The Bretons are descended from Britons who settled in Brittany in the fourth and fifth centuries AD.

▶ *Charles II of France, or Charles the Bald (823–877), fought many wars against his half brothers Louis the German and Lothair. In 843 the Treaty of Verdun gave Charles the rule over the part of the empire that formed the basis for France.*

DID YOU KNOW?

Franks were outnumbered 20 to one by Gallo-Romans – but France is named after them.

▲ *This part of the cathedral in Aachen (Aix-la-Chapelle) was built for Charlemagne between 796–805.*

- **After Clovis's death** in 511, the Merovingian kingdom was divided and weakened. However in about 719, some Merovingian kings allowed a man called Charles Martel ('the hammer') to take control in the north with the title 'Mayor of the Palace'.
- **In 732** Charles Martel defeated a Moorish Muslim army at Tours, and took control of southern France.
- **The greatest** of the Frankish rulers was Charlemagne (Charles the Great), who became King of Italy as well, and was crowned emperor in Rome on Christmas Day 800. His lands became known as the Carolingian empire.

Charlemagne

- **Charlemagne** ('Charles the Great', 742–814) was perhaps the greatest ruler of medieval Europe. He became King of the Franks in 768.
- **His father** was Pepin the Short, son of Charles Martel. Pepin had made sure of his family's hold on power in the Frankish kingdom.
- **Taking his armies** on 53 successful campaigns, Charlemagne was a great military leader. He scored victories against the Moors in Spain, and against Saxons and Avars in central Europe.
- **By 796** Charlemagne had created an empire joining France, Germany, northern Italy and northern Spain.
- **He was a Christian**, and in 800 it was Pope Leo III who crowned Charlemagne 'Emperor of the Romans'. His Carolingian empire was a predecessor of the Holy Roman Empire (962–1806).

▲ *After Charlemagne's death, many legends grew up about him. This beautiful goblet ('Charlemagne's cup') dates back to the time of the Crusaders.*

- **Charlemagne** was a great ruler who set up an effective legal system and introduced the idea of juries in trials.
- **Charlemagne knew** Latin, German and Greek, and he encouraged scholarship, helped by the great teacher Alcuin of York.
- **The palace school** in Charlemagne's capital, Aachen, was the most important school in Europe.

▼ *The scholar Alcuin of York presents manuscripts to the court of Charlemagne, which became an important centre of learning.*

Kingdoms of the Britons

- **After the Romans left Britain**, most of the land was divided into small kingdoms, such as Rheged in the northwest or Elmet in the northeast. These lands were ruled by kings who still followed the Romano-British way of life, and were Christian.
- **In the far north** the Picts ('painted people') had escaped Roman conquest.
- **Attacks on the island of Britain** continued. Germanic invaders (Angles, Saxons, Jutes and Frisians) poured across the North Sea. Irish raiders attacked western shores.
- **The Britons' fight** against the Saxon invaders, ancestors of the English, would continue for many centuries. One legendary figure of this struggle was Arthur. If he existed at all, he would have been a war leader of the early 6th century. Later in the Middle Ages, storytellers hailed Arthur as a great king with many knights. These fanciful tales became popular as far away as France, Germany and Italy.

▼ *Tintagel Castle in northern Cornwall. This area features in the myths and legends about King Arthur.*

▶ *Welsh warriors patrol the borders of the Kingdom of Powys.*

- **Gradually the Germanic invaders** advanced westwards and northwards through Britain, creating 'Anglo-Saxon' kingdoms. British kingdoms became isolated in the far west, in Cornwall, Wales, Cumbria and Strathclyde. The invaders called these western Britons 'Welsh', meaning 'strangers'. The Britons called themselves 'Cymry', meaning 'compatriots'.
- **The ancient British language** had now developed into early forms of Welsh and Cornish. The masterpieces of the earliest Welsh poets, such as the 7th century Aneirin and Taliesin, were written down later in the Middle Ages.
- **Medieval kingdoms** in Wales included Brycheiniog, Ceredigion, Deheubarth, Gwent and Morgannwg. In the long run the northern kingdom of Gwynedd proved the most powerful. Almost all of Wales was united under Llywelyn ap Iorwerth ('the Great', *c*.1172–1240).

Kingdoms of Ireland and Scotland

- **Ireland and most of Scotland** had escaped rule by the Roman empire.
- **The Irish** were converted to Christianity in the 5th century AD, during the mission of a western Briton called St Patrick.
- **At the end** of the Roman era, the greatest ruler of the Gaels was probably Níall of the Nine Hostages, who became High King of all Ireland and died in about AD 405.
- **Níall founded** the O'Neill dynasty, which shaped Irish history through the Middle Ages.
- **In the early Middle Ages** Ireland was divided into five provinces. These later became four – Connacht, Leinster, Munster and Ulster. At this time Ireland produced beautiful books and jewellery.

◀ *The Irish monk St Columba (or Colmcille, 521–597) founded churches in Scotland and preached the Christian faith to the Picts.*

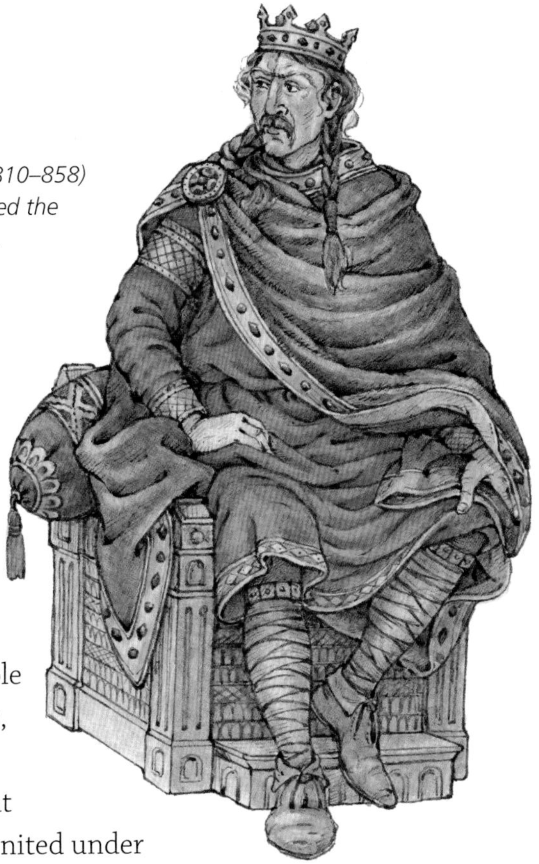

▶ *Legends tell how Kenneth MacAlpin (810–858) united the Picts and the Scots and founded the dynasty that would later rule all Scotland.*

- **Northern Gaels** known as Scoti created a kingdom called Dál Riata, which by the late 6th century stretched from Ulster to the isles and western mainland of what became known as 'Scotland'.
- **The future of Scotland** as a whole would be decided by rival Britons, Scots, Picts, Angles and Norse invaders. It was not until 843 that northern Scotland or 'Alba' was united under Kenneth MacAlpin.
- **In the 900s and 1000s**, many people fought to be king in Scotland. Kenneth III killed Constantine III to become king. Malcolm II killed Kenneth III, and Duncan I who followed him was killed by his general, Macbeth. Macbeth was killed by Malcolm III.
- **Malcolm III's wife** was Saint Margaret (1045–1093), brought up in Hungary where her father was in exile.

Anglo-Saxons

▶ *In 1939, a burial ship, probably of the overlord Raedwald (d. 625), was discovered at Sutton Hoo in East Anglia. This helmet is one of the treasures it held.*

- **The Angles**, Saxons, Jutes and Frisians were Germanic peoples who invaded Britain and settled there in the 5th and 6th centuries AD. Together they are known as 'Anglo-Saxons' and are ancestors of the English.
- **The Britons resisted**, but by 650 they were driven back into the west or made slaves.
- **Angles settled in East Anglia** and the Midlands, the Saxons in Sussex, Essex and Wessex (Dorset and Hampshire). Each group of invaders formed its own small kingdom.
- **Seven leading kingdoms** formed a 'heptarchy' – Essex, Kent, Sussex, Wessex, East Anglia, Mercia and Northumbria.
- **One king was the 'Bretwalda'** (overlord), but the kingdoms vied for power.
- **When Ethelbert of Kent** was Bretwalda, in 597, St Augustine of Canterbury converted him to Christianity. Christianity spread rapidly throughout the Anglo-Saxon kingdoms.

- **A synod** (Christian conference) in Whitby in 664 confirmed the customs of the Roman Church over those of the Celtic Christians. Monks and scholars travelled across Europe.
- **Most Anglo-Saxons** lived in farming settlements. They were fierce warriors, and brilliant craft workers in metal and jewellery
- **In the 9th century** another wave of raiding and invasion began, this time from Scandinavia. Anglo-Saxon England and the Celtic kingdoms of Wales, Scotland and Ireland were attacked by people referred to as Northmen, Danes or Vikings.

▼ Anglo-Saxon buildings were made from materials such as wood, thatch, wattle (interwoven branches) and daub (clay).

Beowulf

- **The Germanic speech** of the Anglo-Saxons became the basis of the English language.
- **The epic poem** Beowulf was written in Old English by an unknown poet in around 700–750.
- **The tale focuses** on the adventures of a Viking hero, named Beowulf. The action takes place in the south of Sweden and Denmark.
- **The poem blends** traditional elements of Norse mythology and warrior culture with belief in a Christian god.
- **Beowulf risks his own life** to help other people by battling three terrifying monsters: Grendel, Grendel's mother, and a dragon.
- **The monster Grendel** is said to bear 'the mark of Cain'. This is a reference to the Bible story in which Adam's son Cain killed his brother Abel.
- **Beowulf is fatally wounded** when all his chosen warriors desert him through fear – except for his courageous nephew Wiglaf.
- **At the end of the poem**, the dead Beowulf is laid to rest in a huge burial mound. A similarly impressive burial mound, dating around AD 650, was discovered at Sutton Hoo in Suffolk in 1939.
- **The oldest manuscript** of Beowulf that exists today was copied from an original version by monks, in about 1000. Many other older copies were destroyed when King Henry VIII ordered the monasteries and their libraries to be closed down in the late 1530s.

The only remaining copy of Beowulf is kept in a controlled environment behind glass in the British Museum, in London, England.

▼ *Beowulf has to descend to the depths of a murky lake to fight the monster Grendel's ferocious mother.*

Alfred the Great

- **Alfred the Great** (849–899) was the greatest of the Anglo-Saxon kings.
- **Alfred became King of Wessex** in 871, at a time when the Danes (Vikings) had overrun East Anglia, Northumbria and Mercia.
- **In 878**, a series of ferocious Danish attacks drove Alfred to hide on the Isle of Athelney, in the Somerset marshes.
- **A legend tells** how Alfred took refuge in a swineherd's cottage. He was so tired he fell asleep by the fire, letting some cakes burn. Not realizing he was the king, the swineherd's wife scolded him.
- **From Athelney**, Alfred secretly assembled an army and emerged to score a decisive victory over the Danes at Edington. The Danes agreed to withdraw to East Anglia and their king Guthrum became a Christian.
- **In 886**, Alfred recaptured London and forced the Danes to stay within an area called the Danelaw.

▶ *This enamel and gold jewel was found near Athelney. It is inscribed with the words* Aelfred mec heht gewyrcan *– Old English for 'Alfred had me made'.*

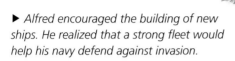

▶ *Alfred encouraged the building of new ships. He realized that a strong fleet would help his navy defend against invasion.*

- **Alfred built forts**, reorganized his army and also created England's first navy to defend the country against invasions.
- **A wise and kindly king**, Alfred created sound laws, protected the weak from corrupt judges and made laws to help the poor and needy.
- **Alfred was a scholar** who encouraged learning. He decreed that all young men should learn to read English, and made important books available in English.

DID YOU KNOW?

Alfred translated many books from Latin into English so that his people could read them.

Early English kings

- **Egbert, King of Wessex** from 802–839, became in effect the first king of England when he conquered Mercia at Ellandun in 829 – but his rule lasted just a year before Mercian king Wiglaf claimed it back.

- **For 100 years**, much of England was lost to the Danes, but Alfred the Great's son Edward and his daughter Aethelflaed gradually drove the Danes out by 918.

- **England's kingship** really began with Athelstan, crowned 'King of all Britain' at Kingston-upon-Thames on 4 September, 925.

- **'Ethelred the Unready'** was King of England between 978–1013 and 1014–1016. *Rede* was old English for advice, and his name meant he was always badly advised.

- **Ethelred created** so much distrust among his subjects that the Danes easily reconquered England in 980.

- **In 1013**, the Dane Sweyn Forkbeard became King of England.

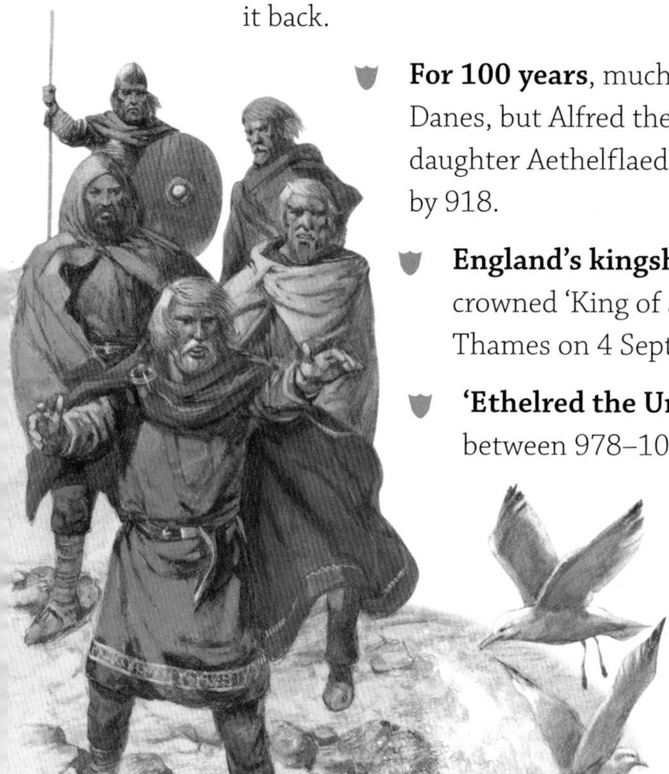

▲ *Canute, or Cnut, ruled England and much of Scandinavia, but was keen to demonstrate that only God ruled the waves.*

- **When Sweyn died**, Ethelred made a comeback until Sweyn's son, Cnut or Canute, drove him out. Cnut became king in 1016 by marrying Ethelred's widow.
- **Cnut ruled well**. A legend tells how he rebuked flatterers by showing how even he could not stop the tide coming in.
- **After Cnut**, in 1035, came Harold I ('Harefoot', 1035–1040), followed by Harthacnut (1040–1042). Ethelred's son, Edward the Confessor, then became king – but the Danes did not want a Saxon king.
- **The Danes called** on their Norwegian allies, led first by Magnus then Harald Hardrada, to win back the throne.

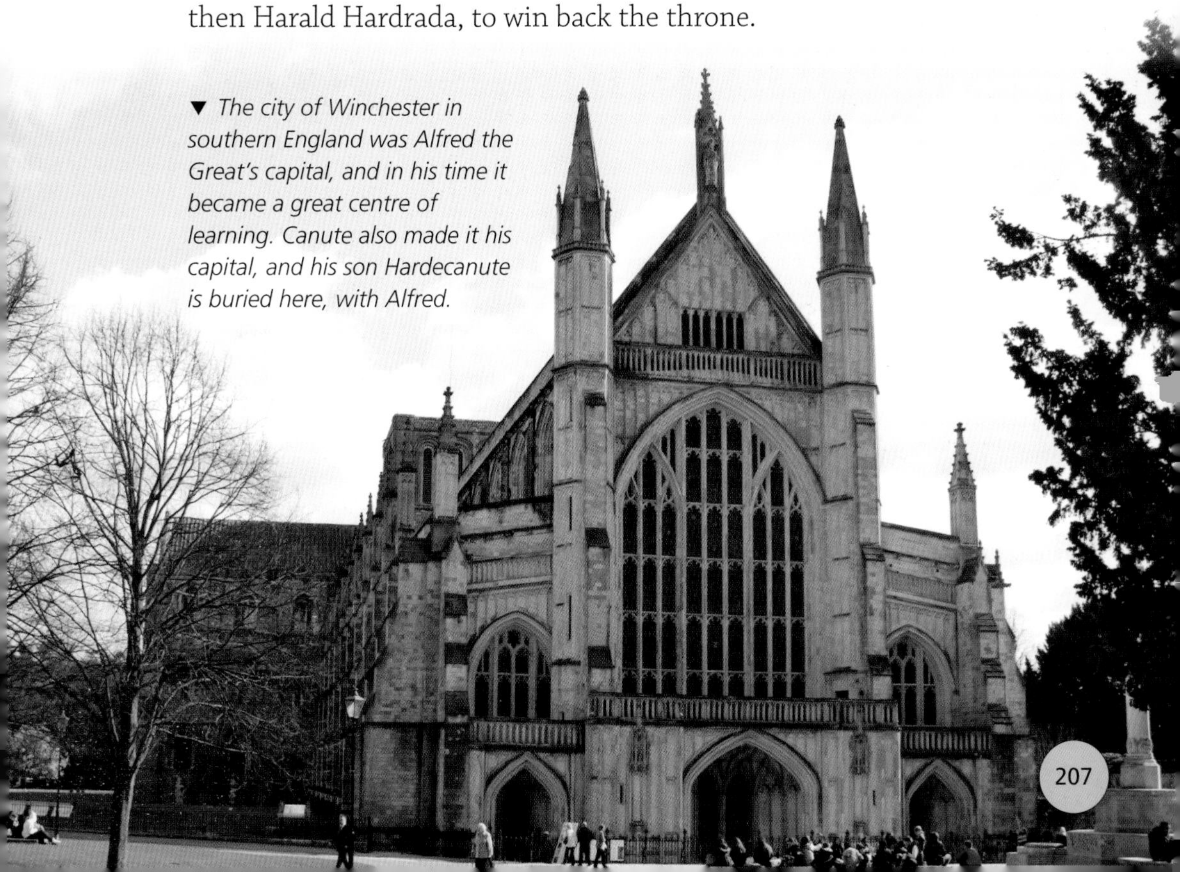

▼ *The city of Winchester in southern England was Alfred the Great's capital, and in his time it became a great centre of learning. Canute also made it his capital, and his son Hardecanute is buried here, with Alfred.*

The Vikings

- **The Vikings were daring raiders** from Norway, Sweden and Denmark. From the 790s onwards they swept in on the coasts of northwest Europe in their longships, searching for rich plunder to carry away.
- **People were terrified** by the lightning raids of the Vikings. A prayer of the time went, 'Deliver us, O Lord, from the fury of the Norsemen (Vikings). They ravage our lands. They kill our women and children'.
- **Vikings prided themselves** on their bravery in battle. Most fought on foot with swords, spears and axes. Rich Vikings rode on horseback.
- **Shock troops** called berserkers led the attack. *Berserk* is Norse for the 'bearskin shirt' they wore. Before a battle, they worked themselves into a rage. They trusted in their god Odin to keep them safe.

▶ *At home, most Vikings were farmers. The women were left in charge when their husbands went raiding.*

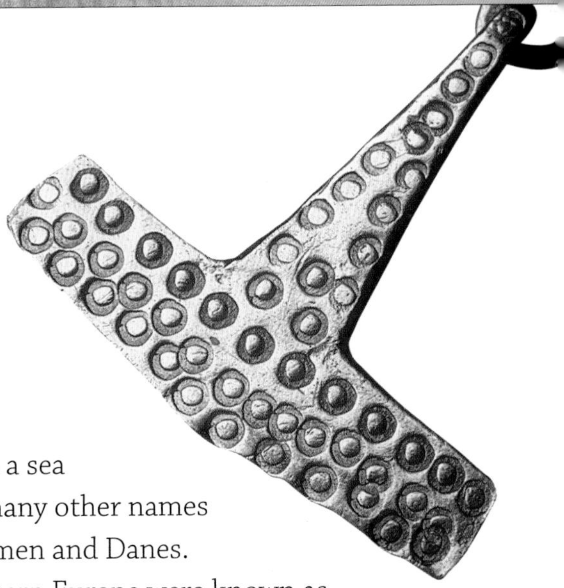

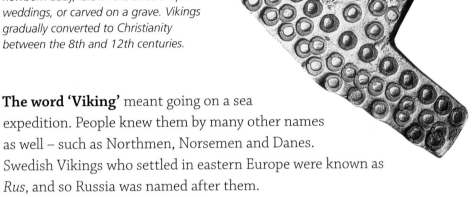

▶ *A hammer symbol represented the Viking god Thor. It would be raised over a newborn baby, laid in the bride's lap at weddings, or carved on a grave. Vikings gradually converted to Christianity between the 8th and 12th centuries.*

- **The word 'Viking'** meant going on a sea expedition. People knew them by many other names as well – such as Northmen, Norsemen and Danes. Swedish Vikings who settled in eastern Europe were known as *Rus*, and so Russia was named after them.

- **When they were not seafaring**, raiding or settling new lands, the Vikings lived by fishing and farming, or by trading. They were fine carvers of wood and walrus ivory, metalworkers and storytellers.

- **Vikings settled permanently** in Britain, Ireland, France, Iceland and Greenland. They raided as far as Gibraltar and into the Mediterranean.

- **In eastern Europe**, the Vikings' ships carried them inland up various rivers. They ventured through the Ukraine into Russia, and served as the imperial guard in Constantinople, which they called Miklagard ('great city').

DID YOU KNOW?
In November 885, Count Odo and 200 knights fought heroically to defend Paris against a Viking army, but the city was reduced to ashes.

- **The Norsemen** who settled in northern France were called Normans. The Norman king, William the Conqueror, who invaded England in 1066, was descended from their leader, Hrolf or Rollo.

Viking society

- **Vikings ate beef**, cheese, eggs and milk from their farms, meat from deer, elks and seals caught by hunters, and fish such as cod, herring and salmon.

- **Viking houses** were one-storey, with no windows. The walls were of timber or stone, with pitched roofs of turf or straw. At the centre was a hearth for warmth and cooking. The man of the house sat on a chair called the high seat; the rest of the family sat on benches.

◄ *Viking women looked after the children and the home, but also had more rights than was common for women at this time.*

◀ *Viking god Odin was said to ride on an eight-legged horse called Sleipnir, accompanied by two ravens that brought him news of any battles.*

- **Men wore trousers** and a long-sleeved smock shirt. Women wore long woollen or linen dresses.
- **Marriages were arranged** by parents, and men were allowed to have two or three wives.
- **A Viking woman**, unusually for the time, could own her own property and divorce her husband.
- **Skalds (Viking poets)** went to battle to report on them in verse.
- **Great storytellers**, the Vikings told of their adventures in long stories called sagas.
- **At first**, sagas were only spoken. From about 1100–1300, they were written down.
- **Vikings were religious** and had several gods. They believed if they died fighting they would go to Valhalla, a special hall in Asgard, home of the gods.

DID YOU KNOW?

Laws were passed and people were judged at a Viking assembly called the Thing.

Viking voyages

- **Great seafarers**, the Vikings made some of the most remarkable voyages of the Middle Ages.
- **The Vikings sailed across** the Baltic Sea and up the Vistula and Dnieper rivers.
- **They also sailed** west around the British Isles, and south around Spain into the Mediterranean.
- **The most daring voyages** were out across the still unknown open waters of the North Atlantic.
- **From 900**, the Vikings sailed to, and settled on islands to the far north – including Iceland, the Faroes and Greenland.
- **In about 800**, Vikings led by Ohthere reached the remote Siberian islands of Novaya Zemlya in the Arctic.
- **In 986**, Bjarni Herjólffson was blown off course sailing home from Greenland and saw an unknown shore.

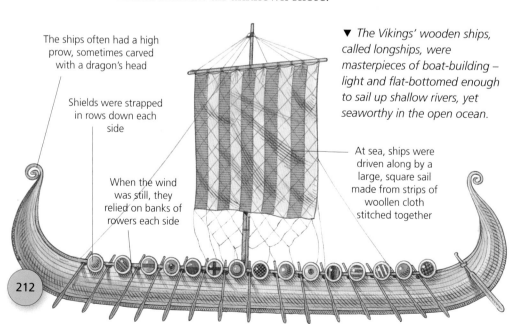

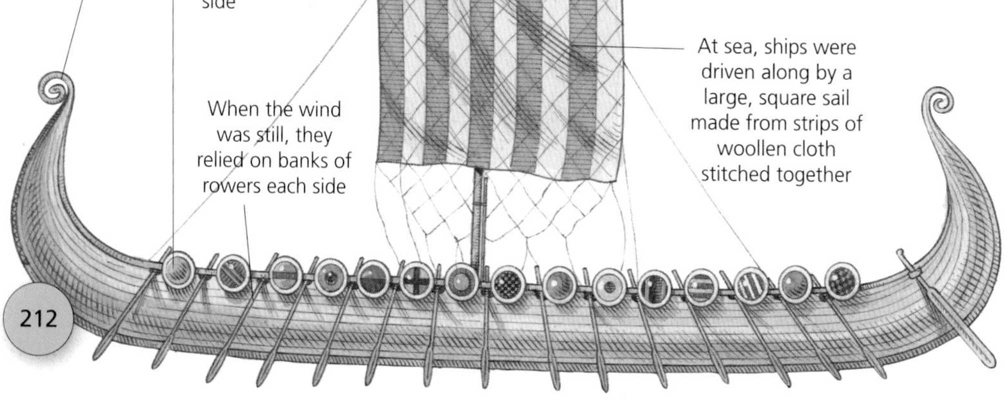
The ships often had a high prow, sometimes carved with a dragon's head
Shields were strapped in rows down each side
When the wind was still, they relied on banks of rowers each side
At sea, ships were driven along by a large, square sail made from strips of woollen cloth stitched together

▼ *The Vikings' wooden ships, called longships, were masterpieces of boat-building – light and flat-bottomed enough to sail up shallow rivers, yet seaworthy in the open ocean.*

- **Leif Eriksson** sailed west to find this shore. The Norse sagas tell how he found a new land. The Vikings called it Vinland, as it was abundant in 'wine berries' (probably cranberries).
- **Most experts** now think Vinland is North America, and that Leif was probably the first European to reach it.
- **In 1004**, Thorfinn Karlsefni took 130 people to settle in Vinland and stayed three years. Remains of a Viking settlement were found in 1963, at L'Anse aux Meadows, on the northern tip of Newfoundland.

▼ *Viking weapons included a spear, knife and protective shield. Vikings held their weapons sacred.*

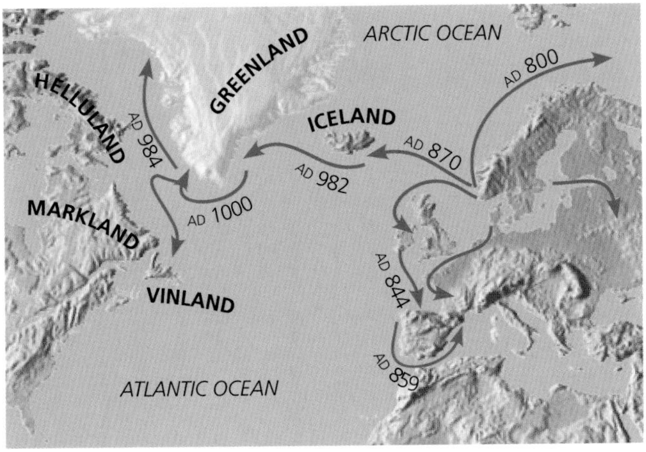

◀ *This map shows just some of the remarkable voyages made by the Vikings, and their approximate dates. The names shown are the Viking names.*

Norse creation myths

- **Norse mythology** tells how in the beginning there was a huge emptiness called Ginnungagap. A fiery southern land called Muspellheim first came into existence, then a freezing northern land called Niflheim.
- **The fires** eventually began to melt the ice, and the dripping waters formed into the very first being: a wicked Frost Giant, named Ymir. More Frost Giants were formed from Ymir's sweat.
- **The next being** that grew from the thawed ice was a cow called Audhumla. Audhumla licked an ice block into a male being called Buri.
- **Buri's grandchildren** were the first three Norse gods: Odin, Vili and Ve. They killed Ymir and threw his body into Ginnungagap. His flesh, blood, bones, hair, skull and brains became the earth, seas, mountains, forests, sky and clouds.
- **Dwarfs came into existence** before human beings. They grew from maggots in Ymir's flesh.
- **Odin, Vili and Ve** created the first man, Ask, from an ash tree and the first woman, Embla, from an elm. The gods gave humans a world called Midgard.
- **The gods tried** to keep the evil giants away by giving them a separate land, Jotunheim.
- **The gods built** themselves a heavenly homeland called Asgard.
- **A rainbow bridge** links the realm of the gods to the world of humans. The god Heimdall was set as watchman to make sure only gods and goddesses could cross.

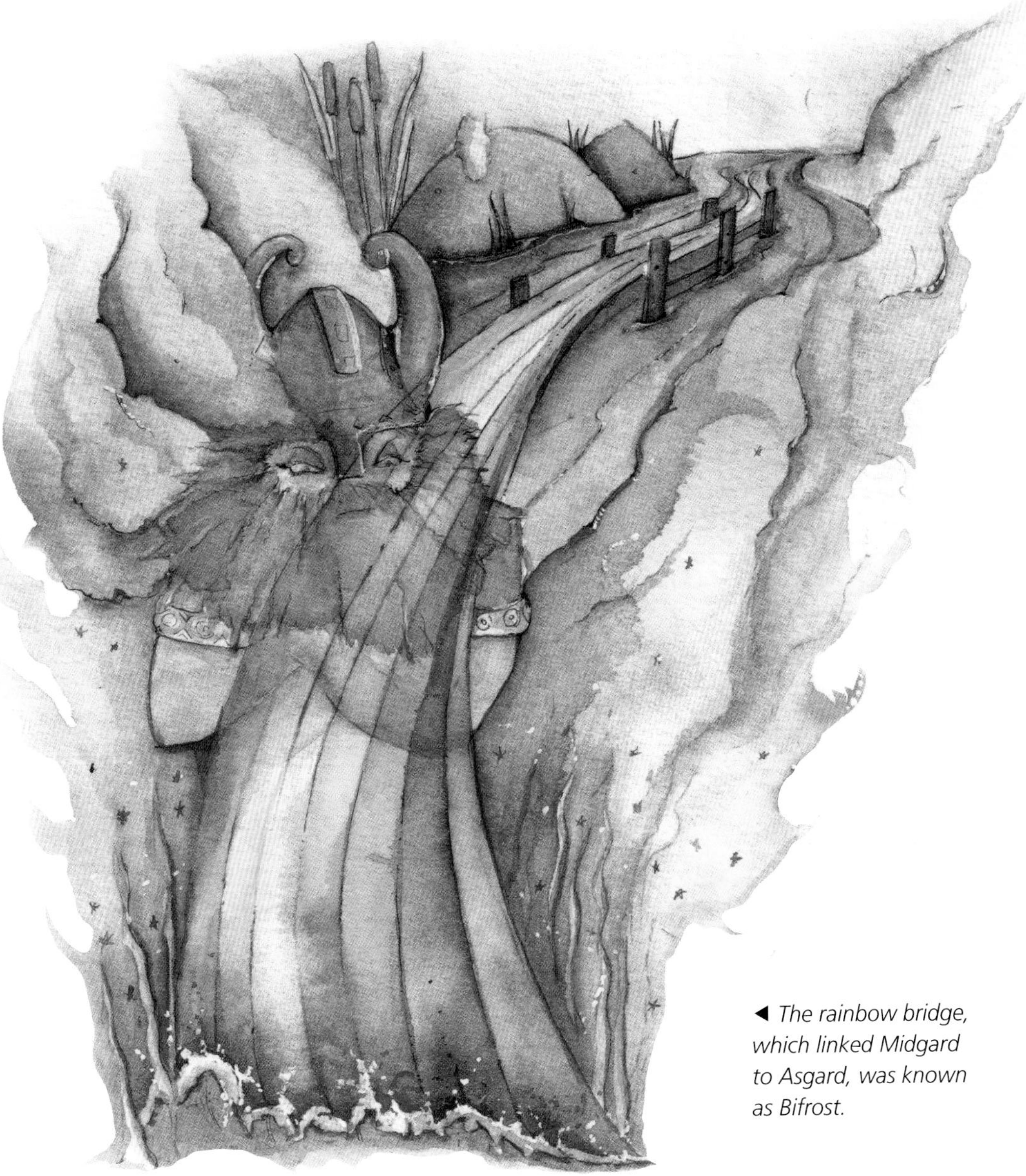

◀ *The rainbow bridge, which linked Midgard to Asgard, was known as Bifrost.*

Warrior gods and goddesses

▲ *The chariot of the goddess Freya was pulled by two cats.*

- **Ancient Norse myths** tell of a race of gods and goddesses called the Aesir.
- **Odin, chief of the gods**, has a high throne called Lidskialf, from which he can see anything happening in the universe.
- **The Norse gods** do not take much notice of humans. They are more concerned with battling giants and dealing with other magical creatures.
- **Odin occasionally** likes to disguise himself as a traveller and wander undetected through the world of humans.
- **The most important** warrior goddesses are Odin's wife, Frigg (a mother goddess with fertility powers),and the beautiful Freya (goddess of love).
- **Norse gods** and goddesses are not immortal. They can be killed by fighting in battle or by cunning magic.
- **The daughters of Odin** were beautiful spirits called Valkyries. They flew over battlefields and took warriors who had died bravely to live happily in Odin's great hall, Valhalla.
- **The Aesir** once fought against gods and goddesses called the Vanir ('shining ones'). They finally made a peaceful alliance against the giants.

- **The ruler of the Vanir** was the fertility god Njord, ruler of the winds and the sea.

- **The Scandinavians** shared their gods with other ancient Germanic peoples, such as the Anglo-Saxons. In English, four days of the week are named after Norse gods. Tuesday is named after Tyr (god of valour), Wednesday after Woden (Odin), Thursday after Thor (god of Thunder), and Friday after Frigg.

▶ *Norse stories said that the thunder god, Thor, raced across the heavens in a chariot pulled by two vicious goats.*

The Viking universe

- **During the early Middle Ages**, poetry and storytelling were performed live, in the great hall of a chief or king. Luckily, much of this material was written down later in the Middle Ages, leaving us some record of this earlier age.
- **Two main written sources** tell us what the Norse people believed about the universe before they became Christians.
- **The *Prose Edda*** is a collection of myths recorded by an Icelander called Snorri Sturluson (1179–1241). The Poetic Edda is a collection of 34 ancient poems recorded in a medieval collection known as the Codex Regius (Royal Book) in the 13th century. This was only discovered in 1649.

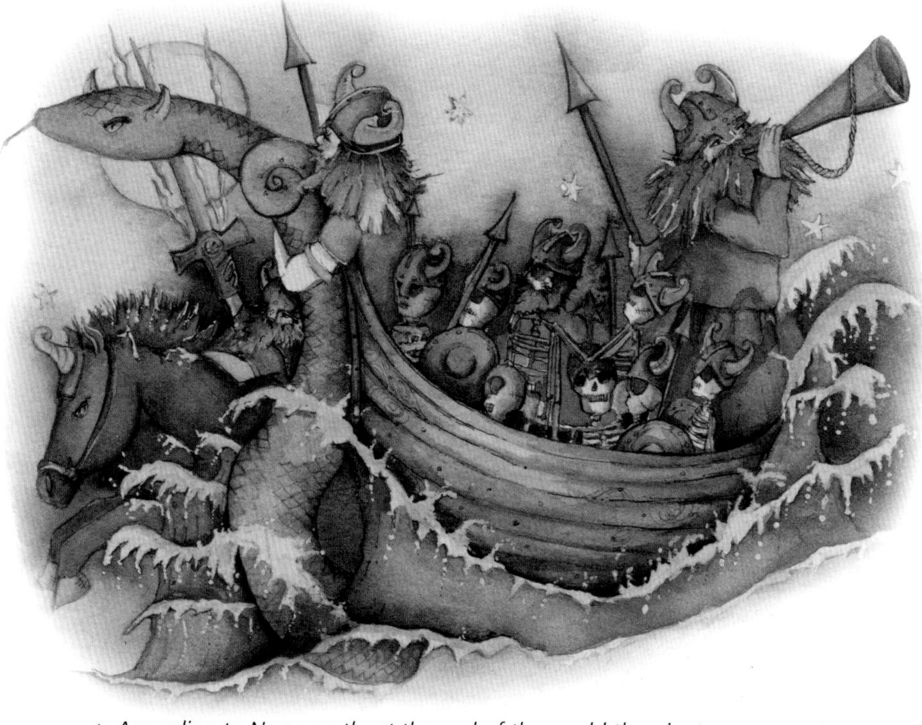

▲ *According to Norse myth, at the end of the world the giant sea-serpent Jormungand will swim ashore to join a battle against the warrior gods.*

▶ *Norse kings had court poets who composed gripping poems about heroes and their battles. The poets performed them as entertainment.*

- **Many Viking carvings** show pictures that also reveal the Norse understanding of the universe.
- **There were nine worlds** arranged on three levels.
- **The uppermost worlds** were Alfheim – home of the light elves; Vanaheim – home of the fertility gods, and Asgard – home of the warrior gods.
- **The middle worlds** were Midgard – home of humans; Nidavellir – home of the dwarfs; Jotunheim – home of the giants, and Svartalfheim – home of the dark elves.
- **Norse myth** said that a giant serpent called Jormungand lived in the sea surrounding the middle worlds, encircling them.

DID YOU KNOW?

Inspiration for the names in JRR Tolkien's The Lord of the Rings trilogy came from characters in the nine Norse worlds.

- **The underworlds** were Muspellheim – a land of fire, and the freezing land of Niflheim, which included Hel – home of the dead.

Holy Roman Empire

- **The Holy Roman Empire** had its origins in the empire of Charlemagne, who was crowned emperor by Pope Leo III in 800.
- **After his death** in 814 the title was contested, but in 962 the German King Otto I was crowned emperor, founding a new empire that covered a large part of Europe. This Holy Roman Empire would survive until 1806.
- **The empire** was really a loose federation of countries. Some of them were large kingdoms, such as Germany, Bohemia, Burgundy and Italy. Others were small duchies, principalities, counties and tiny city states.
- **During the Middle Ages** German influence and settlement moved steadily eastwards into Prussia, Poland and the Baltic lands.
- **The German emperors** often clashed with the Popes in Rome as they vied for political power. In 1076 the emperor Henry IV confronted Pope Gregory VII. He was forced to back down and stand barefoot in the snow for three days at Canossa Castle before the Pope would pardon him.
- **Traditionally the emperor** was elected from among the German princes, but during the 12th century rival dynasties clashed to secure imperial power.
- **Conflict between** the Hohenstaufen family and the Guelphs was resolved under the rule of Frederick I ('Barbarossa'), crowned in 1155.
- **In 1452 Frederick III**, a member of the Austrian-based Habsburg dynasty, was crowned emperor. This same family held the imperial throne until 1740, extending their power across Europe.

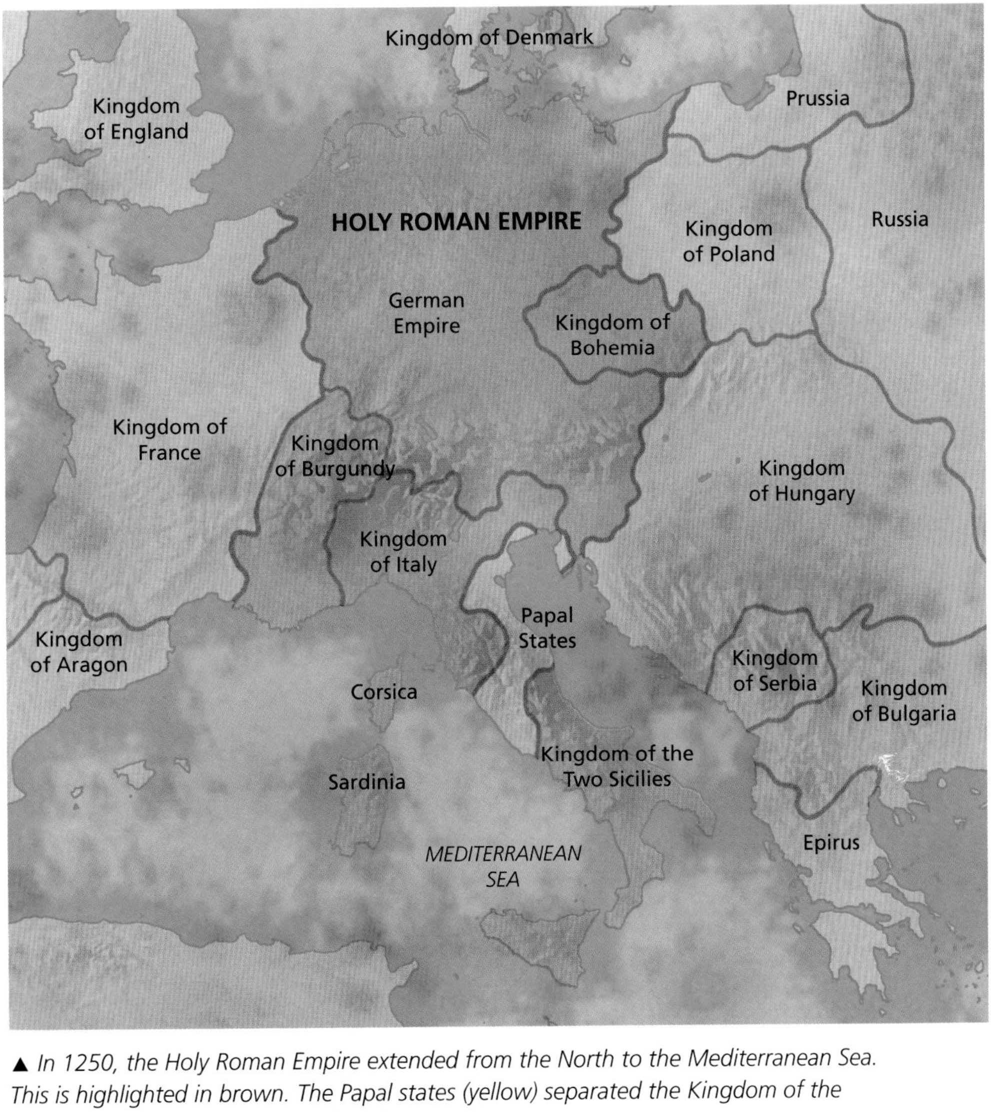

▲ *In 1250, the Holy Roman Empire extended from the North to the Mediterranean Sea. This is highlighted in brown. The Papal states (yellow) separated the Kingdom of the Two Sicilies, which also belonged to the Emperor.*

The Magyars

- **The plains by the River Danube** were settled or conquered by many peoples over the ages – Celts, Dacians, Romans, Ostrogoths (eastern Goths), Huns, Avars and Slavs. In 796, the Avars were crushed by Charlemagne.
- **In about 895** more eastern invaders, the Magyars (or Hungarians), crossed the Carpathian mountains and overran the Danube region. The Magyars were the descendants of people who in ancient times had lived on the Russian steppes, around the River Don.
- **The newcomers formed** a confederation of tribes under the leadership of Árpád. They launched fierce attacks on East Francia and Moravia in central Europe, and raided across Germany, Switzerland, France and Italy. They were halted by Otto I of Germany at Lechfeld in 955.
- **Géza, great-grandson of Árpád**, became a Christian in 975. The lands around the Danube would become a new Hungarian nation, approved by both Pope and Holy Roman Emperor.
- **Its first king** was Géza's son Vajk, crowned as Stephen I by Pope Sylvester II on Christmas Day in 1000, and revered as a saint.
- **Medieval Hungary** became a large and powerful kingdom. In the 1240s it was devastated by Mongol invaders. Hungary was later conquered by the Ottoman Turks and in 1699 came under the rule of the Austrian Habsburgs.

▲ *King Stephen is a famous figure in Hungarian history and his crown became the symbol of the nation.*

The Bulgars

- **The Bulgarians** were a Slavic speaking people. They were descended from Thracians, from early Slavs, and from a Turkic people called the Bulgars who by the 7th century AD were living to the east of the Black Sea and around the Volga River.
- **The Bulgars** were skilled horse-warriors and were ruled by khans (chiefs) and boyars (noblemen).
- **They attacked** the fringes of the Byzantine Empire until they were in turn defeated by another Asian people called the Avars.
- **In 605**, after Kurt or Kubrat became the Bulgar Khan (ruler), the Bulgars re-established themselves on the steppes, but when Kurt died, the Bulgars split into five hordes, or groups.

▲ *In the 800s, the Bulgars were converted to Christianity and adopted the Eastern Orthodox Church of the Byzantines. They began to create icons (religious images) like this.*

- **One of these hordes**, led by Asparukh Khan, advanced westwards into the Danube valley. They overpowered the Slavs living there to create a Bulgarian Empire.
- **Bulgarian Khans** were called emperors (caesars or czars) after helping the Byzantine emperor Justinian II in 710.
- **The Bulgars were more often** at odds with the Byzantines and were usually defeated. However, after one victory, a khan called Krum 'the Fearsome' (reigned 803–814) lined the Byzantine emperor Nicephorus I's skull with silver to make a drinking cup.
- **The Byzantines** sent St Cyril and his brother St Methodius to convert the Bulgar people from a Central Asian religion called Tengrism to Christianity. They succeeded when Czar Boris I was baptized in 864.
- **St Cyril invented** the Cyrillic alphabet, still used by Russians and other eastern Europeans today.
- **The Bulgarian empire** peaked under Simeon I (893–927). Its capital, Preslav, imitated Constantinople in its splendour.

▶ *Devil's Tower Mound in Yelabuga, now in Russia, was built by the Bulgar Khan Ibrahim in 985.*

The East Slavs

- **By the 6th century AD** Slavs were living across East, Central and Southeast Europe.
- **In the 800s**, the Eastern Slavs controlled major trade routes from northwestern Europe to the world's richest cities – Constantinople and Baghdad.
- **They founded towns** such as Novgorod, trading in amber, furs, honey, wax and timber.
- **From around 860**, Viking adventurers raided and traded in the region. They were known as the Varangian Rus. The most famous of them was Rurik, who took over Novgorod.
- **The city of Kiev** grew up further south, on the Dnieper River.
- **Soon the Varangian** Grand Prince of Kiev ruled over a domain called Kievan Rus. This covered what is now Ukraine and western Russia.
- **In about 970** the Eastern Slavs took over the city of Kiev – under Prince Svyatoslav and his son, Vladimir.
- **Legend says** that Vladimir sent people far and wide to study different religions. They were so impressed by the Hagia Sophia in Constantinople that they quickly adopted the Byzantine form of Christianity.
- **The first mention of Moscow**, a timber stronghold on the Moscow River, was in 1147.
- **In the 1200s**, the Eastern Slavs fought off attacks by Swedes and by Germans, but suffered greatly at the hands of Mongol or 'Tatar' invaders, who came to control a vast expanse of Eurasia until the 1480s.

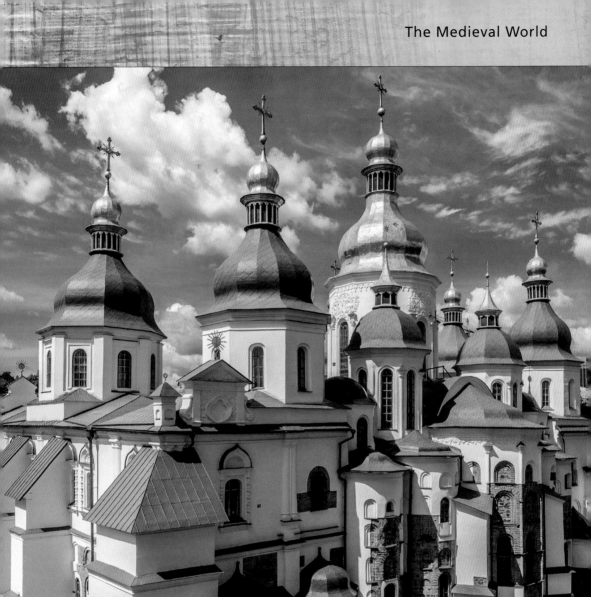

▲ *The beautiful 11th century cathedral of St Sophia in Kiev was inspired by the Hagia Sophia in Constantinople.*

By this time the Grand Duchy of Moscow had grown rapidly in wealth and power, and would eventually become the centre of a Russian empire.

The West and South Slavs

- **The West Slavs** included ancestors of the Czechs, Slovaks, Poles, Silesians and Sorbs.
- **The Czechs lived** on the borders of the Germanic world, in Moravia and Bohemia and Austria. They built a castle at Prague in 880, founding one of Europe's great cities, a centre of learning and culture for many centuries.

▶ *This stone castle was built in Bedzin, in southern Poland in 1348 during the reign of Casimir III ('the Great'). It replaced an earlier one made of timber.*

- **The Czechs fought** alongside the Holy Roman Empire against the invading Magyars. Their Kingdom of Bohemia became an important piece in the jigsaw puzzle of medieval Europe. In the 1200s it was settled by many German immigrants.
- **In the 7th–9th centuries** the ancestral lands of the Slovaks formed part of the Empire of Samo and the Principalities of Moravia and Nitra, but later in the Middle Ages came under Hungarian and then Polish rule.
- **The kingdom of Poland** was formed by West Slavic tribes from the 10th century, with its capital at Kraków. In 1385 Poland's rulers united with the Lithuanians. Their vast territory came under attack from Germany's Teutonic Knights and from invading Mongols.
- **When the West Slavs** converted to the Christian faith they followed the Roman tradition. The South Slavs on the other hand followed Byzantine or Eastern Orthodox forms of worship.
- **In the early Middle Ages** South Slavic tribes peopled the Balkans, the Pannonian Plain and the eastern Alps. They included amongst others the ancestors of the Croatians, Serbians, Bosniaks and Slovenes.
- **The Serbians were allies** of the Byzantine empire and in 1345 formed a regional empire under Stefan Dusan. This was defeated by the Ottoman Turks at the Battle of Kosovo in 1389.

Muhammad

- **Muhammad** (*c.*AD 570–632) was the Arab prophet whose teachings form the basis of the Islamic faith.
- **Muslims (followers of Islam)** believe Muhammad was the last and greatest prophet, a messenger of God, whom they call Allah.
- **Muhammad was born in Mecca**, in what is now Saudi Arabia.
- **His father died** before he was born and his mother died when he was a child. He was raised by his grandfather and uncle, tending sheep and camels.

▼ *Each year, many thousands of Muslims from all over the world travel to Mecca, to perform the pilgrimage, or Hajj.*

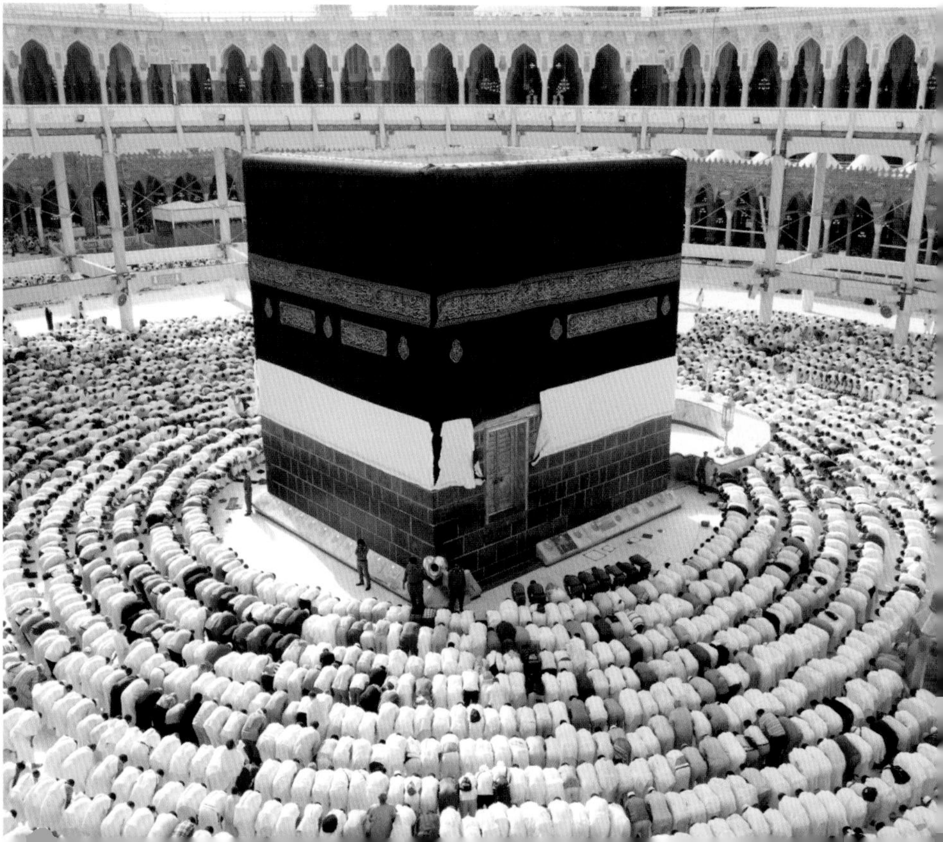

▲ *The Qu'ran is Islam's holy book. Muslims believe it reveals the word of God, as taught by Muhammad.*

- **At the age of 25**, Muhammad entered the service of a rich widow of 40 called Khadija and later married her. They had two sons and four daughters.
- **When he was 35**, Muhammad was asked to restore a sacred stone that had been damaged in a flood. He had a vision that told him to become a prophet and proclaim the word of God.
- **The people of Mecca** resented Muhammad's preaching, and in 622 he emigrated to Medina, in Saudi Arabia.
- **In Medina**, he attracted many followers. The Meccans went to war against Medina, but were driven back.
- **In 630**, Muhammad re-entered Mecca in triumph, pardoned the people and set up a mosque there.

DID YOU KNOW?

The Muslim year begins with the day of Muhammad's escape to Medina, called the Hegira.

The spread of Islam

- **The Islamic faith** spread rapidly after the death of Muhammad in 632. The first Muslims were Arabs. However the Islamic world soon contained many other peoples too.
- **The first Muslims** were guided by leaders called caliphs, meaning 'successors'.
- **Islam expanded** by conquest, led by zealous Arab armies. However they worshipped alongside people of other faiths, such as Jews and Christians. Later in the Middle Ages there were fierce wars between Christians and Muslims.
- **Muslim Arabs** conquered Iraq in 637, Syria in 640, Egypt in 641 and Persia (Iran) in 650.
- **By 650** Islam had also reached China, along the trading routes of the Silk Road.

▼ *Five times a day, devout Muslims face the holy city of Mecca to pray.*

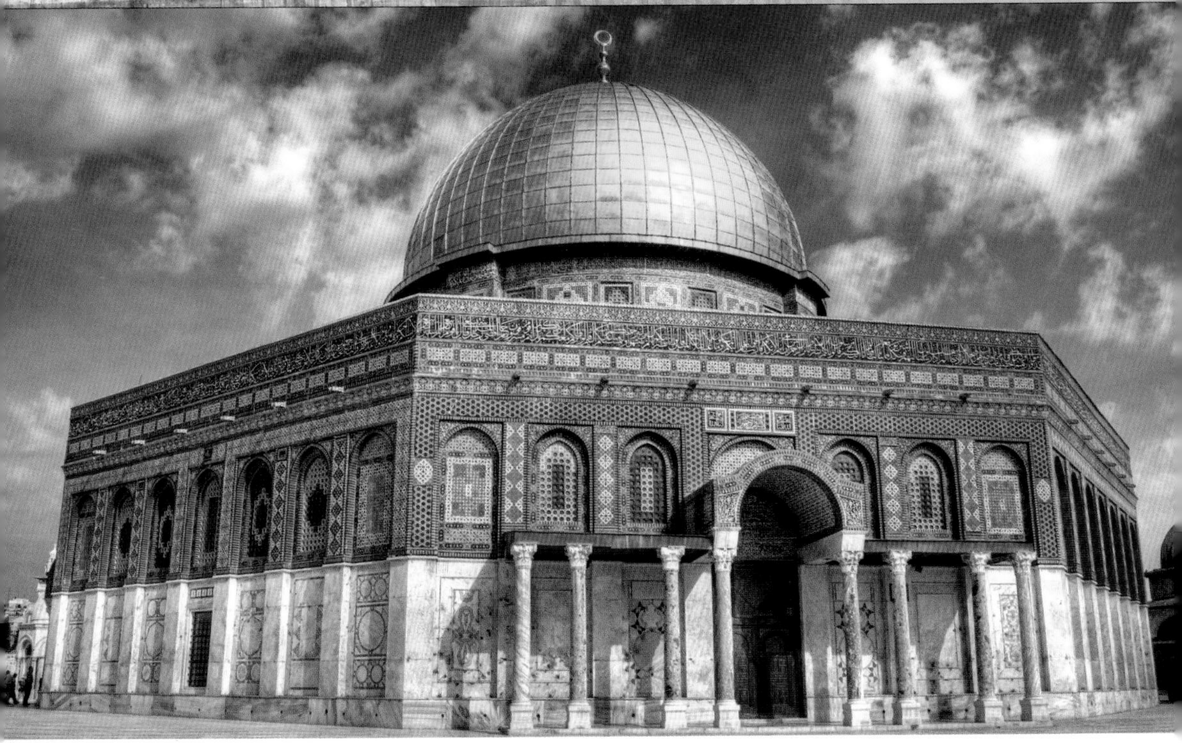

▲ *The Dome of the Rock in Jerusalem, built for Abd al-Malik in 691, was one of the first examples of beautiful Islamic architecture.*

- **By 661**, a great Islamic Empire stretched from Tunisia to India. Its capital was at Damascus. The arts, scholarship and sciences flourished.
- **In 711 Muslim armies** crossed into Spain from Morocco. By the 900s Islam had reached West and East Africa. Northern India first came under Muslim rule under the Delhi Sultanate (1206–1526). Islam also spread through many islands of Southeast Asia from the 1200s to the 1600s.

DID YOU KNOW?

In just 100 years, the empire of Islam became bigger than the Roman Empire at its height.

The caliphs

- **The caliphs** were the leaders of Islam following the death of Muhammad in 632.
- **The choice of caliphs** to succeed Muhammad soon divided the Islamic world.
- **The first caliph** was Muhammad's father-in-law, Abu Bakr. After that came Umar, Uthman and Ali, referred to by Sunni Muslims as Rashidun (the 'rightly guided').
- **Other Muslims**, known as Shi'ites, only recognized Ali (Muhammad's cousin and son-in-law) and his successors as imams, true leaders chosen by God.

▼ *Jabir ibn Hayyan was born in Persia. Between 721–815 he became a leading scholar of the Islamic world. He was an astronomer, chemist, doctor, geographer and engineer.*

▶ *Under the Abbasid caliphs, Islamic artists made beautiful ceramic tiles and glassware.*

- **Most Muslims** followed the Umayyad family, who became caliphs in Damascus from 661.
- **The 14 Umayyad caliphs** expanded the Islamic empire by conquest through North Africa and into Spain, but it proved too be too ambitious.
- **In 750**, the last of the Umayyad caliphs – Marwan II – was beaten at the Battle of the Great Zab by the rival Abbasids, who were descended from Muhammad's uncle.
- **The Abbasid caliphs** turned their attentions eastwards and made a new capital at Baghdad, which soon became the richest city in the world.
- **Under the Abbasids**, Islam became famous for its science, learning and art, especially during the time of Harun al-Rashid.
- **One Umayyad** escaped to set up a rival caliphate in Spain (756–1031).
- **Descendants of Muhammad's daughter** Fatimah became caliphs in Egypt, creating the great city of Cairo.

Harun al-Rashid

- **Harun al-Rashid** (766–809) was the most famous of all the caliphs.
- **In Harun's time**, Baghdad became the most glamorous city in the world, famed for its luxury as well as its poetry, music and learning.
- **Harun was famous** far and wide. He sent ambassadors to the Chinese emperor and an elephant to Charlemagne.
- **Zubaydah, Harun's wife**, would only drink from silver and gold cups studded with gems.
- **A great patron of the arts**, Harun gave lavish gifts to poets and musicians. Yet he also enjoyed watching dogs fight – and often had people executed.
- **Stories tell how Harun** would wander in the moonlight with his friend Abu Nuwas, the brilliant poet, as well as Masrur the executioner.
- **Harun has become famous** because he features in the famous collection of tales known as *One Thousand and One Nights*, or *The Arabian Nights*. Many of these tales may have originated in India or Persia.
- **The tales include** such famous characters as Aladdin and his genie, Ali Baba and Sinbad the Sailor.
- **The tales begin** with King Shahriyar of Samarkand feeling distraught by his wife's unfaithfulness. He vows to marry a new girl each night and behead her in the morning.

The lovely princess Scheherazade insists on marrying the king, then at night tells him a tale so entertaining that he lets her live another day to finish it. One story leads to another for 1001 nights, by which time the king has fallen in love with her.

▼ *Scheherazade tells her tales to the king. The* One Thousand and One Nights *collection has remained popular into modern times.*

North Africa and Spain

- **The original inhabitants** of North Africa are known as Berbers.
- **Over the ages** many invaders came to their lands, including Carthaginians, Romans, Vandals and Byzantines.
- **In the 7th century AD**, Arab armies invaded North Africa. Many Berbers became Muslims. The Berbers adapted Islam to their own traditions They based their religion around marabouts – holy men who lived very frugally and morally.
- **In 711** Muslim forces (known to the Europeans as 'Moors') crossed the Strait of Gibraltar and invaded Spain. Their troops included both Arabs and Berbers.
- **The lands they invaded** became known as al-Andalus. It was a place of learning and fine craftwork, with mosques, palaces and gardens. One of the finest buildings is the Alhambra, in Granada.

- **In the 11th century** a new Berber dynasty called the Almoravids came to rule all of al-Andalus and Morocco. A second Berber dynasty, the Almohads, seized power in the 12th century.
- **In the 1300s** Ibn Battuta, a Berber from Tangier, travelled the world, from Spain to China and Southeast Asia. He wrote a fascinating account of his travels.
- **For most of the Moorish occupation**, Christian armies from the north were attempting to reconquer Spain. This process took nearly eight centuries, with Granada finally falling to the Christians in 1492.

▼ *The North African Berbers survived repeated invasions by withdrawing to the harsh wilderness of the Sahara desert.*

African empires

- **During the Middle Ages**, Muslim Arab and Persian ships visited the islands and coasts of East Africa.
- **The African peoples** from the coast traded goods from the interior, such as gold and ivory. Thriving ports grew up such as Zanzibar and Kilwa. The coastal culture became known as Swahili.
- **Inland, the city of Great Zimbabwe** (the name means 'house of stone') flourished within its huge granite walls. It is now a ruin, but in the 1400s, gold made this city the heart of the Monomatapa Empire.
- **Further inland**, by the lakes of Uganda, were the extraordinary grass palaces belonging to the Bugandan kings.
- **In West Africa**, trade across the Sahara made kingdoms like Ghana flourish. Two great empires grew up – first Mali (1240–1500) and then Songhai, which peaked in the 1500s.

▶ *The splendid ancient city of Great Zimbabwe, now in ruins, flourished in southern Africa and gave its name to modern Zimbabwe. At its height, the city's population was up to 18,000.*

▶ *A bust made by the Edo people of Benin, Africa's greatest city during the 1600s.*

- **The Mali Empire** centred on the city of Timbuktu.
- **Timbuktu's glory** began in 1324, when King Mansa Musa went on a grand trip to Mecca with camels laden with gold and brought back the best scholars and architects.
- **Timbuktu means** 'mother with a large navel', after an old woman said to have first settled there. But from 1324–1591 Timbuktu was a splendid city with what may have been the world's biggest university, catering for up to 25,000 students.
- **The Songhai Empire** in the 1400s stretched right across West Africa from what is now Nigeria to Gambia. It reached its peak under the rule of Sunni Ali, from 1464–1492, who conquered Timbuktu, and his son Askia the Great, from 1493–1528.

African mythology

▲ *Wild animals feature prominently in African culture. The chameleon, with its highly developed ability to change colour, features in tales from the forest kingdoms of West Africa.*

- **The peoples and languages** of Africa are numerous and varied, but they have many shared beliefs. Sometimes these are reflected in their rich mythology, their legends and folk tales.
- **Many traditional African cultures** believe in one supreme creator god who judges people wisely, as well as many minor gods.
- **Many myths** say that the creator god grew weary of constant demands from people, so he left the Earth and went to live in heaven.
- **The Yoruba people** of Nigeria believed that in the beginning the universe consisted of the sky, ruled by the chief god Olorun, and a watery marshland, ruled by the goddess Olokun.
- **The Yoruba believed** that a god called Obatala shaped the Earth with the help of magic gifts from other gods.

- **The Fon people**, of what is now the Benin Republic, believed that the world was created by twin gods: the moon goddess Mawu and her twin brother Lisa, the Sun.
- **The Dogon people** of Mali believed that the creator god moulded the Sun, Moon, Earth and people out of clay.
- **The Pygmies believed** that the first man and woman were brought forth by a chameleon that released them from a tree in a gush of water.
- **The Yoruba believed** that the chief god, Olorun, breathed life into the first people, who were modelled from mud.

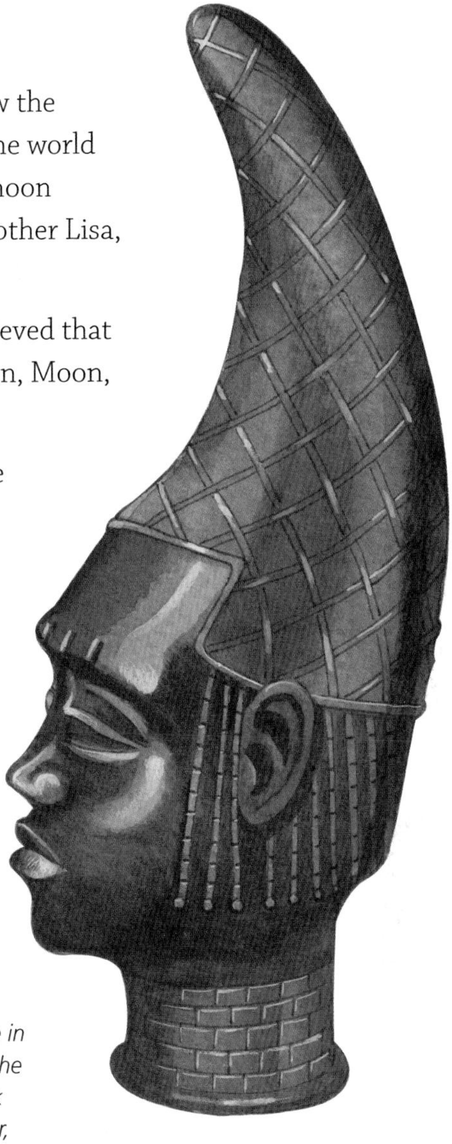

▶ *Benin, a kingdom of the Edo people in what is now Nigeria, developed from the 11th–17th century. This fine brasswork represents the head of a queen mother, and was made to honour royal ancestors.*

Gassire's Lute

- **An African people** called the Soninke have an epic poem called *Gassire's Lute*. It was composed between AD 300–1100 as part of a group of songs called the *Dausi*.
- **Most other songs** in the *Dausi* have been forgotten.
- ***Gassire's Lute*** is a tale about the ancestors of the Soninke, a tribe of warrior horsemen called the Fasa.
- **The Fasa lived** around 500 BC in a fertile area of sub-Saharan Africa bordered by the Sahara desert, Senegal, Sudan and the river Nile.
- **The hero of the legend**, Gassire, is a Fasa prince who longs for his father to die so he can become a famous king.
- **The heroes of other epic poems** usually put their lives at risk trying to help other people. This epic is strikingly different, because the hero puts his own desires in front of everything else.
- **Gassire realizes** that all things die, and that the only way to win lasting fame is to be remembered as a hero in battle songs.
- **He has a lute made** so he can sing of his own adventures. However, the lute will only play once it has been soaked with blood in battle.

▶ *Gassire's lute would have been a stringed instrument like the kora.*

▲ *The Fasa ancestors of this Soninke woman were like medieval knights. They fought on horseback with spears and swords, not just in battle but also for sport.*

- **Gassire leads his eight sons** and followers into war against an enemy tribe. It is only when all but one of Gassire's sons have been killed that his lute finally sings.
- **Gassire grieves** for the dead, but is filled with joy now he has a great battle song to bring him fame.

Sui and Tang China

- **In AD 581**, Yang Jian seized the throne in the north of China and founded the Sui dynasty.
- **Yang Jian**, known as the Emperor Wen of Sui, conquered the south and reunited China for the first time since the fall of the Han in AD 220.
- **Under the second Sui emperor**, Yangdi, China's Grand Canal was rebuilt on a huge scale, linking China's main rivers north and south. Other canals extended the network.
- **Yangdi was betrayed** by one of his 3000 mistresses and was strangled in 618. Li Yuan, an ambitious Sui minister, then seized the throne and became known as Emperor Gaozu of Tang.
- **Under the Tang dynasty**, trade along the Silk Road reached its high point. China became rich again and the arts and sciences flourished.
- **By 751**, China was the world's largest empire and the capital, Chang'an (modern Xi'an), was the world's largest city, with over one million inhabitants and many foreign residents.
- **Poets such as Li Bai** (701–762) wrote of his love of wild mountains and the fleeting nature of happiness. China's tradition of great landscape painting began and one of the earliest printed books, *The Diamond Sutra*, was made in 868.
- **By 800**, the Tang dynasty was beginning to break up, Chang'an declined and China descended into turmoil.

▶ *Gunpowder was invented in the Tang era. The Chinese used it first to make fireworks, and later weapons.*

Song China

- **After almost a century of chaos**, the Song dynasty of emperors came to power in China in 960.
- **They ruled** from Kaifeng in northern China until 1127, but then ruled from Hangzhou in the south after the north had fallen to the Jin dynasty. In the early 1200s Mongol invaders also attacked.
- **Despite this**, the Song era could be seen as a golden age of Chinese civilization.
- **The Song rulers** renounced the war-like policies that had kept China in strife, and brought peace by paying tribute money to the nomadic warriors to their the north. The Song had a huge army, but this was partly to give jobs to thousands of poor Chinese.
- **The Song slowly got rid** of soldiers from the government and replaced them with civil servants.

▼ *A finely illustrated scroll shows life during the Song dynasty. A family returns to Kaifeng, after tending their ancestors' graves for the Spring Festival.*

- **In earlier times**, only aristocrats tended to hold key posts in government, but under the Song, anyone could enter for the civil service exams. Competition to do well in the exams was intense, and the main yearly exams became major events in the calendar.
- **The civil service exams** stressed not practical skills but the study of literature and the classic works of the thinker Confucius. So the Song civil service was full of learned, cultured men, known in the west as mandarins.
- **Ouyang Xiu** (1007–1072) was a typical mandarin – statesman, historian, poet, philosopher, wine and music connoisseur and brilliant player of the chess-like game Go (weiqi).
- **Under the Song**, the population soared, trade prospered and advances were made in science and technology – from printing with moveable type to machines used to make silk textiles. Technologically, China was about 500 years ahead of Europe.
- **The Song period** is also known for its exquisite landscape paintings and fine porcelain, known in English as chinaware – or just 'china'.
- **By 1275**, Hangzhou was the world's largest city, with a population of one million. Its warm climate encouraged a lively, leisurely lifestyle. The city was full of luxury shops, bars, restaurants, tea-houses and clubs where girls sang. Often, people went out to stroll in the gardens by the West Lake or lazed over long meals on the lake's scores of floating restaurants, pushed along by poles. Marco Polo later complained that the people here were 'anything but warriors; all their delight was in women, nothing but women.'

The Mongol Khans

- **The Mongols were nomads** who lived in gers (round tents made of felt) in central and northeastern Asia.
- **In 1180**, a 13-year-old Mongol boy called Temujin was made khan (chief) of his tribe. He soon became a great leader, and in 1206 he was hailed as Genghis Khan (Chief of all Men).
- **Genghis Khan** was a brilliant and ruthless soldier. His armies terrified their enemies, and butchered anyone they met.
- **Genghis's horse archers** could kill at 180 m while riding at full gallop. They once rode 440 km in just three days.
- **Within four years** (1210–1214), Genghis Khan conquered northern China, much of India, and Persia. His empire stretched right through Asia, extending from Korea to the Caspian Sea.

▶ *Genghis Khan was a man of incredible physical strength and willpower. He could be tyrannical and cruel, yet philosophers would travel from far away to talk with him about religion.*

- **After Genghis Khan died** in 1227, his son Ögedei ravaged Armenia, Hungary and Poland.
- **Genghis Khan's grandson**, Kublai Khan, conquered the rest of China in 1265 and made himself the first of a line of Mongol emperors of China called Yuans. The Yuan dynasty lasted until 1368.
- **Kublai's rule** in China was harsh, but he was greatly admired by the Venetian traveller, Marco Polo.
- **Kublai Khan created** a grand new capital called Dadu ('Great Capital') or Khanbaliq – now Beijing.
- **Kublai Khan adopted** Chinese ways of government and ruled with such efficiency that China became very rich.

▲ *A man of vision, energy, and a certain ruthlessness, Kublai Khan encouraged the arts and sciences, rebuilt Beijing and made Buddhism the state religion – suppressing Daoism in the process. First emperor of the Yuan dynasty, he gave China a strong separate identity and led a glittering court that was famed far and wide.*

Marco Polo

- **Marco Polo** was an Italian traveller. Born in about 1254 in Venice, he spent many years in China at the court of Kublai Khan.
- **In the 1200s**, most of Europe knew China only as the romantic land of 'Cathay'. But Marco's father Niccolo and uncle Maffeo were well-travelled merchants who had already been there.
- **In 1271**, Niccolo and Maffeo invited 17-year-old Marco to come with them to Cathay again.

- **The Polos** took four years to reach China, travelling on foot and horse along the 'Silk Road' – a network of routes through Central Asia, used by merchants bringing silk and other precious goods from China to Western Asia and Europe.
- **Kublai Khan** welcomed the Polos. Marco had a gift for languages and became one of the Khan's diplomats.

◀ *While in China, Marco Polo is said to have served as governor of Yangzhou.*

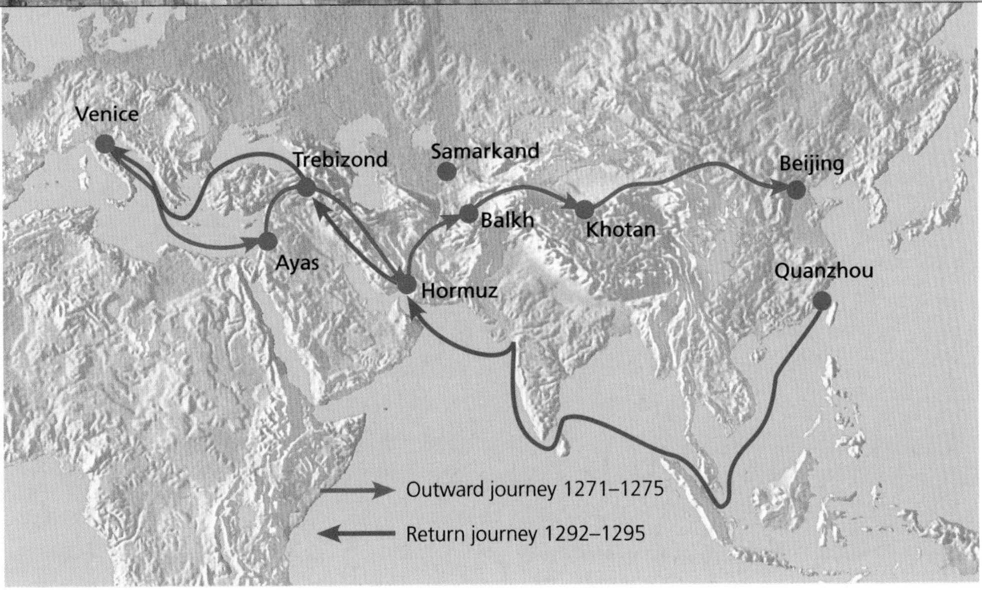

▲ *Marco Polo was one of the few Europeans to journey all the way to China and back in the Middle Ages.*

- **After 17 years**, the Polos decided to return, but the Khan would only let them go if they took a princess, who was to be wed to the Khan's great-nephew in Persia.
- **The Polos arrived** back in Venice in 1295, laden with jewels, silks and spices.
- **Marco Polo later** wrote an account of his time in China while a prisoner of war in Genoa, dictating it to a man called Rustichello.
- **Marco's tales** were so fantastic that some called the book *Il Milione* ('The Million' – perhaps referring to 'a million lies'). Some experts think that he reported the truth. Others think he just recycled other travellers' tales.
- **Christopher Columbus** was just one of many people who were inspired by Marco Polo's accounts.

Fujiwara Japan

- **The Fujiwara clan** rose to power during the 7th century AD, in the Asuka period. They dominated Japan during the Heian period (794–1185).
- **The Fujiwara were not emperors** themselves, but were close advisers.
- **They maintained** their position by marrying daughters of their family into the imperial family, creating the role of an all-powerful *kampaku* (chancellor) or *sessho* (regent). These officials effectively ran Japan, while the emperors just dealt with religious matters.
- **Their dictatorial powers** peaked with Fujiwara no Michinaga (966–1028).
- **Michinaga's mansions** were more splendid than palaces. Lavish banquets, concerts, poetry and picnics took place there.
- **Many women** of the court were novelists and poets, and love affairs were conducted via cleverly poetic letters.
- **The brilliant court life** of Michinaga was captured in the famous novel *The Tale of Genji* by Lady Murasaki.
- **During Michinaga's reign**, warrior families gained the upper hand by quelling rural rebellions, eventually bringing about the Fujiwara clan's downfall.

DID YOU KNOW?

Sei Shonagon, a lady at Michinaga's court, wrote a famous Pillow Book – a diary of daily court life.

▶ The Tale of Genji *is thought to be the world's oldest full-length novel. It was written in about the year 1000 by Murasaki Shikibu, a lady-in-waiting to the empress of Japan. It tells the story of Prince Genji and his various loves.*

The Khmer

- **Southeast Asia** had come under southern Indian influence as early as AD 100, when the Hindu Funan kingdom was founded in Cambodia. It was followed by the Chenia state.
- **In 802** the Khmer people of this region founded a great Hindu-Buddhist empire that dominated Southeast Asia until 1431. They ruled what is now Cambodia as well as parts of Laos, Thailand and southern Vietnam.
- **The empire's golden age** began in the 12th century when the spectacular temple now known as Angkor Wat was built in honour of the god Vishnu. It remains the world's largest religious monument.

▶ *Angkor Wat was built by the Khmer ruler Suryavarman II, who reigned from about 1113–1150. It began life as a Hindu temple but later became devoted to the Buddhist faith. It has become a symbol of the Khmer culture and of Cambodia.*

- **The Khmer people** lived by farming and fishing. They were great architects and carvers of stone.
- **The empire's greatest ruler** was Jayavarman VII, who ruled from 1181–1219. He built a large new city called Angkor Thom near the old capital of Yasodharapura.
- **The empire went into decline** during the 1300s. Its rival for power was the Thai kingdom of Ayutthaya, founded in 1350. The Thais attacked Angkor and sacked it in 1431. The great city was abandoned and left to the jungle.

The Maoris

- **The final phase** of Polynesian expansion around the Pacific islands came in the 12th–13th centuries, when settlers left eastern Polynesia in fleets of large canoes.
- **Their legendary navigator** was Kupe, a powerful chief from an island referred to in myth as Hawaiki.
- **Their final discovery** was a group of uninhabited islands, which became known as Aotearoa (sometimes translated as 'land of the long white cloud') or New Zealand.

▼ *A Maori chief stands in his canoe. Both the prow and the meeting house on shore are elaborately carved.*

▶ *The beautiful Pacific island of Tahiti is a tropical paradise. It is one of several possible starting points for voyages by the ancestors of the Maoris, and may represent their mythical homeland of Hawaiki.*

- **The settlers** are known as Maoris, a name they began to use when European settlers first arrived in the late 18th century.
- **The Maoris lived** mostly near the coast or by rivers. They survived by hunting seals and huge flightless birds called moas, which soon became extinct. They ate fish and shellfish, and grew yams and kumara (sweet potatoes).
- **Fierce warriors**, Maoris built stone forts called *pa*.
- **Maoris tattooed** their bodies and wore kilts and cloaks made of New Zealand flax. They were skilled carvers in wood and built beautiful wooden houses and canoes.

The Toltecs

▲ *Toltec temples in Tollán were guarded by stone statues of warriors wearing breastplates as armour and feathered headdresses.*

By 900, the great Mexican city of Teotihuacán was destroyed and much of the land was in the hands of warrior tribes from the north.

- **Legend says** that Teotihuacán was destroyed by one of these warrior tribes, known as Toltecs. The Toltec leader was named Mixcóatl, meaning 'Cloud Serpent'.
- **Under Mixcóatl's son**, Topiltzin, the Toltec were said to have built an empire and a capital at Tollan, now thought to be Tula, 45 km north of Mexico City.
- **Topiltzin introduced** the cult of the god Quetzalcóatl ('Feathered Serpent'). Later tales conflate the man with the god, so he may have taken the name himself.
- **The Toltecs** were not only great warriors but fine builders and craftsmen. Tollan was full of pyramids, temples and other huge, impressive buildings.
- **Legends tell how** Topiltzin/Quetzalcóatl was driven out of Tollan by jealous rivals – including the priests of the god Tezcatlipoca ('Smoking Mirror').
- **After leaving Tollan**, Quetzalcóatl sailed east into the Gulf of Mexico, vowing to return one day.
- **The Aztec people** were greatly influenced by the Toltecs. They took the custom of human sacrifices from the priests of Tezcatlipoca. Some Aztecs believed that, when Spanish invaders arrived in 1519, it was Quetzalcóatl returning to seek vengeance.
- **The Toltec empire** broke up in the 12th century and Tollan vanished.

DID YOU KNOW?

Tollán, or Tula, had an area of about 14 sq km and was home to about 40,000 people.

The Cahokia era

- **The period before** the coming of Christopher Columbus to the Americas in 1492 is often called the pre-Columbian era.
- **However the first European** contact with native peoples actually occurred from the 980s to the 1000s, when Vikings settled in Greenland, Labrador and Newfoundland.
- **Many different cultures** thrived across North America in the centuries before 1492.
- **New waves of settlement** by whale hunters (the 'Thule culture') spread across the Arctic from Alaska to Greenland, from the 900s to the 1100s.
- **In the Northwest**, Pacific coast peoples lived by hunting and fishing and were skilled wood carvers.
- **In the dry Southwest**, in Arizona, New Mexico and Colorado, peoples of the Ancient Pueblo (or Anasazi) cultures made advances in irrigation and agriculture. They wove baskets and made pottery. Pueblo is the Spanish word for 'village'. Dwellings of earth and stone were often built into cliffs, which were easy to defend from attack. Major centres included Mesa Verde and Chaco Canyon.
- **The largest town in pre-Columbian** North America was Cahokia, built in a farming region beside the Mississippi River. It developed between AD 600–1400 and originally covered about 16 sq km. Cahokia was also a ritual centre, which included over 100 earthen mounds.

▶ *The Cahokia mounds provide evidence of an urban centre that in the 1200s may have had a population of up to 40,000. It was a centre of trade, crafts, tool-making and farming.*

Serfs and lords

- **A new way of ordering society** developed in Europe during the early Middle Ages. It was called the feudal system.
- **A king or overlord** gave a lord a fief (a grant of land). In return, the lord swore to train and fight for the king as a knight (horse warrior). Land was security rather than money, because it could not be moved. Any lord who held a fief was called his king's vassal.
- **Feudalism reached** its high point in western Europe from the 8th century onwards, under Frankish and Norman rulers.
- **The feudal system** had a pyramid structure, with many levels. The king held the land from God, and the nobles from the king or from other nobles.
- **The arrangements** could become quite complex. The Count of Champagne had 2017 vassal knights, but he himself was vassal to ten overlords, including the King of France.

▶ *Most people in medieval Europe were poor serfs tied to their lord. They lived in basic huts clustered around the lord's manor house and scraped a meagre living.*

- **The feudal system** soon controlled most of the land in Europe, as kings tied their subjects by grants of land. There was a saying: 'No land without a lord; and no lord without a land'.
- **With so much land** held in fiefs, most peasants were serfs, legally bound to their lords by the 'manorial' system, which centred on the local manor house or castle.
- **In return for working** their lord's land, serfs were given small plots of land to live off. Serfs could not be evicted, but had few rights. They could not leave the village, marry or sell their possessions without their lord's permission.
- **The feudal** and manorial systems reached a peak in the 1100s but then began to decline. Serfs were not freed in Russia until 1861.

▼ *In return for basic food and housing, serfs worked their lords' lands and had virtually no personal freedom. In the Middle Ages, most people in Europe worked on the land. Almost everything they owned, from food and clothing to land and animals belonged to the local lord.*

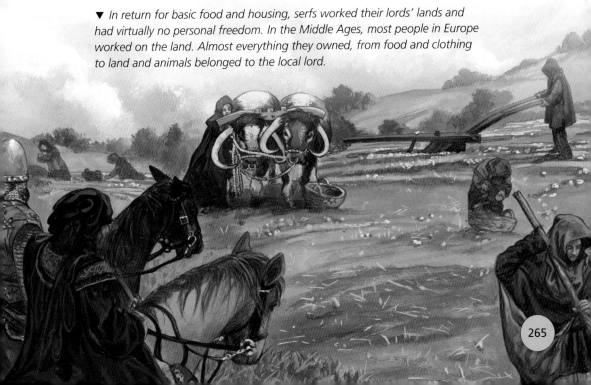

Norman invasions

- **In 911**, the West Francian King Charles III, weary of attacks by the Vikings, granted a large area of northern France to the Viking leader, Hrolf or Rollo. This became known as the Duchy of Normandy, land of the Northmen or Normans.
- **The Normans intermarrried** with the Franks and came to speak a dialect called Norman French. Norman knights were ruthless warriors who overran large areas of Europe and the Near East.
- **The Normans won land** in southern Italy. They captured Sicily and Malta, and attacked the Byzantine empire.
- **On 5 January, 1066**, the English king Edward the Confessor died. As he died, he named as his successor Harold Godwinson – the powerful earl of the kingdom of Wessex.
- **Harold's claim** to the English throne was challenged by William, Duke of Normandy. William claimed that Edward had already promised him the throne.

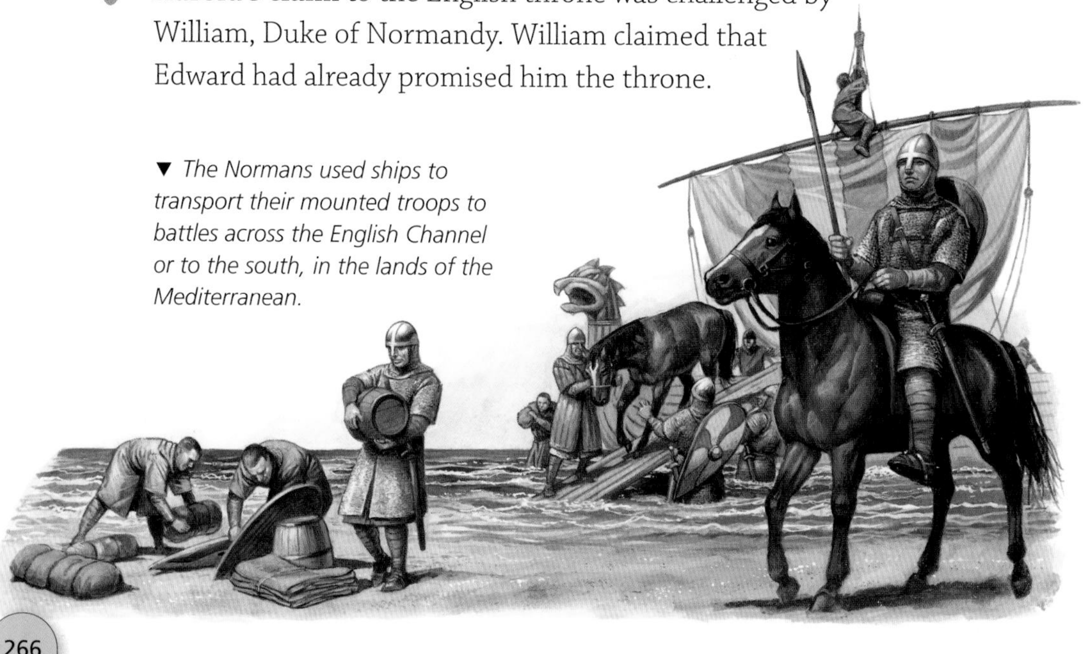

▼ *The Normans used ships to transport their mounted troops to battles across the English Channel or to the south, in the lands of the Mediterranean.*

▲ *The Normans commemorated their victory at the Battle of Hastings with a famous tapestry. It may have been made in England, but has been at Bayeux in France since at least 1476.*

- **On 28 September**, William's Norman army of 7000 crossed from France and landed in southern England.
- **Harold had just fought off** an attack in the north by the King of Norway. He now had to march his army south to meet the Normans. He was killed in a great battle near Hastings, and William 'the Conqueror' was crowned King of England.
- **England was parcelled out** between Norman feudal lords, and resistance was crushed. In the next two centuries, descendants of the Norman knights attacked and seized parts of Wales and Scotland and also intervened in Irish wars and settled there.

The age of castles

- **Fortifications had been part** of warfare and defence since ancient times. However the strongholds built under the feudal system often had an additional purpose.
- **These castles** were the residences of feudal lords or kings and queens, and were designed to impress and oppress local populations.
- **Castles became a symbol** of the high Middle Ages. Their ruins can still be seen across Europe and southwest Asia. Castles of a rather different design were also built in feudal Japan.
- **The first European castles**, built by the Normans in the 10th and 11th centuries, were wooden towers set on a mound called a motte, surrounded by a yard called a bailey and protected by palisades.
- **Timber is easily destroyed by fire**, so castles were soon being built of stone, with square and later round stone towers called keeps. These were surrounded by courtyards called wards, by very thick walls and moats full of water.
- **Sieges were common**. The attackers would attempt to cut off the castle's supplies of water and food. They would batter the walls with huge catapults called mangonels and trebuchets. They would try to smash down the gatehouses and doors, or undermine them.
- **The defenders** would fire arrows and crossbow bolts at the attacking army, or hurl boulders at them.
- **As the Middle Ages** came to a close, castles were no longer built. The feudal system had collapsed, the rulers now wanted to live in luxurious palaces, and warfare too had changed as cannon became bigger and more effective.

1 Arrow loops Archers could shoot arrows through loops – narrow slits in the castle walls.

2 Outer walls Thick stone walls were fireproof and hard to knock down.

3 Battlements The walls were topped by battlements. These walkways were defended by stone blocks called merlons and firing gaps called crenels.

4 Machicolations Chutes overhung the outer walk, for dropping missiles on the enemy.

5 Gatehouse A strong gate called a portcullis could be dropped to seal off the entrance to the castle.

▲ *Castles were built with rings of defences and were garrisoned by foot soldiers, archers and men-at-arms. They also included living quarters, chapels, kitchens, and a great hall for banquets and meetings.*

Knights

- **Knights were the elite** fighting men of Europe's Middle Ages, highly trained for combat both on horseback and on foot.
- **Knights always wore armour**. At first, the armour was simply shirts of mail, made from linked rings of iron. By the 1400s, most knights wore full suits of plate armour.
- **A knight rode** into battle on a horse called a destrier, or warhorse, and usually had an easy-going horse called a palfry just for travelling, plus a packhorse called a sumpter.
- **Chivalry** was the knights' strict code of honour. It comes from *chevalier*, the French for 'horseman'.
- **The ideal knight** was meant to be bold but good and gentle – fighting only to defend his lord, his lady and the Church. But in reality many were just brutal combatant.

▶ *Medieval knights were always ready to fight to defend their own honour and that of their lord.*

- **Training to be a knight** was a long and costly process, so most were from wealthy families.
- **A young boy** began training to be a knight at seven years of age as a page to a lord. Then he became a knight's squire (apprentice) at 14.
- **A squire's task** was to look after his master's armour, dress him for battle and serve his food.
- **A squire who passed** all the tests was dubbed a 'knight' at about 21 years old.
- **Knights took part** in mock battles called tournaments, often involving 'jousts', where two knights would charge at each other with lances.

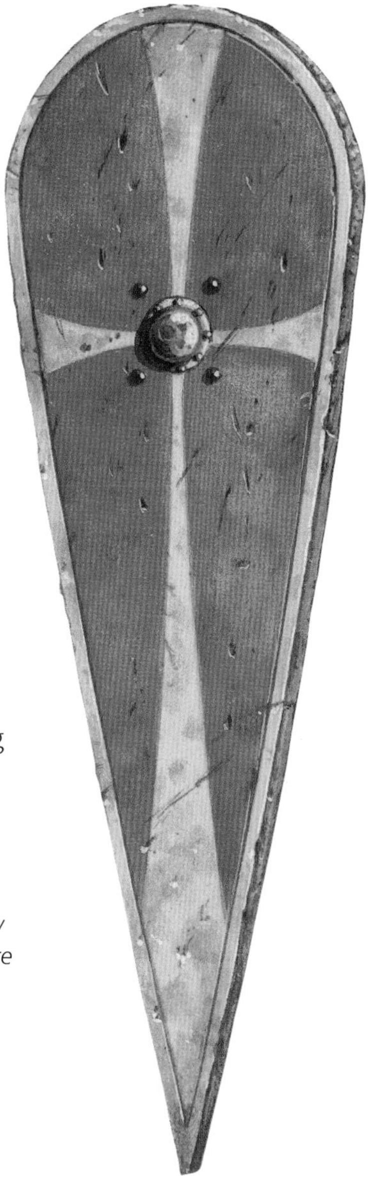

▶ *This is a typical design of an 11th-century shield. As knights wore more and more plate armour, their shields were made smaller.*

Christendom

By the later Middle Ages, most of Europe and parts of Western Asia shared the Christian faith. These lands were known as 'Christendom'. Latin was the common language of worship and scholarship.

Beautiful stone cathedrals were built in cities across Europe, with massive towers or soaring spires and windows of stained glass. Chimes of bells called people to prayer.

There were however, many divisions amongst Christians. In the 11th century the Roman Church and the Eastern or Byzantine Church disagreed bitterly and separated.

▶ *The impressive Palace of the Popes in Avignon, southern France, was built between 1314–1370. It was the home of the French Popes for 100 years during the time of the Great Schism.*

- **Core Christian beliefs** were unchallenged by most people, but there were powerful debates among leading churchmen. In the 1200s Bernard of Clairvaux emphasised the importance of faith, while scholars such as Roger Bacon and Peter Abelard called for questioning and reason.
- **Some Christians** such as the Cathars of southern France had views that were not accepted by the Church. They were persecuted and thousands of them were killed between 1209–1229.
- **Kings and emperors** all vied with the Popes for political power. In 1302 Pope Boniface VIII declared that all were subject to him. In 1309 Pope Clement V moved from Rome to Avignon in France. From 1378–1418 there was a Great Schism or split, as rival factions declared for different Popes.
- **In England** the followers of John Wycliffe (1320–1384) argued that the Church's political power, its wealth and its corruption went against the spirit of Christianity. After Wycliffe died his work was taken up by a Czech priest from Prague, Jan Hus (*c.*1370–1415). Hus was burnt at the stake for his views.

The Crusades

- **The word 'crusade'** comes from the Latin *crux*, meaning 'cross'. It refers to holy wars fought by knights from all over Christendom, between the 11th and late 13th century.
- **In 1095**, an army of the Muslim Seljuks (a Turkish-Persian dynasty) were just outside Constantinople, the centre of Christianity in the east. The Byzantine emperor Alexius I Comnenus appealed to Pope Urban II for help.
- **Urban II** held a meeting of church leaders at Clermont in France. He called for Christian warriors to drive back the Turks and reclaim the Holy Land.
- **In 1096**, armies of French and Norman knights set out on the First Crusade. At Constantinople, they joined forces with the Byzantines. Despite quarrelling on the way, they captured Jerusalem in 1099 and then set about massacring both Jews and Turks.
- **After capturing Jerusalem**, the Crusaders divided the Holy Land into four parts, together known as Outremer, which meant 'land beyond the seas'. The Crusader kingdoms ruled Outremer for 200 years and built great castles like Krak des Chevaliers in Syria.

▶ *When the Crusader knights set out to fight for control of Jerusalem, in the Holy Land, they went with different motives. Some were courageous, with a deep sense of honour and a holy purpose. Others were adventurers, out for personal gain or glory. This Crusader wears the famous uniform of the Knights Templars.*

DID YOU KNOW?

The most famous Crusader in England was King Richard I, known as the Lionheart for his bravery.

- **Two orders** of soldier-monks were formed to protect pilgrims journeying to the Holy Land – the Knights Hospitallers of St John and the Knights Templars. The Hospitallers wore black with a white cross. The Templars wore a red cross on white.
- **By 1144**, Crusader control of Outremer had weakened, and the Turks advanced. King Louis VII of France and King Conrad of Germany launched a Second Crusade. But by 1187, the Muslim leader Saladin had retaken most of the region.
- **In 1190**, the three most powerful men in Europe – Richard I of England, Philip II of France and Frederick Barbarossa (Holy Roman Emperor) – set off on the Third Crusade. Barbarossa died on the way and Philip II gave up. Only Richard went on, and secured a truce with Saladin.

- **On the Fourth Crusade** (1202–1204) the Crusaders turned aside to attack and loot Constantinople. This act of treachery was disastrous for the Byzantine Empire and for Christian unity.
- **A fervour for crusading** was whipped up by fanatical preachers. It led to mass movements of ordinary people setting out for the Near East. The chaotic People's Crusade of 1096 and Children's Crusade of 1212 ended in enslavement, kidnapping and death before they had even left Europe.
- **Some crusades** were fought against pagans in eastern Europe and the Baltic region. The Christian fight against the Moors in Spain was also seen as a crusade.

Saladin

- **Salah ad-Din Yusuf ibn Ayyub**, known in Europe as Saladin, was perhaps the greatest Islamic leader of the Middle Ages. To his people he was a hero. Even his Christian enemies were awed by his honour and bravery.
- **He is famed** as a brilliant soldier, but Saladin was also deeply religious. He built many schools, mosques and canals.
- **Saladin was a Kurd**, born in Tikrit, now in Iraq, in 1137, but he was brought up in Syria.
- **He became a soldier** at the age of 14. Right from the start he had an intense belief in the idea of jihad or 'struggle' – in this case an armed struggle to defend the Islamic faith.
- **Saladin's leadership** brought him to prominence and in 1169 he was effectively made Sultan (ruler) of Egypt.
- **By diplomacy** and conquest, he united the different Muslim peoples, which had been torn apart by rivalries for the 88 years since the Crusaders captured Jerusalem in 1099.
- **In 1187**, with Islam united, Saladin was able to turn his attentions to driving the Crusaders out of the Near East.
- **On 4 July 1187**, Saladin routed the Crusaders at Hattin, in what is now Israel. This victory was so devastating to the Crusaders that within three months the Muslims had recaptured almost every bit of land they had lost.
- **Shocked by the fall of Jerusalem**, the Christian countries threw themselves into yet another crusade, led in part by the great Richard I ('Lionheart') of England.

Such was Saladin's leadership that the Muslims fought off the Crusaders' onslaught. Eventually, Richard and Saladin drew up a truce that ended the crusade.

▼ *The Battle of Hattin in 1187 was a decisive victory for Saladin and a turning point in the Crusades.*

Magna Carta

- **Under King Henry II** of the Plantagenet dynasty, England ruled a large area of Europe, from the Scottish borders to southwestern France. It was called the Angevin Empire.
- **However** Henry nicknamed his son John 'Lackland'. Unlike his older brothers Richard and Geoffrey, John did not inherit land to provide him with an income.
- **When Richard I** became king, he went off on the Third Crusade. John was left to manage the kingdom. He behaved as if he was already king. He imposed heavy demands on his leading nobles (the barons) for tax and military service.
- **John did come to the throne** in 1199 and ruled until 1216. During his reign he lost Normandy to the French.
- **On 15 June 1215**, rebellious barons compelled John to meet them at Runnymede beside the River Thames, and agree to their demands by placing his seal of approval on a Magna Carta ('Great Charter') which contained 36 clauses.

▶ *The barons compelled King John to put his seal (wax stamp) on the Magna Carta at Runnymede in 1215.*

- **Magna Carta** may not have been a Bill of Rights in the modern sense, but it did confirm legal reforms made by Henry II, offer protection to free citizens and place limits on royal power.
- **Under Magna Carta** even the king had to obey the law. At a time when the power of kings or queens was absolute, this was a sign of progress.
- **John got the Pope to annul** (cancel) the document three days later, but it was reissued in 1225, after John's death.

Europe's monasteries

- **European monasteries** were no longer the small religious settlements of the early Middle Ages. By the 1200s orders of monks and nuns had become landowners, with immense power and wealth.
- **In England alone**, monasteries owned one-third of all the land and one-quarter of the country's wealth. Monasteries were Europe's biggest single employers.

▼ *Like many monasteries in England and Wales, the great 12th-century Cistercian monastery at Tintern was destroyed by Henry VIII.*

▶ *St Francis of Assissi (c.1181–1226) was an Italian monk who rejected wealth and valued the simple life. He founded three religious orders.*

- **The most famous** monastery was Cluny in France, but there were thousands of others. Most had a church called an abbey, some of which are among the most impressive medieval buildings.
- **Monasteries were places** where the poor went for welfare and they were also the only hospitals. They were also used by scholars to study. They had the only libraries in existence. Most great works of medieval art, literature and scholarship came from monasteries.
- **However, many monasteries** oppressed the poor by taking over land and imposing a heavy toll in tithes (church taxes). Many became notorious for the indulgences of their monks in fine food and high living.
- **New orders of monks** attempted every now and then to go back to a simpler life, like the Cistercians from Cîteaux in France and the Premonstratensians of Laon in France.
- **Cistercians founded monasteries** in barren places, such as Fountains Abbey in Yorkshire. But even they grew rich and lazy.

Battles for power

▶ *The story goes that, while in hiding, Robert Bruce was inspired to go on fighting after seeing a spider struggle up its thread again and again – and eventually succeed.*

- **The later Middle Ages** saw many kingdoms in Western Europe grow larger. Some defeated their neighbours in battle and annexed their lands. Others used marriage to unite rival dynasties and increase their domain.
- **France won the Duchy of Burgundy** at the Battle of Nancy in 1477, and won Brittany through the marriage of Anne of Brittany to Charles III in 1491.
- **Spain began to take on** its modern shape in 1479, when Ferdinand II of Aragon married Isabella I of Castile, uniting the two kingdoms.
- **England finally conquered** Wales in 1286, when Llywelyn II ap Gruffudd, the 'Last Prince', was killed in a skirmish at Cilmeri. Several uprisings followed, most notably under Owain Glyndŵr between 1400 and 1415. Wales and England were formally united by Acts of Union in 1536 and 1542.
- **In 1171 King Henry II** of England landed in Ireland, to be followed by his descendants King John and Richard II, all wishing to reinforce English control. In reality, English rule of medieval Ireland was limited to a small region around Dublin, known as the Pale. Beyond the Pale were the Irish-speaking Gaels, and descendants of the first Norman invaders.

In 1286 King Alexander III of Scotland died, and his grand-daughter Margaret died just four years later. As 13 rivals claimed the throne, Edward I of England tried to take advantage, marching into Scotland. A long war for Scottish independence began, with William Wallace defeating the English at Sterling in 1305. In 1314 Robert Bruce led the Scots to victory against Edward II at Bannockburn, regaining Scottish freedom.

DID YOU KNOW?
At Bannockburn, just 9000 Scots may have routed an English army of 25,000.

▼ *Scottish hero Robert Bruce freed the Scots from English control at the Battle of Bannockburn, in 1314.*

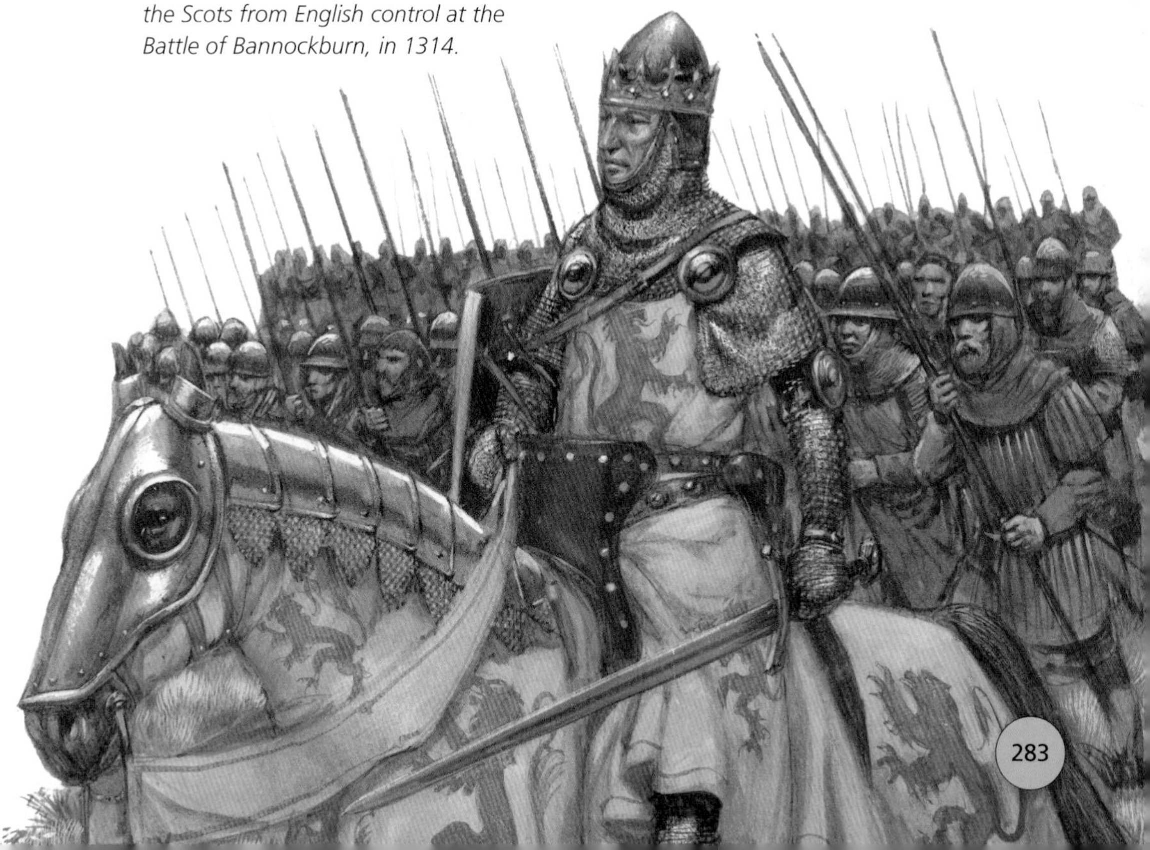

The Black Death

- **The Black Death** was one of the worst global diseases or pandemics ever to have struck humanity. It was a form of the bubonic plague, passed on by rat fleas.
- **The disease may have started** in China in the 1330s. It spread eastwards to Korea and westwards into Central Asia, along the trading routes of the Silk Road. It devastated Persia and Syria.
- **The plague may have been passed on** to Europeans when Mongol raiders catapulted infected corpses into a Genoese trading centre in the Crimea.

▼ *The plague brought death so close to people that they began to think of it as a real person.*

DID YOU KNOW?

More than one-third of all Europeans may have died from the plague in just four years.

- **The disease reached** the Italian port of Genoa in 1347 and spread west and north, reaching Portugal, Spain, France and Britain in 1348. From 1349–1351 it spread into Scandinavia and northwest Russia.
- **Worldwide**, it is estimated that the Black Death killed between 75–200 million people.
- **Afterwards** there was such a shortage of labour that wages soared and many serfs gained their freedom.

▲ *Plague returned to Europe many times over the centuries. This is London's Great Plague of 1665, during which houses of plague victims were marked with a cross.*

Money and trade

- **During the 1300s**, Europe's feudal system, under which people fought or worked in exchange for land, was replaced by an economy based on wages and finance.
- **Kings began to rely** on paid armies. They turned to newly rich merchants to pay for their wars. The Italians invented banks to give loans.
- **From the 1300s**, many serfs gained freedom and became prosperous 'yeoman' farmers. They needed merchants to sell their produce.
- **After the Crusades**, silks, spices and riches from the east were traded in the Mediterranean region for cloth, hides and iron. In northern Europe, the wool trade thrived.
- **In the 1300s and 1400s**, powerful trading towns grew up across western Europe – at Antwerp, Bruges, Bristol, Norwich, York, Florence, Venice, Milan and many others.

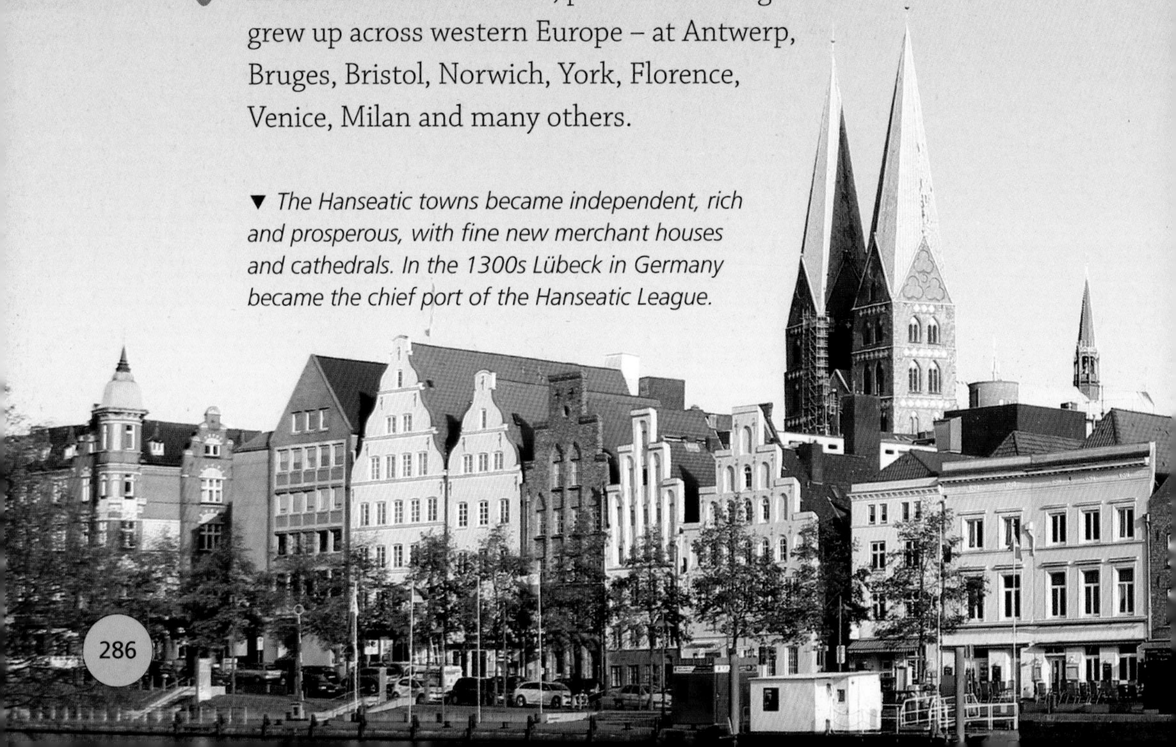

▼ *The Hanseatic towns became independent, rich and prosperous, with fine new merchant houses and cathedrals. In the 1300s Lübeck in Germany became the chief port of the Hanseatic League.*

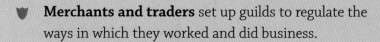

- **Merchants and traders** set up guilds to regulate the ways in which they worked and did business.
- **In 1241**, the German ports of Hamburg and Lübeck set up a Hanse (guild) to protect merchants against pirates. This alliance prospered and grew into the powerful Hanseatic League, which traded across the Baltic and the North Sea.
- **The Hanseatic League** set up special areas and warehouses in cities across northern Europe and controlled most trading routes. The League sometimes went to war to protect its interests, or put financial pressure on rulers to prevent wars that disrupted trade.
- **Many in society** remained desperately poor. Unfair taxation sparked rebellions and uprisings such as the French Jacquerie of 1358 and the English Peasants' Revolt of 1381.

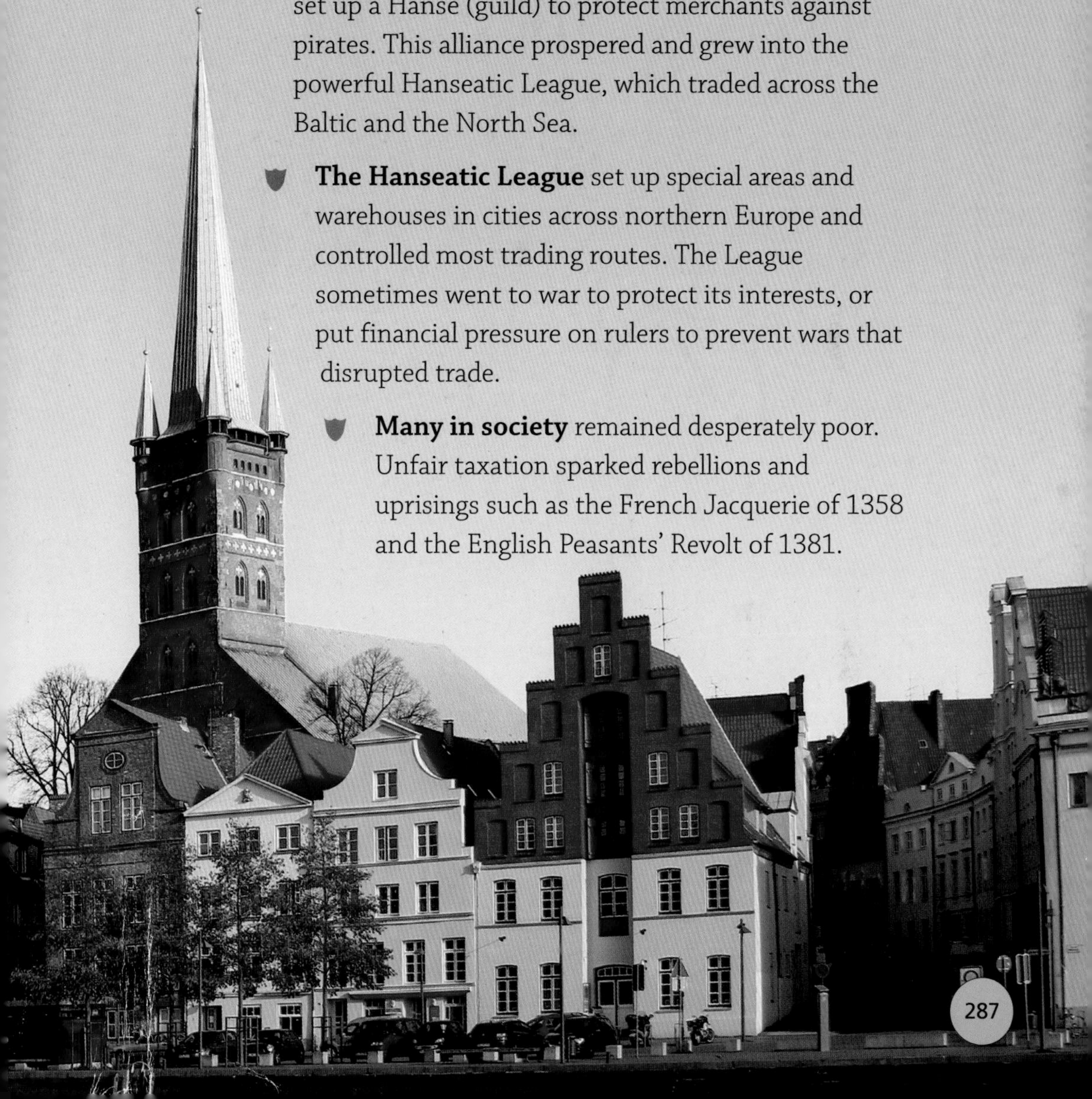

The Hundred Years' War

- **The Hundred Years' War** actually lasted for 116 years, from 1337–1453 – and was a series of conflicts rather than a single war.
- **The rivals** were the kingdoms of England and France, but warfare also affected the Welsh, Scots, Bretons, Burgundians, Spanish and the people of the Low Countries.
- **The reasons for war** were many. There was a dispute over Guyenne (English land in southwest France), over English claims to the French throne, over French support for the Scots, and over French efforts to block the English wool trade.
- **In 1337**, French King Philip VI tried to take over Guyenne. The English King Edward III, whose mother was sister to three French kings, retaliated by claiming the French throne.
- **In 1346**, Edward's archers – outnumbered three to one – used deadly longbows to rout the greatest French knights at Crécy. Armoured knights no longer seemed invincible.

DID YOU KNOW?
The tide turned for the French in 1429, when Joan of Arc led them to victory at Orléans.

▶ *The greatest knight of the war was Edward the Black Prince (1330–1376), hero of the Battles of Crécy, Poitiers and Navarette.*

▲ *In the Battle of Agincourt (1415), the French failed to learn lessons from previous defeats and Henry V won a glorious victory.*

- **In 1347** Edward III took the port of Calais. In 1356, Edward III's son, the Black Prince, won a great victory over the French at Poitiers.
- **England's last great victory** was under Henry V at Agincourt in 1415.
- **Despite these successes**, the better resourced French won the war as a whole.

Joan of Arc

- **St Joan of Arc** (*c*.1412–1431) was a peasant girl who saved France from defeat in the Hundred Years' War, and was burned at the stake for her beliefs.
- **Joan was called Jeanne d'Arc** in France. She called herself Jeanne la Pucelle (Joan the Maid).
- **She was brought up** in the village of Domrémy, in northeastern France, as a shepherd girl.
- **By the age of 13**, Joan was having visions and believed that God had chosen her to help the French king Charles VII to beat the English. At that time Charles was uncrowned and French fortunes were at their lowest point.

▼ *It was said that a short-haired, armour-clad Joan, flying her own flag, pushed back the English at Orléans, in 1429. She then took the Charles to Rheims to be crowned.*

▶ *Known traditionally as the Maid of Orléans, Joan was made a saint in 1920.*

- **Joan tried to see the king** but was laughed at until she was finally admitted to the royal court, in 1429.
- **To test Joan**, the king stood in disguise amongst his courtiers but Joan recognized him instantly. She also told him what he asked for in his secret prayers.
- **Joan was given armour** and an army to rescue the town of Orléans from the English. She succeeded in just ten days.

- **Joan then led Charles VII** through enemy territory to be crowned at Rheims cathedral.
- **In May 1430**, Joan was captured by the English and accused of witchcraft.
- **Joan insisted** that her visions came from God, but a tribunal condemned her as a heretic. She was burned at the stake in Rouen on 30 May 1431.

Wars of the Roses

- **Throughout the Middle Ages**, European wars were often fought not so much between 'nations' as between powerful dynasties.
- **The Wars of the Roses** devastated England in the 1400s. Two branches of the Plantagenet dynasty fought for the throne.
- **On one side** was the House of York, with a white rose as its emblem. On the other was the House of Lancaster, with a red rose as its emblem.
- **The wars began** in 1453, when Lancastrian King Henry VI became insane. With the country in chaos, Richard Neville, Earl of Warwick (the 'Kingmaker') set up Richard, Duke of York as Protector in Henry's place.
- **In 1455**, Henry VI seemed to recover and war broke out between Lancastrians and Yorkists. Richard was killed at the Battle of Wakefield in 1460, but Henry VI became insane again.
- **A crushing Yorkist victory** at Towton, near York, in 1461, put Richard's son on the throne as Edward IV.
- **Edward IV** made enemies of his brothers Clarence and Warwick, who invaded England from France in 1470 with Henry VI's queen Margaret of Anjou and drove Edward out.

◀ *The white – and red – roses were emblems of the rival houses of York and Lancaster. When Henry VII married Elizabeth of York, he combined the two to make a 'Tudor' rose.*

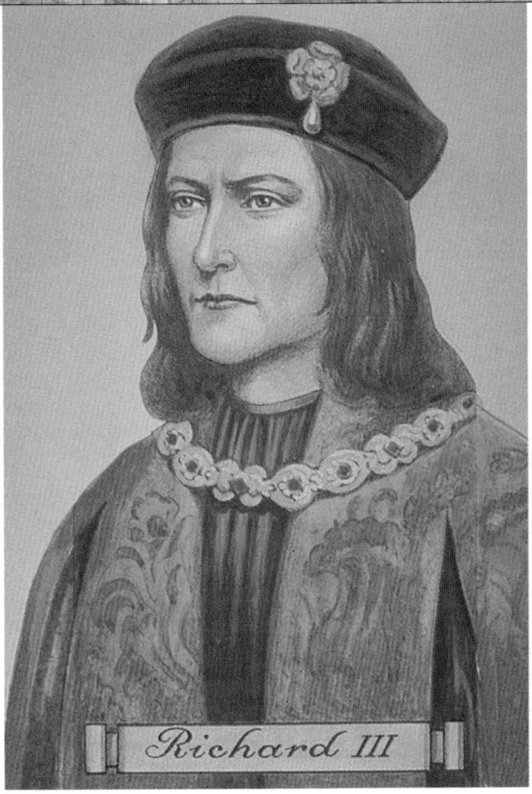

◀ *Richard III's remains were discovered in Leicester in 2012.*

- **Henry VI** was brought back for seven months before Edward's Yorkists defeated the Lancastrians at Barnet and Tewkesbury. Henry VI was murdered.
- **When Edward IV died** in 1483, his son Edward V was still a boy. When young, Edward and his brother vanished – probably murdered in the Tower of London – their uncle Richard III seized the throne.
- **Richard III** made enemies among the Yorkists, who sided with Lancastrian Henry Tudor. Richard III was killed at the Battle of Bosworth Field on 22 August 1485. Henry Tudor became Henry VII and married Elizabeth of York to end the wars.

In the early modern period, humanity discovered new lands, sciences and arts.

AFRICA

1500
Europeans build forts in West and East Africa.

1500s
Golden age of the Benin or Edo empire, Nigeria.

1517
Egypt becomes part of the Turkish Ottoman empire.

c.1520
Beginnings of the trans-Atlantic slave trade out of West Africa.

1550s
Piracy and slave raids from the 'Barbary' (Berber) coast, North Africa.

1608
Growing power of the Oyo empire of the Yoruba in West Africa.

1623–1626
The Portuguese fight against Queen Nzinga of the Ndongo.

1652
The Dutch found Cape Colony, South Africa.

EUROPE

1470s–1500s
High point of the Renaissance in Italian states such as Florence and Pisa.

1490s–1600s
European seafarers led by Spain and Portugal explore the world and acquire great wealth.

1517
German priest Martin Luther's 95 Theses mark the start of the Protestant Reformation.

1520
Suleiman the Magnificent rules the Ottoman empire from Istanbul.

1568–1648
Dutch War of Independence against Spain. Rise of the Netherlands.

1618–1648
The Thirty Years' War devastates Germany and Central Europe.

1643–1715
Reign of Louis XIV, the 'Sun King', in France.

1649
King Charles I is tried and executed in England. A Commonwealth (republic) is declared.

ASIA

1521
Explorer Ferdinand Magellan claims the Philippines for Spain.

1526–1857
The Mughal empire rules in India.

1584–1640
The Russian conquest of Siberia.

1587–1629
Shah Abbas I rules Persia's Safavid empire, a great age of culture and crafts.

1600s
European powers set up companies to dominate shipping and trade in southern Asia.

1603
Tokugawa Ieyasu becomes Shogun (military leader) in Japan.

1644
In China, Manchurian rebels overthrow the Ming dynasty and found the Qing.

1683
The Turkish Ottoman empire is at its greatest extent, extending to the Persian Gulf.

Age of Discovery

NORTH AMERICA

1534
French explorer Jacques Cartier explores the Gulf of St Lawrence in Canada.

1565
The Spanish found St Augustine, Florida.

1585
English explorer Sir Walter Raleigh attempts to found a colony at Roanoke Island, now in North Carolina.

1600s
Rise of the Iroquois League, a union of northeastern Native American nations.

1620
The founding of Plymouth Colony in Massachusetts by English settlers (the 'Pilgrim Fathers').

1626
The Dutch establish New Amsterdam. In 1664 it came under English rule as New York.

1670
The English found Hudson's Bay Company to control trading and government in a large area of Canada.

1682
The French establish the colony of Louisiana, part of a vast territory known as New France.

CENTRAL AND SOUTH AMERICA

1492
Christopher Columbus' first voyage starts the European exploration and colonization of the Americas.

1492–1600s
Caribbean islands colonized by Europeans. Indigenous peoples enslaved and murdered, replaced by slaves from West Africa.

1500
Portuguese navigator Pedro Álvares Cabral claims Brazil for Portugal.

1519–1521
Spanish conquistador Hernan Cortés defeats Mexico's Aztec empire.

1520
Ferdinand Magellan navigates the Strait of Magellan, from the Atlantic to the Pacific Ocean.

1532
Spanish conquistador Francisco Pizarro defeats the Inca empire in Peru.

1566
Spanish treasure fleets start to ship the riches of the New World back to Europe.

c.1630
Dutch, English and French colonies established on South America's north coast.

OCEANIA

c.1500
Start of the Classic period of Maori culture in New Zealand, finely made weapons and ornaments.

c.1500
Maoris settle the Chatham Islands, start of the Moriori culture.

1526
The island of New Guinea is first sighted by Portuguese explorer Jorge de Meneses.

1606
Dutch navigator Willem Janszoon explores Australia's Cape York peninsula.

1616
Dutch captain Dirk Hartog reaches the western coast of Australia.

1642
Dutch captain Abel Tasman charts the coasts of Tasmania and New Zealand.

1643
Tasman is the first European to visit the island of Fiji.

1699
William Dampier's expedition to Western Australia provides first detailed record of plant and animal species.

The Renaissance

▲ *This portrayal of God's creation of man comes from the great Renaissance artist Michelangelo's famous paintings on the ceiling of the Sistine Chapel, in Rome.*

- **The Renaissance** was a great revolution in arts and ideas that began in Italy between the 1300s and the 1500s.
- **Renaissance is French** for 'rebirth', and refers partly to a revival of interest in the works of the classical world of Greece and Rome.
- **During the Renaissance** many scholars began to question aspects of Medieval Christian teaching and to focus more on the nature of humanity. They gradually developed the idea of 'humanism'.
- **A spur to the Renaissance** was the fall of Constantinople to the Ottoman Turks in 1453. This sent Greek scholars fleeing to Italy, where they set up academies in cities like Florence and Padua.

- **Artists in the Renaissance**, inspired by classical examples, began to try and put people at the centre of their work – and to portray people and nature realistically rather than as religious symbols.
- **In the 1400s** brilliant artists like Donatello created startlingly realistic paintings and sculptures.
- **Perhaps the three greatest artists** of the Renaissance were Leonardo da Vinci (1452–1519), Raphael (1483–1520) and Michelangelo (1475–1564).
- **The Renaissance saw** some of the world's greatest artistic and architectural masterpieces being created in Italian cities such as Florence and Padua.
- **During the late 1400s**, Renaissance ideas spread to northern Europe.

▶ *Many Renaissance painters ran studios where a team of artists worked on a 'production line' principle, so that the painter himself was not wholly responsible for the work.*

The Medicis

- **The Medici family** of Florence, a city-state and republic in Italy, were one of the most powerful families in Europe between 1400 and 1700.
- **The Medicis' fortunes** began with the bank founded by Giovanni de' Medici in 1397. The Medicis became staggeringly rich.
- **Giovanni's son**, Cosimo, built up the bank and there were soon branches in major cities across Europe.
- **By 1434**, Cosimo was so rich and powerful that he became ruler of Florence. Except for brief periods, the Medicis then ruled Florence for 300 years.
- **The Medicis were famed** for paying huge sums of money to commission fine works of art.
- **The artist Michelangelo** worked for the Medici family from 1515–1534 and created the fabulous Medici Chapel for them.

◀ *Lorenzo de' Medici was a tough ruler who put down opposition brutally. But he was also a scholar and a fine poet.*

▲ *During the 1400s, art and architecture in Florence flourished under the Medicis' patronage. The great dome of the city's cathedral was the work of Filippo Brunelleschi.*

- **The most famous** Medici was Lorenzo (1449–1492), known as 'the Magnificent'. Under him, Florence became Europe's most splendid city, full of great works of art.
- **Lorenzo may have been called** the Magnificent, but he managed to bankrupt the Medici bank.
- **Three Medicis** became Popes – Leo X (from 1513–1521), Clement VII (from 1523–1534) and then Leo XI (from 1605).
- **Two Medicis became** queens of France. One of these was Catherine de' Medici (1519–1589), queen of Henry II.

Rise of the Ottomans

- **In 1453**, Byzantine Constantinople fell to the Ottoman Turks under Mehmed II. The city became their new capital, Istanbul. By 1458 the Turks had captured Athens and most of Greece.
- **Who were the Ottomans?** The name came from the Osmanli dynasty, which back in 1281 had ruled a Turkish state called Sögüt.
- **The Ottomans** now came to rule a large Muslim empire. This would include North Africa, Western Asia, and southeastern Europe.

▲ *Oruç Reis ('Barbarossa', c.1474–1518) was a piratical governor on the Barbary Coast. His brother Hayreddin (c.1478–1546) became admiral of the Ottoman fleet.*

- **Beautiful mosques** were built in Istanbul, and a luxurious palace, Topkapi Saray. Turkey was famous for its bazaars, its rich silks and carpets, its pottery and metalwork, and its coffee and spices.
- **Ottoman power peaked** in the 1520s under Suleiman, known as Qanuni ('law-giver') by Turks and 'the Magnificent' by Europeans because of his splendid court.
- **In 1522**, Suleiman captured the island of Rhodes. In 1529 he took all Hungary and attacked Vienna. There was constant fighting between Turkish and Christian shipping across the Mediterranean.

- **In the 1500s** the Berber rulers of the 'Barbary' (Northwest African) coast became virtually independent of the Ottomans and engaged in piracy, aided by renegade European pirates.
- **When the Turks attacked** Cyprus in 1571, Venetian, Spanish and Papal fleets combined to crush them at the naval battle of Lepanto.
- **Ottoman power declined** after 1683, when the Turks were again defeated outside Vienna, by Polish hero John III Sobieski.

▼ *Lepanto was the last great battle between fleets of galleys – warships powered by huge banks of oarsmen.*

Voyages of exploration

During the late Middle Ages, turmoil across Asia cut off Europe's overland trading routes with India and China. European merchants needed to find new routes by sea. Bold seafarers set out from Portugal and Spain to find a way to the east by sea.

▼ *Many European explorers sailed in caravels. These ships were rarely more than 20–30 m long and weighed under 150 tonnes. But they could cope with rough seas and head into the wind, so could sail in most directions. They were also fast – vital when crossing vast oceans.*

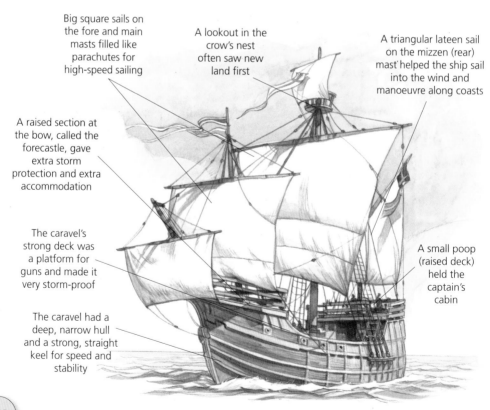

Big square sails on the fore and main masts filled like parachutes for high-speed sailing
A lookout in the crow's nest often saw new land first
A triangular lateen sail on the mizzen (rear) mast helped the ship sail into the wind and manoeuvre along coasts
A raised section at the bow, called the forecastle, gave extra storm protection and extra accommodation
The caravel's strong deck was a platform for guns and made it very storm-proof
A small poop (raised deck) held the captain's cabin
The caravel had a deep, narrow hull and a strong, straight keel for speed and stability

DID YOU KNOW?
A treaty signed at Tordesillas in 1494 divided all new discoveries in the world between Spain and Portugal.

- **Many early voyages** were encouraged by Portugal's Prince Henry ('the Navigator', 1394–1460). In 1488, Bartolomeu Dias sailed around Africa's southern tip and into the Indian Ocean. In 1497, Vasco da Gama sailed around Africa to Calicut in India, and returned laden with spices and jewels.
- **In 1492** the Genoese sailor Christopher Columbus set out across the open Atlantic. He hoped to reach China by travelling westwards around the world. Instead, he found the whole 'New World' – North and South America.
- **Columbus only landed** on Caribbean islands at first. Even when he reached South America on his last voyage, he thought he was in Asia. The first to realize that it was an unknown continent was the Florentine explorer Amerigo Vespucci, who landed there in 1499. A map, which was made in 1507, named North and South America after him.
- **In 1497** Venetian John Cabot set out from Bristol in the service of England and reached Labrador in North America.
- **In 1519–1522**, Ferdinand Magellan sailed across the Atlantic, around the southern tip of South America, across the Pacific and back around Africa to Spain. Although this Portuguese explorer was killed in the Philippines, his surviving crew and one ship went on to complete the first round-the-world voyage.
- **In the 1500s and 1600s** navigators from England, France and the Netherlands also sailed the world's oceans from the Arctic to Australia, discovering new lands.

Christopher Columbus

- **Christopher Columbus** (1451–1506) was the Genoese sailor who crossed the Atlantic and 'discovered' North and South America for Europe.
- **Columbus was not** the first European to cross the Atlantic. The Vikings had briefly settled in Newfoundland in 1004. However it was the voyages of Columbus that would have a lasting impact on the Americas.
- **Other sailors** were trying to find their way to China and the east by sailing south around Africa. Columbus, aware that the Earth is round, wanted to strike out west across the open Atlantic Ocean and reach China that way.
- **After years spent trying** to get backing, Columbus finally got support from the Spanish monarchs Ferdinand and Isabella.
- **Columbus set sail** from southwestern Spain on 3 August, 1492, in three caravels – the Santa Maria, the Niña and the Pinta.

▼ *The beautiful shores of the Bahamas were probably those first spotted by Columbus on his voyage westward.*

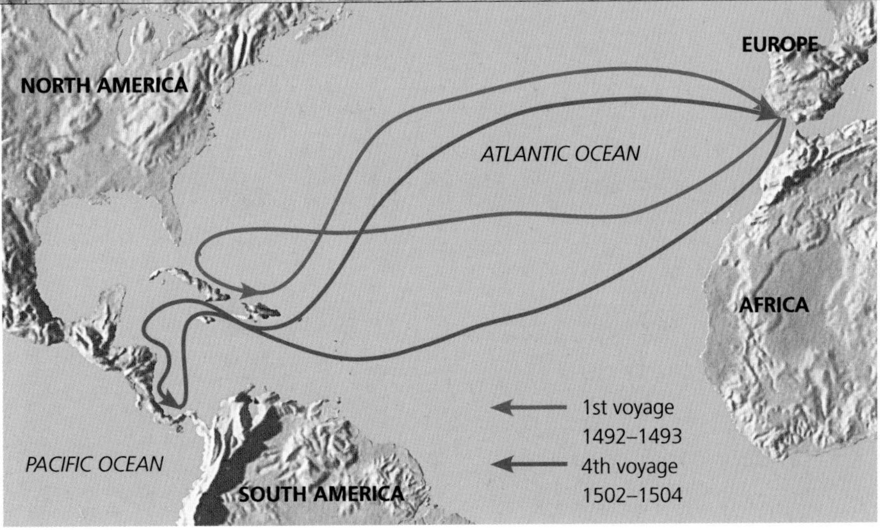

▲ *Columbus made four voyages across the Atlantic, and they are all given great significance today. He died in 1506, still refusing to believe the New World existed.*

- **They sailed west** into the unknown for three weeks, by which time the fearful sailors were ready to mutiny.
- **On 12 October**, a look-out spotted the Bahamas. Columbus thought he was in the Indies (hence the name 'West Indies'). He called the native peoples 'Indians'.
- **Columbus left 40 men** on a large island that he called Hispaniola and went back to Spain a hero.
- **In 1493 and 1498**, he set off on two more voyages with large fleets, as Viceroy of the Indies. He set up a colony on Hispaniola, but it was a disaster. The Spaniards complained of his harsh rule and many native Americans died from cruelty and disease. Columbus went back to Spain in chains.
- **Columbus was pardoned**, and began a fourth voyage in 1502. He died in Spain in 1506, still thinking his journeys had taken him along the east coast of Asia.

The Aztecs

- **In the year 1502** the most powerful empire in Mexico was that of the Aztecs.
- **Their original homeland** had been in the northwest, but in about 1100 they had started a southward migration in search of better land – guided, they believed, by their god Huitzilopochtli. Nearly 100 years later they entered the Valley of Mexico.
- **In 1325**, on an island on a lake, the Aztecs founded their capital, Tenochtitlán. Linked to the shores by causeways, it grew into a splendid city with canals, gardens, temples, palaces and schools.

▶ *The 25 tonne Sun Stone or Calendar, discovered in the centre of Mexico City, shows the gods and cosmos of the ancient Aztec religion.*

- **By 1428** the city was joined with Texcoco and Tlacopan in a Triple Alliance. The empire grew and grew.

DID YOU KNOW?

Every year Tenochtitlán took in 9000 tonnes of corn, beans and seeds in taxes.

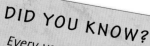

- **Aztec society** was headed by a powerful ruler, and by nobles and priests. The Aztecs built vast pyramids topped by temples, where priests made bloody human sacrifices.

- **Farmers grew tomatoes**, squash, sweet potatoes and maize. Cocoa beans were used not only to make chocolate drinks but also as a form of money in big markets, as at Tlatelolco.

- **Warriors fought with spears**, wooden swords, clubs, bows and arrows. Cutting edges were of razor-sharp obsidian rather than metals.

- **Central American peoples** like the Aztecs played a sacred ball game. Teams had to hit a rubber ball through a small ring, using hips, knees and elbows.

- **In 1519** Spanish ships arrived on the east coast of Mexico. The days of the mighty Aztec empire were numbered.

Aztec myths

- **It was said** that the Aztecs founded Tenochtitlán on the island in the lake because priests saw an eagle land there, on a cactus plant growing from a rock. This was interpreted as a sign from the gods.
- **The Aztecs shared** the same mythology as the earlier Toltec civilization. Their first ruler claimed to be a descendant of the chief Toltec god Huitzilopochtli.
- **In the beginning**, the gods created and destroyed four worlds one after another, because humans did not make enough sacrifices.

▲ *The Aztecs' feathered serpent god, Quetzalcóatl was also worshipped by many earlier peoples of the region. This is his temple at Teotihuacán.*

- **In order to create** a sun for the fifth world, two gods sacrificed themselves by jumping into a flaming bonfire.
- **At first**, the fifth world consisted only of water with a female monster goddess floating in it, eating everything. The mighty gods Quetzalcóatl and Tezcatlipoca ripped the goddess apart and turned her body into the Earth and the heavens.
- **The Aztecs believed** that the sun god and the earth monster needed sacrifices of human blood and hearts in order to remain fertile and alive.
- **Human beings** were created by Quetzalcóatl, from the powdered bones of his dead father and his own blood.

▲ *This magnificent manuscipt or 'codex' was prepared by Aztec priests at about the time of the Spanish invasion. It shows the god Quetzalcóatl.*

- **Quetzalcóatl and Tezcatlipoca** brought musicians and singers from the House of the Sun down to Earth. From then on, every living thing could create its own kind of music.
- **Like the Toltecs**, the Aztecs built huge pyramid temples. Modern Mexico City is built on the ancient site of Tenochtitlán.
- **We know about Aztec myths** from an ancient Aztec calendar, and a document that explains how Aztec gods fit into the calendar.

The Incas

- **In South America**, the Inca culture reached its peak about 1500.
- **The Incas were a tribe** from the highlands of Peru, who built their capital at Cuzco in about 1200.
- **In 1438**, Pachacuti Inca Yupanqui became their Sapa Inca (king) and they built up a huge empire that controlled lands northwards to Colombia and south to Chile, a distance of 4000 km. It was known as Tawantinsuyu.
- **Inca builders** cut and fitted huge stones with astonishing precision to create massive buildings.
- **Inca engineers** built 30,000 km of roads across the empire, spanning deep ravines with dizzying suspension bridges. They also built irrigated terraces for farming high into the Andes mountains.

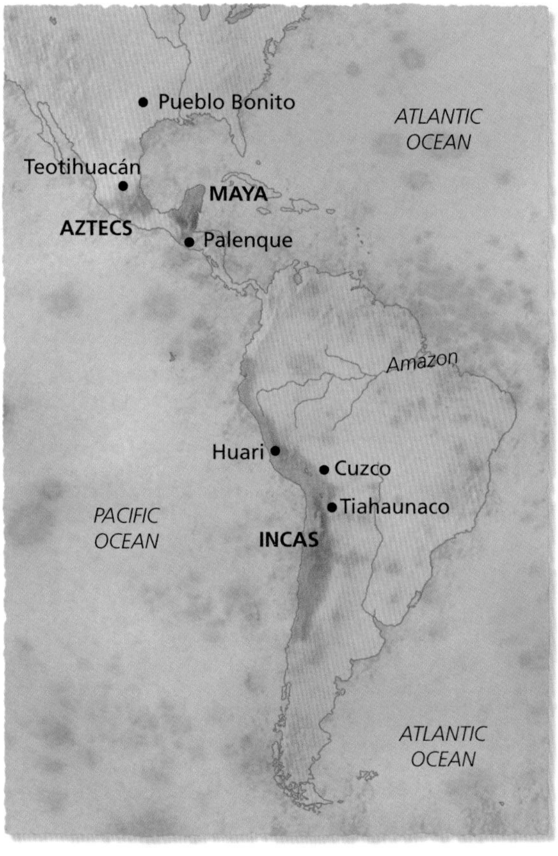

▶ *The darker brown area shows the extent of the Inca empire at the height of its power.*

▲ *The remains of Inca buildings at Pisac, in modern-day Peru. The Incas built impressive palaces, temples, fortresses and warehouses, and covered some buildings in sheets of beaten gold.*

- **The Incas communicated** across their vast empire by relays of runners 2.5 km apart. A message could travel 250 km in less than one day.
- **The royal palace** had a garden full of life-like corn stalks, animals and birds made of solid gold and silver. Gold was a symbol of the sun god, and silver of the moon goddess.

DID YOU KNOW?

The Inca capital was called Cuzco, which means 'navel', as it was the centre of their world.

The conquistadors

- **Conquistadors** ('conquerors') were soldiers from Spain and Portugal who landed in the Americas in the 1500s. They attacked indigenous peoples.
- **Some conquistadors** were greedy for land and riches, while some wished to spread the Christian faith. These were daring, tough and violent men, who often fought amongst themselves.
- **The invaders brought** with them deadly European diseases such as smallpox. With their firearms, horses and ships, even a few conquistadors could defeat whole populations.

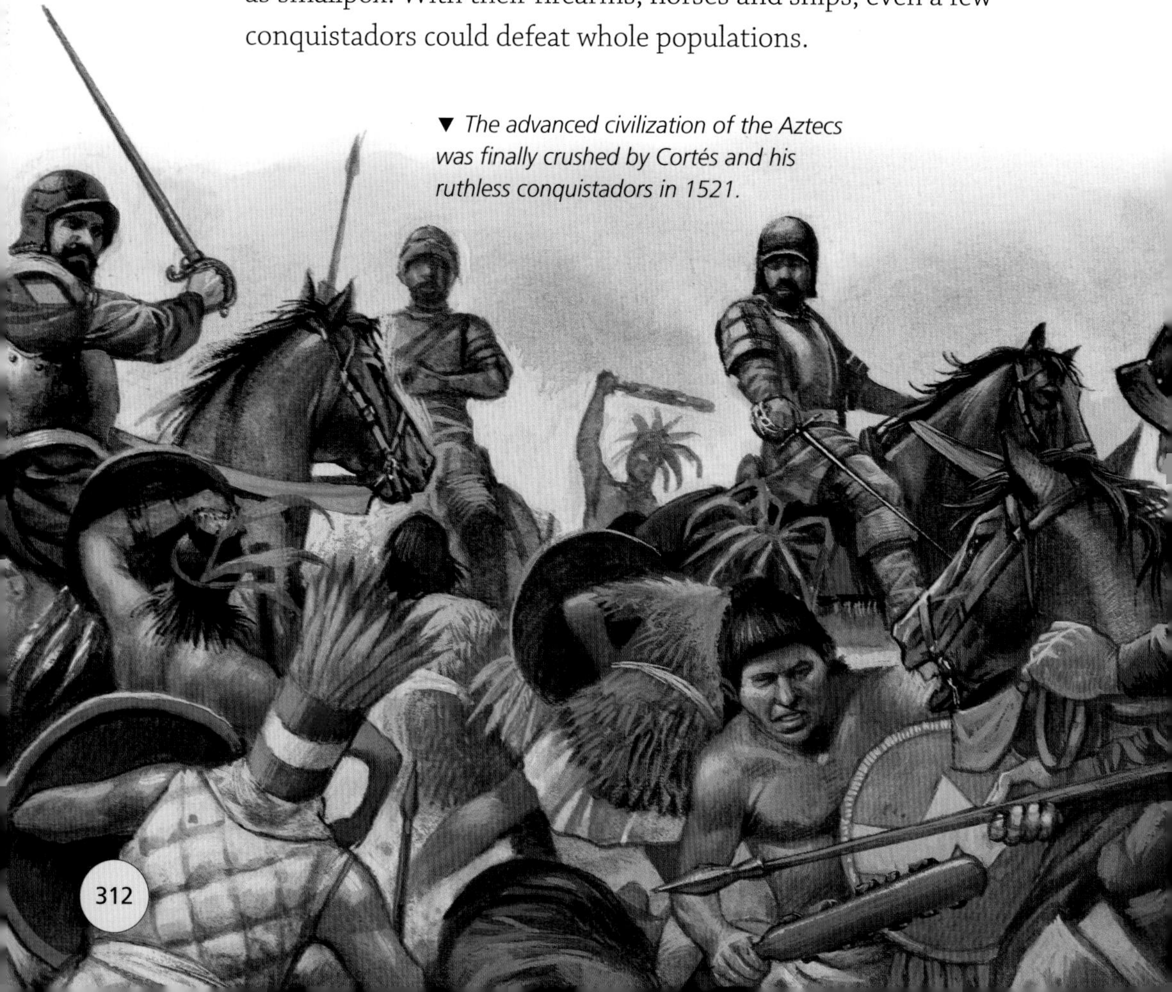

▼ *The advanced civilization of the Aztecs was finally crushed by Cortés and his ruthless conquistadors in 1521.*

▶ *A statue in Peru represents Francisco Pizarro. He was assassinated by rival conquistadors in 1541.*

- **Hernán Cortés** (1485–1547) landed in Mexico with 500 men in 1519. Joining with rebels against the Aztecs, he marched to Tenochtitlán.
- **The Aztec leader** Moctezuma welcomed the Spaniards, but was taken captive. Six months later the Aztecs rebelled and Cortés fled, only to return and destroy the city.
- **Francisco Pizarro** (*c.*1478–1541) set off to find the Incas in 1524. When he reached Peru, the Incas had been fighting a civil war. Pizarro captured the ruler Atahualpa, ransomed him for a vast amount of gold and then killed him anyway.

DID YOU KNOW?
When Spaniards got off their horses, the Incas thought they were beasts splitting in two.

- **Pizarro took Cuzco** in 1533, but resistance to Spanish rule continued until 1572.

The Spanish Empire

- **Within half a century** of Columbus's arrival in America in 1492, Spanish conquistadors had conquered the Americas from California to Argentina.
- **Thousands of Spaniards** came to colonize Latin America in the 1500s, creating cities such as Cartagena in Colombia and Guayaquil in Ecuador.

▼ *Once a year, two Spanish treasure fleets would leave from Havana in Cuba guarded by the galleons of the Armada de la Guardia. Galleons were the biggest warships, 35 m long and weighing around 500 tonnes.*

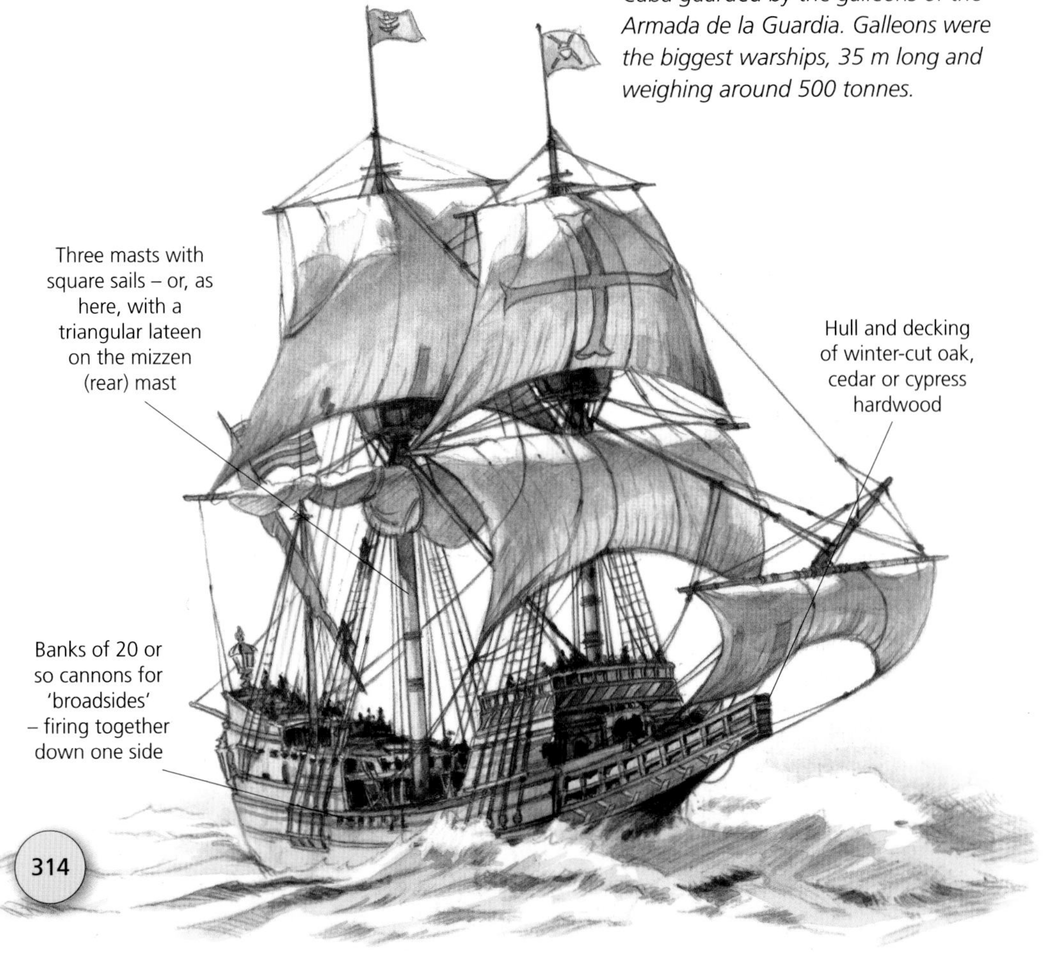

DID YOU KNOW?
The Spanish brought new foods such as tomatoes, potatoes and chocolate back to Europe from their American empire.

- **Spanish rulers** tried to deal with local people through the encomienda system, whereby indigenous peoples ('Indians') were assigned to Spaniards who were supposed to look after them in return for taxes and labour.
- **Many of these people** were cruelly abused by their masters. In 100 years, the indigenous population dropped from 50 million to 4 million, through cruelty, poverty and diseases brought in by Europeans.
- **Some Spanish Dominican friars** condemned the encomienda – especially Bartolomé de Las Casas – and fought unsuccessfully for better conditions for Native Americans.
- **Indians mined silver**, gold and gems in huge amounts in South America. The Muzo and Chivor mines in Colombia were famous for their emeralds.
- **Every year**, in the calm months between March and October, ships laden with treasure left the Americas bound for Spain.
- **By the 1540s**, the Spanish ships were suffering pirate attacks, so the ships crossed the Atlantic every year in two great fleets protected by an armada of galleons (warships).
- **Besides American treasure**, Spanish ships carried cargoes of spices from the East Indies and silks from China. These were shipped across the Pacific from the Philippines to Mexico, then carried overland to be shipped from the Caribbean to Europe.

The Reformation

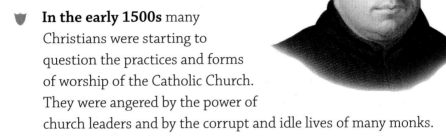

▶ *Martin Luther was the monk whose radical views sparked off the Protestant reformation, dividing Christians in Europe into Catholics and Protestants.*

- **In the early 1500s** many Christians were starting to question the practices and forms of worship of the Catholic Church. They were angered by the power of church leaders and by the corrupt and idle lives of many monks.
- **Martin Luther** (1483–1546) was the son of a poor miner from Saxony, in Germany. As a monk at Wittenberg University, he earned a reputation for his great biblical knowledge.
- **Luther attacked** the sale of 'indulgences' (officially issued pardons for sins) by Pope Leo X. He was selling them to raise money to build St Peter's basilica in Rome.
- **In 1517** Luther nailed a list of grievances to the door of the chapel at Wittenberg Castle, hoping to start a debate.
- **The Pope responded** by issuing a bull (demand) that Luther withdraw his theses or face expulsion from the Church. Luther burned the bull – and the Church expelled him in 1521.
- **The development of printing** in Europe at this time meant that pamphlets explaining Luther's views could be read by thousands. Support grew rapidly.

- **Luther set up** his own church, whose members became known as Protestants. Protestants wanted the Latin scriptures translated into languages people spoke every day. They wanted simpler churches and less ritual.
- **Other radical rebels** joined the cause, such as the Swiss pastor Ulrich Zwingli (1484–1531) and the French theologian John Calvin (1509–1564).
- **The movement** gathered pace across northern Europe, and the split with the Catholic Church seemed permanent. It became known as the Reformation.

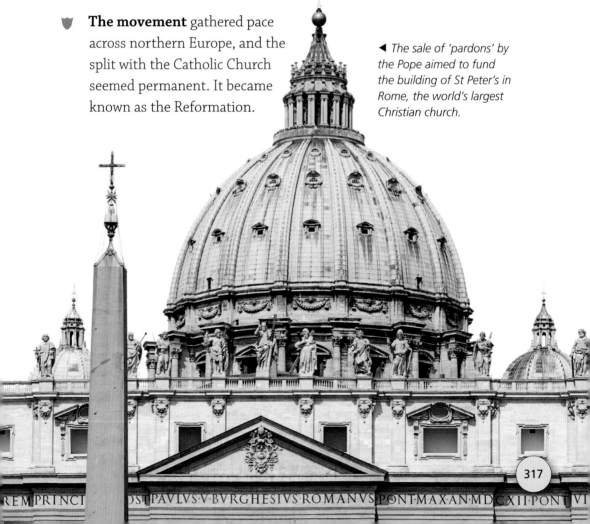

◀ The sale of 'pardons' by the Pope aimed to fund the building of St Peter's in Rome, the world's largest Christian church.

Henry VIII of England

- **Henry VIII** of the Tudor dynasty became King of England at the age of 18, in 1509. He was handsome and athletic, spoke several languages, played the lute well and was keen on new humanist ideas.
- **Henry engaged in war** with Scotland and France. He was a faithful Catholic, indeed he was given the title 'Defender of the Faith' by Pope Leo X. However he soon fell out with the Church for personal reasons.
- **A Spanish Catholic** called Catherine of Aragon was Henry's first wife, and she bore Henry a daughter, Mary, but not a male heir.
- **The Pope refused** a divorce, so Henry broke with Rome to be declared head of the Church in England.

▶ *We have an astonishingly clear picture of what Henry and his court looked like from the brilliant portraits of Hans Holbein. This picture is based on Holbein's striking painting of Henry from 1537.*

- **Unlike some of his subjects**, Henry was no radical Protestant and he continued with Catholic tradition whilst opposing Rome.
- **Henry divorced Catherine** and banished her from court, marrying Anne Boleyn. She too bore a daughter, Elizabeth, and she was beheaded in 1536. Of Henry's four other wives, one died, one had her marriage to him anulled, one was beheaded and one outlived him.
- **Henry seized the property** of the Catholic Church, destroying and looting monasteries and giving the land to his supporters.
- **Clever ministers** such as Thomas Wolsey and Thomas Cromwell served Henry, but many were executed when things went wrong. Henry faced several rebellions and uprisings.
- **As Henry grew old**, he became grossly fat, riddled with sickness and inclined to terrible outbreaks of anger. Hed died in 1547.

▶ *Catherine Parr (1512–1548) – the last of Henry's six wives.*

Catholics *vs* Protestants

- **In the 1500s**, the Roman Catholic Church was determined to fight against the Protestant Reformation and other threats. Their fight is called the Counter-Reformation.
- **In 1534**, St Ignatius Loyola founded the Society of Jesus (Jesuits) to lead the Counter-Reformation.
- **Investigative bodies** called Inquisitions were set up to seek out and punish heretics – anyone who held views that did not agree with those of the Catholic Church.
- **From 1483**, the Spanish Inquisition became a byword for terror, swooping on suspected heretics – Protestants and Jews alike – torturing them and burning them at the stake.
- **The battle between** Catholics and Protestants created many victims and many martyrs in the late 1500s.

▶ *Thomas More (1478–1535) was executed when he refused to acknowledge Henry VIII as head of the English Church.*

▲ *The Spanish Inquisition was notorious for public burnings of anyone considered to be dangerously anti-Catholic. Their activities continued until the 1800s.*

- **In the St Bartholomew's Day massacre** in 1571, up to 70,000 French Protestants, called Huguenots, were killed on the orders of the Catholic queen Catherine de' Medici.
- **English Protestants** were burned during the reign of Catholic Queen Mary I, earning her the name 'Bloody Mary'. English Catholics such as Edmund Campion were hanged, drawn and quartered in Protestant Queen Elizabeth I's reign.
- **In Germany**, a terrible Thirty Years' War was started in 1618 as rivalries between Catholics and Protestants flared up.

DID YOU KNOW?

Catholic houses in England in the late 1500s had hiding places for priests called 'priest holes'.

Dutch independence

- **In 1500**, there were 17 provinces making up what is now Belgium, the Netherlands and Luxembourg. The most important was Holland.
- **The provinces came under** Spanish rule in 1516, when their ruler the Holy Roman Emperor Charles V also became the King of Spain (Charles I).
- **Holland's capital Amsterdam** became the leading commercial centre of Europe. With the growth of trade, Protestant ideas started taking hold.
- **Charles's son Philip II** and his deputy the Duke of Alba tried to crush the Protestants by executing their leaders. As Alba became more ruthless, opposition spread.
- **In 1566**, William, Prince of Orange, led the Dutch in revolt. Although the Dutch controlled the sea, they gradually gave way before the Spanish army.
- **In 1574**, the Dutch opened dikes holding back the sea to sail over the flood to Leiden and rescue the besieged.
- **Protestants retreated** to the northern provinces, and in 1581 declared themselves the independent Dutch Republic. The fighting ceased, but it was 1648 before the nation was recognized legally.
- **The 1600s** proved to be a 'golden age' for the Dutch Republic.
- **The Dutch merchant fleet** became the biggest in Europe. Dutch banks and businesses thrived and Dutch scientists like Antonie van Leeuwenhoek and Christiaan Huygens made great discoveries.

▼ *The Low Countries became a centre of painting in the 15th century. This painting is by Jan Van Eyck. In the following centuries Dutch artists like Jan Steen, Johannes Vermeer and Rembrandt van Rijn created vibrant, technically brilliant paintings, often of everyday scenes.*

Elizabethan England

- **Elizabeth I (1533–1603)** was one of England's greatest rulers. Under her strong and intelligent rule, England became an enterprising and artistically rich nation – and increasingly a global power to rival Spain.
- **Elizabeth was the daughter** of Henry VIII and his second wife Anne Boleyn, who was beheaded when Elizabeth was three.
- **She was a brilliant scholar**, fluent in many languages by the time she was 12.
- **When Henry VIII died**, Elizabeth's nine-year-old half-brother became King Edward VI, but he died in 1553. He was succeeded by his and Elizabeth's older sister 'Bloody' Mary I.
- **Mary was staunchly** Catholic. For a while Elizabeth was locked up, suspected of involvement in a Protestant plot.

◀ *Elizabeth loved the theatre. Here, Shakespeare himself (at the front of the action) performs in a play in front of the queen.*

▶ *William Shakespeare's plays are still performed all over the world today.*

- **In 1558**, when Mary died, Elizabeth became queen. At once Elizabeth strengthened her power by bringing back the Act of Supremacy, confirming her as head of the Church. She effectively founded the moderately protestant Church of England.
- **Elizabeth was expected** to marry, and she encouraged foreign suitors when it helped diplomacy. But she remained single, earning her the nickname 'The Virgin Queen'.
- **Elizabeth sent troops** to help Protestants in Holland against their Spanish rulers, and secretly urged Francis Drake to raid Spanish treasure ships.
- **In 1588** Spain sent an Armada to invade England. Elizabeth proved an inspiring leader and the Armada was repulsed and scattered by storms.
- **Elizabeth's reign** is famed for the poetry and plays of great writers such as Edmund Spenser, Christopher Marlowe and William Shakespeare.

Mary, Queen of Scots

- **Scotland was ruled** by the Stewart (later, Stuart) dynasty. James IV ruled from 1488 and married Margaret Tudor, sister of Henry VIII of England. James died fighting the English in 1513.
- **His son**, James V, married Mary of Guise, a French Catholic. After his death in 1542 his wife sent their baby daughter Mary, Queen of Scots, to be raised at the French court.
- **Mary married** the French King Henry II's son Francis at the age of 15 and was briefly Queen of France, but Francis died in 1560.
- **In 1561**, Mary returned to Scotland. By this time, many Scots had become Protestants, while Mary remained a Catholic.

▼ *Linlithgow Palace in Scotland was the birthplace of Mary, Queen of Scots, in 1542.*

- **In 1565**, Mary fell in love with her cousin Henry Stuart, Earl of Darnley. She married him and they had a child, but Darnley was only interested in power. Led by Darnley, Protestant nobles assassinated Mary's Catholic secretary, David Rizzio.

- **The Earl of Bothwell** was in love with Mary and murdered Darnley. He married Mary three months later. The Scots were so outraged by this that Mary had to flee to England.

- **After Elizabeth**, Mary was next in line to the English throne. Many Catholics felt she was first in line, since they did not recognize Henry VIII's marriage to Anne Boleyn.

- **Mary posed a danger** to Elizabeth, so she was kept under house arrest. She became the focus for plots against Elizabeth. Elizabeth's spy-master Walsingham trapped Mary into going along with one of these. Mary was found guilty of treason and beheaded at Fotheringay in 1587.

▲ *Mary, about to meet her death at the executioner's block. Her presence in England had made her a dangerous focus for Catholic plots against Elizabeth I.*

Ireland and the English

- **During the Middle Ages**, Norman barons from England had intervened in Irish wars and settled in Ireland. Their growing power worried the English crown and in 1171 Henry II of England landed in Ireland and brought the land under his control.
- **Anglo-Norman power** in Ireland weakened, and many of the invaders adopted Irish ways. By the 1400s, the English controlled only a small area around Dublin, called the Pale.
- **The phrase** 'beyond the Pale' originally meant those lands beyond the rule of English law.
- **To regain control**, the English began the 'plantation of Ireland' – granting land to English settlers. This policy would lead to centuries of conflict and war.
- **In the late 1500s**, Elizabeth I tried to set up Protestantism in Ireland by force. The Irish in Ulster revolted, led first by Shane O'Neill and later his nephew Hugh O'Neill, but Elizabeth crushed the rebellion in 1603.

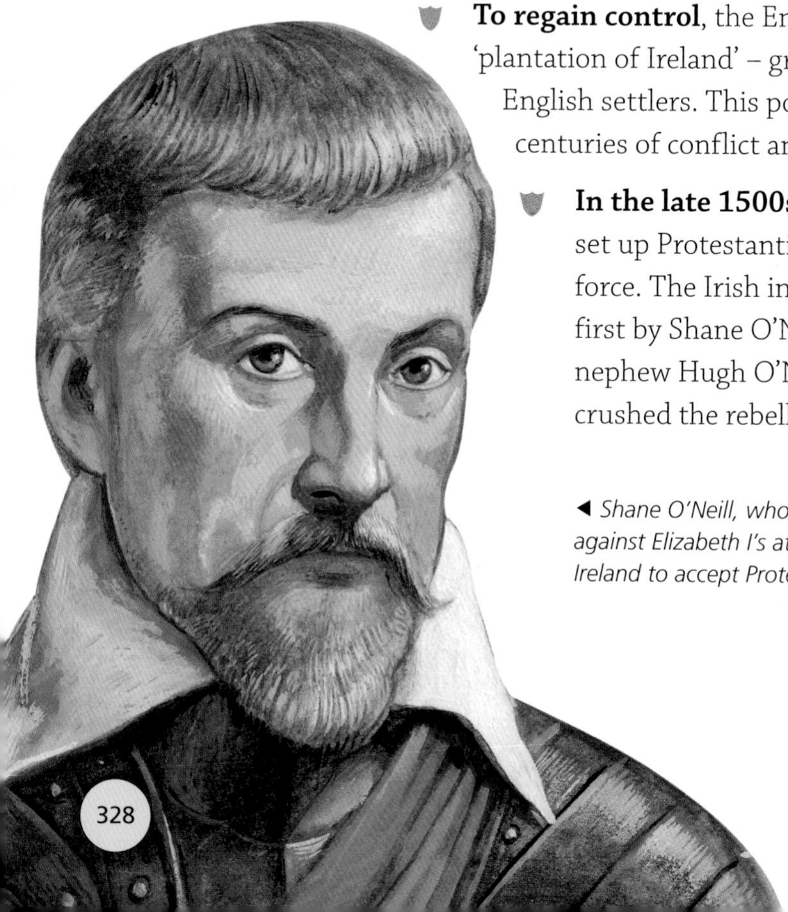

◄ *Shane O'Neill, who led Irish revolts against Elizabeth I's attempts to force Ireland to accept Protestantism.*

▲ *In July 1690, William III of England fought the former King James II for the English crown at the Battle of the Boyne in Ireland.*

- **An Irish rebellion of 1641** led to an invasion by the radical Protestant forces of the English Parliament during the Civil War. Oliver Cromwell's reconquest was brutal.
- **After the defeat** of James II at the Battle of the Boyne in 1690, Irish Catholics lost more land to English and Irish Protestants. By 1704, they owned just 15 percent of Ireland.

Russia of the Tsars

- **Towards the end** of the Middle Ages, the Tatar (Mongol) grip on Russia weakened. In 1453, Ivan III 'the Great', Grand Prince of Muscovy (the state of which Moscow was the capital), was strong enough to drive out the Tatars.
- **Russians were Christians** of the Eastern Church. When Constantinople fell to the Turks in 1453, Ivan III called for Moscow to be the Third Rome. He wed a Byzantine princess, and his grandson Ivan IV (1544–1584) took the title 'tsar', after the Roman Caesars.
- **Ivan's ambitions** created a need for money and food, so he forced thousands of peasants into serfdom – at the very time when peasants in western Europe were gaining their freedom. Those who would not submit fled to the southern steppes, where they became known as Cossacks.
- **The armies of Ivan IV** pushed eastwards, conquering Kazan, Astrakhan and much of Siberia – creating the first Russian Empire.

▼ *Ivan rebuilt Moscow's Kremlin as a vast, walled complex of palaces and churches. It has remained the centre of Russian government ever since.*

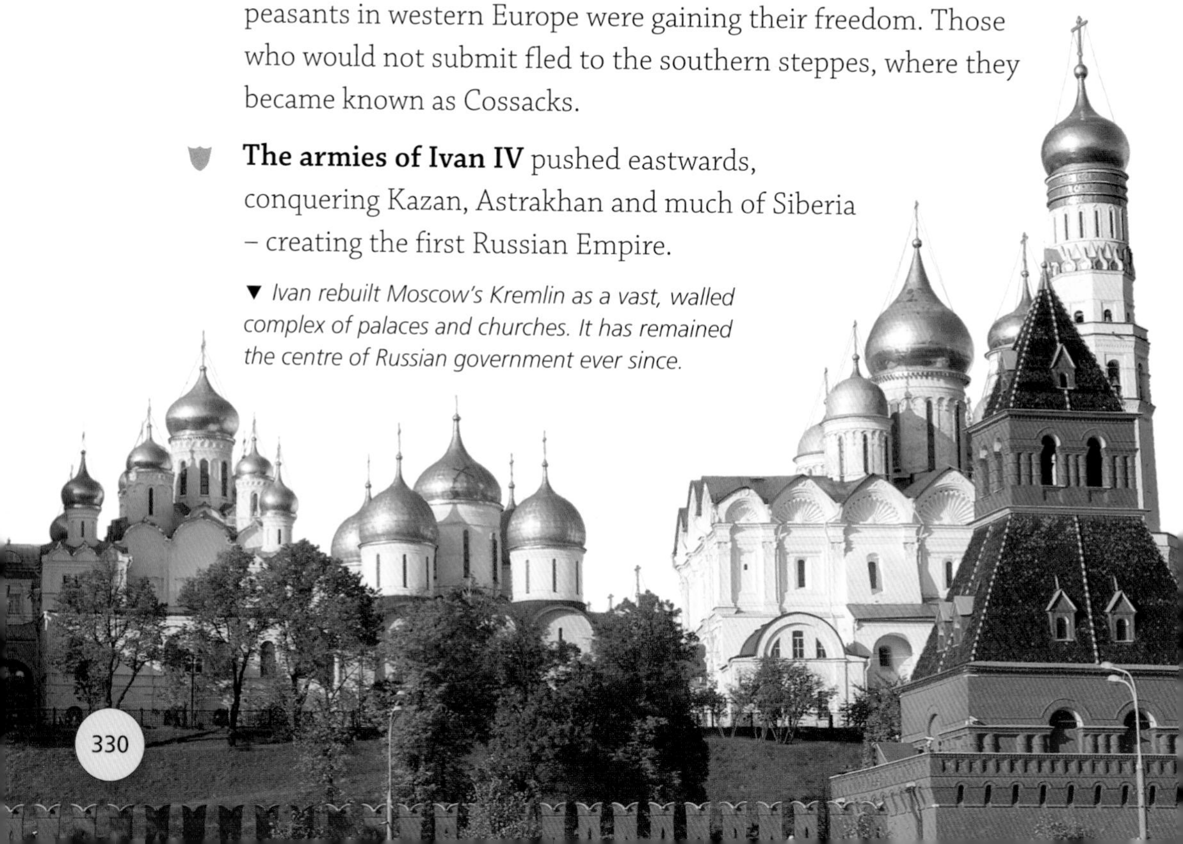

▲ *Under Ivan the Great (red boundary) and his grandson Ivan the Terrible (yellow boundary), the Russian empire expanded greatly.*

- **Ivan IV was an effective ruler**, who encouraged scholars and brought Moscow its first printing presses.
- **However he was also brutal and disturbed**, given to rages. He became known in history as Ivan the Terrible. He formed the *Oprichniki* – a police force to control the people – and he had hundreds of boyars (aristocrats) murdered. He even beat his son Ivan to death in a fit of rage.
- **Fyodor, Ivan IV's second son**, was intellectually disabled, and his wife's brother Boris Godunov seized the throne in 1598.
- **When Godunov died** in 1606, Moscow fell into a period of chaos that is called the 'Time of Troubles'. A monk named Gregory Otrepiev claimed to be Dmitry, another of Ivan IV's sons who was thought to have died. He invaded Moscow with a Polish army and rebellious Cossacks, and Russia was torn apart by a civil war.
- **The Romanov dynasty** was established in 1613 under young Mikhail I, a reluctant tsar. Despite many crises, the Russian empire grew over the centuries, and the Romanov family continued to rule Russia until 1917.

Japan's samurai

▶ *Samurai warriors dominated Japan for centuries.*

- **In the 12th century**, Japan's Fujiwara rulers were replaced by powerful warrior clans from country areas – notably the Taira and Minamoto.
- **In 1185**, the Minamoto Yoritomo crushed the Taira clan and made himself ruler of Japan as sei-i-dai-shogun, which means 'barbarian-conquering great general'.
- **Shoguns were officially** appointed by the emperors, but in practice they held the real power. These military commanders effectively ruled Japan until 1868.
- **The most powerful shoguns** included Toyotomi Hideyoshi (*c*.1536–1598) and Tokugawa Ieyasu (1543–1616). Ieyasu founded his capital at Edo (modern Tokyo).
- **The elite warriors** or knights of the shogun period were known as bushi ('warriors') or samurai, meaning 'those who serve'. Samurai followed a strict code of conduct, called Bushido ('the way of the warrior').

- **Samurai warriors** lived to fight and were highly trained.
- **A samurai's prized possession** was his massive two-handed sword, which was sharpened and honed to such an extent that a skilled samurai could slice a man in half with a single stroke.
- **The philosophy** of the samurai was closely linked with Buddhism, especially with the practice of Zen meditation, which originated in China and developed in Japan during the Middle Ages.

▼ *The simple lines of this Zen Buddhist garden promote calm feelings of peaceful meditation. Samurai valued these techniques to calm and focus their minds.*

Toyotomi Hideyoshi

- **Toyotomi Hideyoshi** (*c*.1536–1598) was the great Japanese shogun who unified Japan.
- **Hideyoshi was the son** of poor, hard-working peasants.
- **As a boy**, Hideyoshi believed that if he became a shogun, he'd make sure peasants wouldn't have to work so hard.
- **As a man**, Hideyoshi became a soldier for shogun Oda Nobunaga, who was trying to unify Japan through force.

▼ *Hideyoshi did much to develop international trade, but in 1597 became the first person in Japan to ban the Christian religion on political grounds.*

◀ *Hideyoshi helped to perfect the Japanese art of making and taking tea.*

- **Legend says that one day** Hideyoshi warmed Nobunaga's shoes for a winter walk. Nobunaga made him a general.
- **Hideyoshi proved himself** a brilliant general, and when Nobunaga was murdered, Hideyoshi carried on his work in unifying Japan – but by good rule as well as by arms.
- **By 1591**, Hideyoshi had unified Japan, but he kept warriors and peasants firmly separated as classes.
- **To establish** a mystique for his court, Hideyoshi had the Zen master Sen No Rikyu perfect the elaborate rituals known as the 'tea ceremony'.
- **Later**, Hideyoshi became paranoid. Suspecting his chief adviser Hidetsugu of plotting, he had Hidetsugu's family killed – including the beautiful Princess Komahime.
- **Komahime's father**, Yoshiaki, sided decisively with Hideyoshi's enemy, the heroic Tokugawa Ieyasu, in the great battle that led to Hideyoshi's downfall.

The Moghul Empire

- **The Moghuls**, or Mughals, formed a dynasty that ruled most of northern India from 1526–1748.
- **The Moghuls were descended** from Genghis Khan via Tamerlane – the great Mongol conquerors of the Middle Ages. Their way of life was Persian.
- **The first Moghul emperor** was Babur (1483–1530), who invaded India on swift horses that completely outran the Indians' slower elephants.
- **Babur** was a brave and brilliant leader, as well as a famous poet and diarist.
- **He created beautiful gardens** and held garden parties there when they were finished.
- **After Babur** came a string of remarkable emperors: Humayun, Akbar, Jahangir, Shah Jahan and Aurangzeb.

▸ *Babur, or Zahir-ud-din Muhammad Babur in full, became the first Moghul emperor, occupying Agra and Delhi in 1526.*

▶ *Akbar (1542–1605) was one of the great Moghul emperors, bringing in an age of prosperity, great art and literature.*

- **Akbar (1556–1605)** was the greatest of the Moghul emperors – conquering most of India and setting up a highly efficient system of government.
- **Jahangir (1569–1627)** was a great patron of the arts – but suffered from an addiction to drugs and alcohol. He was also attacked for being under the thumb of his Persian wife, Nur Jahan.
- **The Moghul Empire** reached its peak under Shah Jahan (1592–1666), when many magnificent, luxurious buildings were built – most notably the Taj Mahal.
- **Aurangzeb (1618–1707)** was the last great Moghul emperor, ruling over perhaps 250 million people. After his death the European powers closed in on Indian trade.

DID YOU KNOW?
The Taj Mahal, completed in 1653, is one of the world's most beautiful buildings. It took around 20 years to build.

Ming China

- **In China**, Mongol power was ended by a new Han Chinese dynasty called the Ming. It was founded by General Zhu Yuanzhang, who became the Hongwu emperor.
- **The Ming dynasty** ruled China from 1368–1644. This long period was one of stability, with the emperors remaining very powerful.
- **China traded internationally**, and during the 16th century even the produce of the Americas such as chilli peppers and potatoes began to reach the region.
- **Ming China made porcelain** of the highest quality and from the 1570s exported a large amount of it to Europe. Priceless examples survive today in museums and galleries.
- **Between 1405–1433**, a Chinese Muslim admiral called Zheng He led seven voyages of discovery, trade and diplomacy around Southeast Asia, the Indian Ocean, Arabia and East Africa.
- **Zheng's first fleet** was made up of 317 ships and 28,000 crew. The ships were far bigger than anything Europe could build at the time.

◄ Zheng He's great voyages increased China's power and prestige in Asia and East Africa.

▲ *North of Bejing, gateways and sacred paths lined by statues lead to the tombs of the Ming emperors.*

- **The Ming period** saw a great flowering of poetry, fiction, Chinese opera, music and painting.
- **In the later Ming period** China became more inward-looking and conservative. Imperial power was weakened by rebellions and foreign attacks. In the 1630s there were mutinies of troops and peasant uprisings.

Manchu China

- **In 1644**, the last Ming emperor hanged himself as the bandit Li Zicheng and his rebels overran Beijing.
- **Guarding the Great Wall** were Manchu troops, from Manchuria in the far northeast. A desperate Ming general invited them to help get rid of Li Zicheng.
- **The Manchus marched** into Beijing and proclaimed their own child-emperor as the 'Son of Heaven', setting up the Qing dynasty of emperors.

◀ *Hongli, the Qianlong emperor, ruled China from 1735–1799 and greatly increased the size of the empire.*

▲ *Plantations in southern China exported large amounts of tea to Europe, where the drink was becoming hugely popular.*

- **Resistance to the Manchu emperors** went on in the south for 30 years, but was eventually suppressed.
- **At first**, the Qing forced Chinese men to put their hair in pigtails to show they were inferior to Manchus.
- **Manchus and Chinese** were also made to live separately and were not allowed to marry each other.
- **In time, the Qing adopted** Chinese ways, and even Manchu civil servants had to learn the classic works of Confucius, just like the Chinese.
- **Under the Qing**, China reached its greatest extent.
- **In the 1800s**, the power of the Qing was weakened by rebellions, Muslim uprisings and growing European intrusion into Chinese affairs.

North American colonists

- **During the 1500s and 1600s**, Europeans colonized an ever-growing part of North America.
- **The Spanish explored** California in 1535 and founded St Augustine in Florida in 1565.
- **The French were in Canada** by 1534, and by 1682 they had established the territory of Louisiana in the south. The vast swathe of their North American 'possessions' was known as New France.

▼ *'Pilgrims' on their way to church. Pilgrims were Puritans (radical Protestants) who had been persecuted for their beliefs in England and so set up their own colony in North America.*

▶ *Daughter of a Native American chief, Pocahontas wed prominent Virginian colonist John Rolfe.*

- **The Dutch founded** the city of New Amsterdam in 1626. In 1664 it was ceded to the English, who renamed it New York.
- **In 1585** the English attempted a colony at Roanoke, now in North Carolina. It failed, but in 1607 the London Company founded Jamestown, in the colony of Virginia.
- **In December 1620**, 102 'Pilgrims' arrived from Plymouth, England, in the *Mayflower* and set up a new colony near Cape Cod. They survived thanks to help from Wampanoag Indians.
- **In November 1621**, the Pilgrims invited the Wampanoags to celebrate their first harvest. This first Thanksgiving Day is now celebrated every year in the USA.
- **By 1733** the British ruled 13 colonies along the Atlantic coast.

DID YOU KNOW?

Pocahontas died of influenza while in London, raising money for the colonists.

Native Americans

- **When European colonists** arrived in North America, there were perhaps 1.5 million Native American inhabitants.
- **Sometimes the settlers** cooperated with these 'Indians', but often they made war and stole their land. They were recruited to fight in wars between the colonizing nations.
- **There were many different languages** and customs among the indigenous population. Some tribes were allied, such as the Iroquois nations, who formed a Confederacy in the 1600s and 1700s.
- **Cultural regions included** Southwest, Great Plains, Far West, Plateau, Northwest, Eastern Woodland and Northern.
- **Southwest peoples** lived by growing corn, beans and squash. Plains tribes like the Blackfoot, Comanche and Cheyenne hunted buffalo.
- **Amongst Woodland tribes** such as the Delaware, the men hunted deer and fished while the women grew crops. Northern tribes like the Cree were caribou hunters.
- **Plateau and Northwest** Native Americans like the Nez Percé and the Kwakiutl lived by fishing and gathering berries.
- **Native Americans travelled** by foot or canoe. Horses were introduced by Spanish settlers and by the 1680s were being used by the Plain Indians.

◀ *Native American warriors and hunters often wore 'buckskin' clothes – made from the tanned hides of deer. Feathers indicated rank and status.*

DID YOU KNOW?

Woodland tribes lived in wigwams, domes of sticks covered in hide and moss.

▶ *Native Indians who lived on the Plains were often on the move, looking for buffalo to hunt. As they went from camp to camp they made tepees – large tents built with poles and covered by buffalo skins.*

English Civil War

- **The English Civil War** was part of a series of conflicts that took place between 1639–1651. They spread across Britain and Ireland and together are referred to as Wars of the Three Kingdoms.
- **After Elizabeth I died** without children in 1603, rule passed to the Stuart dynasty, uniting the thrones of England and Scotland.
- **After Charles I** came to the throne in 1625 there was growing unrest. Anglicans, and the more radical Protestants known as Puritans, were worried by his marriage to a Catholic.
- **There were other problems**, too. Parliament was now a force to be reckoned with, but Charles treated it with contempt. He believed he had a god-given right to rule and to levy taxes.
- **Charles I** also reserved the right to decide how people worshipped, angering Scottish Protestants.

◄ *The civil war was a series of bloody battles, shifting alliances and political intrigue. It divided families, communities and classes across the British Isles.*

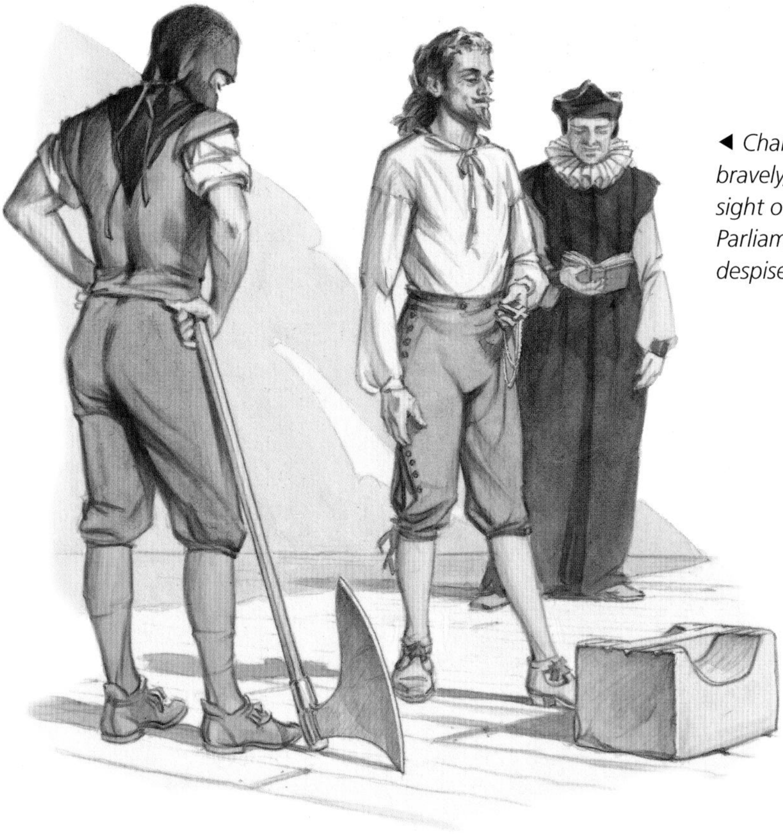

◀ *Charles I died bravely, within sight of the Parliament he despised.*

- **Civil war broke out** in 1642. Those loyal to the crown ('Cavaliers') included many wealthy aristocrats. Parliamentarians ('Roundheads') included some aristocrats too, but also merchants, poor people and revolutionary groups such as the Diggers and the Levellers.
- **Parliament's New Model Army**, under Oliver Cromwell, was victorious.
- **After a public trial**, Charles I was executed in 1649, an act which sent shockwaves across Europe.

Parliament or monarch?

- **For 11 years** after the execution of Charles I in 1649, England was without a king.
- **At first it became a republic**, known as the Commonwealth of England. This was governed by Parliament and its Council of State. Fighting continued in Scotland and Ireland.
- **In 1653** Oliver Cromwell was declared Lord Protector of the Commonwealth of England, Scotland and Ireland. Army officers governed regions.
- **Cromwell's Protectorate** became unpopular. When he died in 1658, the army removed his son Richard as successor and called for Charles I's exiled son Charles II to be recalled as king.
- **The Restoration** of Charles II took place in May 1660.

▶ *The sedan chair was a popular way for the rich to get about in the years after the Restoration.*

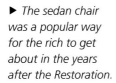

▶ *Exiled after his father's death, Charles II first attempted to bring back the monarchy in 1651 but was defeated. After nine more years in exile, he was finally invited to return as king.*

- **Charles II was more tolerant** than his father, attempting to ease tensions between rival religious groups. However there was still great suspicion of his Catholic sympathies.
- **Charles II** was known as 'the Merry Monarch', because of his love of partying, theatre, horse-racing and women contrasted with the years of grim Puritan rule.
- **Bans on Christmas celebrations** were lifted. Plays such as William Congreve's *Way of the World* made Restoration theatre lively and outrageous.
- **Of Charles II's many mistresses**, the most famous was Nell Gwyn, an orange-seller who became an actress.
- **His own wife**, the Portuguese Catholic Catherine of Braganza, bore no children, so Charles's brother James was the heir – and he too was a Catholic.

DID YOU KNOW?

During the Great Fire of London in 1666, Charles II personally organized the fire-fighting.

The Glorious Revolution

◀ *Mary sided with her Protestant husband, William, against her Catholic father James II.*

- **James II of England** (VII of Scotland) became king when his brother Charles II died in 1685. He upset people by giving Catholics key jobs. He jailed bishops who refused to support his Declaration of Indulgence in favour of Catholics.
- **In 1688**, James II and his Catholic wife Mary had a son. It seemed England was set to become Catholic.
- **Leading Protestants decided** to invite the Dutch Prince William of Orange to help. William was married to James II's Protestant daughter, Mary (1662–1694).
- **William landed with his army** at Brixham in Devon on November 5, 1688. James's army refused to obey its Catholic generals and so he was forced to flee to France. Parliament offered the throne to William and Mary.

- **James tried a comeback**, landing in Ireland with French troops. Defeat came at the Battle of the Boyne in July 1689.
- **These events are known** as the 'Glorious Revolution'. They left a lasting legacy of religious conflict, but they did result in the Bill of Rights (1689), which reasserted parliamentary rights above those of the monarch, an important step on the road to democracy.

◀ *William III, or William of Orange (1650–1702), suffered much political opposition and countless assassination plots in the latter years of his reign.*

DID YOU KNOW?

Some Ulster Protestants are called Orangemen as their ancestors supported William of Orange.

The Thirty Years' War

- **The Thirty Years' War** was made up of a series of conflicts across Central and Western Europe, lasting from 1618–1648.
- **It was a period** of horrific violence, devastating battles, homelessness, looting, famine, and diseases such as typhus, scurvy and plague.
- **The population plummeted** and the European economy was damaged. Society collapsed. There was a crazed persecution of innocent people accused of witchcraft.
- **The war began** when the Habsburg Archduke Ferdinand II tried to suppress Protestantism in Bohemia. Soon the Catholic and Protestant states of the Holy Roman Empire were at war.
- **The war soon ignited rivalry** between the Habsburg dynasty and France. It drew in most of the great powers of Europe – the Danes, the Swedes, the French, the Spanish and the Ottoman Turks.
- **The commander** of the Habsburg forces was a brilliant, ambitious general called Albrecht von Wallenstein. He fell out with the emperor and was assassinated in 1634.

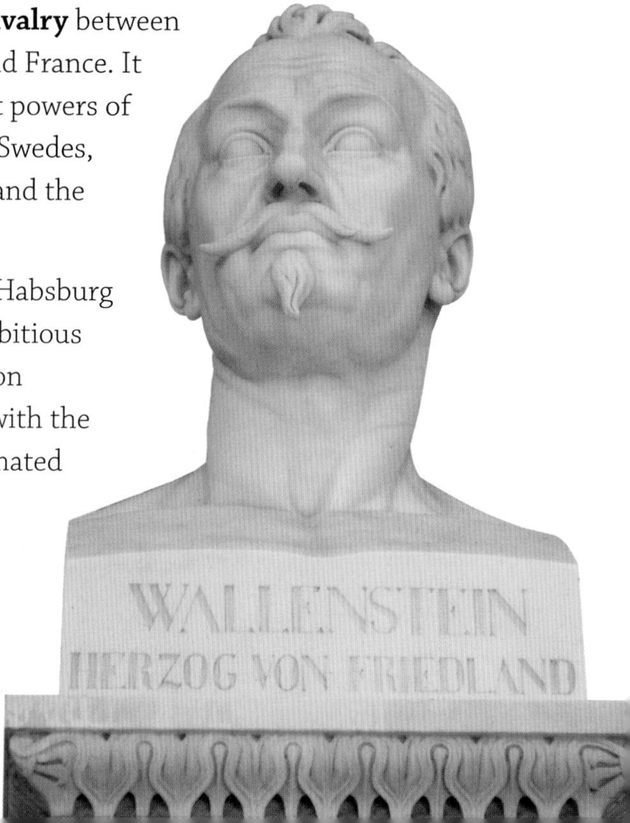

▶ *The Bohemian general Albrecht von Wallenstein (1583–1634) made too many powerful enemies on his own side.*

▲ *In 1632 King Gustavus Adolphus of Sweden died at the Battle of Lützen, a major Protestant victory.*

- **The greatest Protestant commander** was King Gustavus Adolphus of Sweden, a military genius whose greatest victory was at Breitenfeld near Leipzig in 1631. In the following year he was killed at the Battle of Lützen.
- **The war ended** with the Peace of Westphalia. It left the Habsburgs weakened, the Holy Roman empire fragmented, and Spain in decline. It heralded Sweden as a rising power, and left France as the strongest nation in Europe.

Gustavus Adolphus

- **Gustavus Adolphus** (1594–1632) was Sweden's greatest king and military leader.
- **He was a brilliant speaker** and inspiring general who always led his men into battle from the front.
- **Gustavus had a perfect ally** in his chancellor Axel Oxenstierna. Gustavus ran the foreign wars while Oxenstierna ran Sweden.
- **When Gustavus came to the throne** at the age of 17, Sweden was involved in three wars: with Denmark (1611–1613), Russia (1611–1617) and Poland (1626–1629).
- **Gustavus quickly made peace** with Denmark and Russia.
- **In skirmishes** with the Poles, Gustavus began to develop the first modern army – a large, highly mobile force combining foot soldiers and horsemen.
- **Gustavus was a devout Protestant**. When he saw the German Protestants facing defeat in the Thirty Years' War against the Catholic Austrian emperor Ferdinand II, he decided to intervene.
- **In July 1630**, Gustavus' armies landed in Germany. In 1631 Gustavus won a great victory over Ferdinand's army at Breitenfeld near Leipzig.
- **On 6 November, 1632**, the Swedes scored a crucial victory over Bohemian general Wallenstein, but Gustavus himself was killed leading a charge.

▶ *Gustavus's great flagship, the* Vasa, *sank on its maiden voyage in 1628, but it has been recovered almost intact and can now be seen in Stockholm.*

Scandinavia

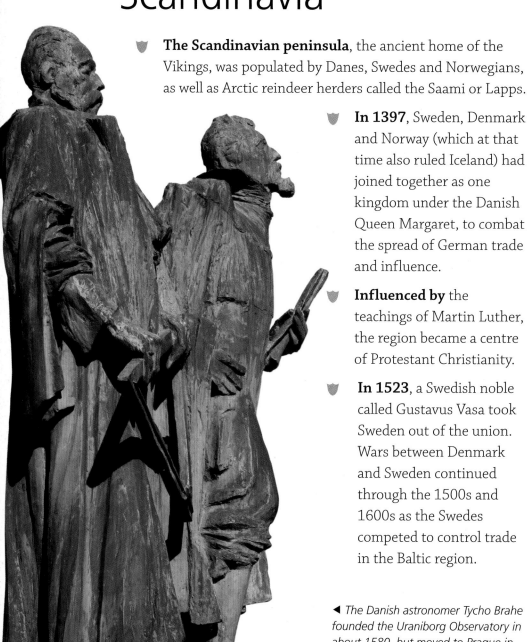

- **The Scandinavian peninsula**, the ancient home of the Vikings, was populated by Danes, Swedes and Norwegians, as well as Arctic reindeer herders called the Saami or Lapps.
- **In 1397**, Sweden, Denmark and Norway (which at that time also ruled Iceland) had joined together as one kingdom under the Danish Queen Margaret, to combat the spread of German trade and influence.
- **Influenced by** the teachings of Martin Luther, the region became a centre of Protestant Christianity.
- **In 1523**, a Swedish noble called Gustavus Vasa took Sweden out of the union. Wars between Denmark and Sweden continued through the 1500s and 1600s as the Swedes competed to control trade in the Baltic region.

◄ The Danish astronomer Tycho Brahe founded the Uraniborg Observatory in about 1580, but moved to Prague in 1597, working with Johannes Kepler.

- **Sweden became** one of Europe's major powers, gaining Finland in 1540, and other eastern Baltic lands in the 1600s, under Gustavus Adolphus. His part in the Thirty Years' War (1618–1648) brought Sweden fame and prestige.
- **In 1665** the Swedish King Charles X declared war on Poland, making enemies of Russia, Austria and Denmark. In the Great Northern War of 1700–1721, Sweden was defeated by Russia at the Battle of Poltava and lost territory in the eastern Baltic.
- **Norway and Denmark** remained united until 1819. After the Napoleonic Wars, Norway was ceded to Sweden and did not become independent until 1905.
- **Denmark was home** to pioneering astronomer Tycho Brahe (1546–1601). He founded the Uraniborg Observatory and carried out detailed, scientific study of the Solar System.

▶ *In 1585 King Frederick II of Denmark handed over the medieval church of St Peter's to the German-speaking community in Copenhagen.*

France's Sun King

- **Louis XIV (1638–1715)** was King of France for 72 years, a longer reign than any other European monarch
- **Louis came to the throne** in 1643, when he was five. The first minister Cardinal Mazarin effectively ruled France on his behalf.
- **In 1648**, heavy taxes and other grievances inspired a rebellion – the Fronde – against the hated Mazarin.
- **During the Fronde**, Louis was forced into hiding, and vowed never to let the same happen again.

▼ *Court life at the magnificent palace and gardens of Versailles, just outside Paris, formed the stunning centrepiece of the Sun King's reign.*

- **Louis declared** 'L'état c'est moi' ('I am the State') and believed it was his god-given right to have total command over his subjects.

DID YOU KNOW?
Louis' magnificent new palace at Versailles took 36,000 workers 47 years to build.

- **When Mazarin died** in 1661, Louis decided to run the country himself, and devoted huge energy to administering every detail of the nation's business.
- **Louis made France** the most efficiently run country in Europe. It hummed with new industries, linked by roads and canals.
- **He turned the French court** into a stage for glittering spectacles and banquets – to distract nobles from thoughts of rebellion.
- **Great writers of the age** included the popular playwright Molière (1622–1673), and the founders of classical French theatre, Pierre Corneille (1606–1684) and Jean Racine (1639–1699).

◀ *Louis was known as 'The Sun King' because of his favourite dance role, that of Apollo the Sun God. He adopted the Sun as his personal emblem.*

Piracy

▲ *Grim pirate flags in red or black were designed to terrify. They became known as 'blackjacks' or 'Jolly Rogers'.*

- **In the 1500s** some 'seadogs' (experienced seafarers) were regarded as heroes by one nation but as common pirates by their enemies. Queen Elizabeth I of England secretly encouraged Sir Francis Drake to attack Spanish shipping.
- **'Privateering'** was a kind of legalized piracy, where a captain was issued with official 'letters of marque', permitting him to raid enemy ships.
- **In the 1630s**, Caribbean islands such as Hispaniola and Tortuga became the haunt of poor adventurers from all over Europe – mutineers, escaped slaves, outlaws and murderers. Some of them lived by hunting feral pigs.
- **They became known** as buccaneers, named after the boucan, a frame on which they smoked their meat.
- **Soon the buccaneers** were using canoes and small ships to attack Spain's treasure fleets.

- **When the British seized** the island of Jamaica from the Spanish, it was in British interest to encourage attacks on Spain. So Welsh adventurer Henry Morgan was richly rewarded when he led buccaneer armies against ports on the Spanish 'Main' (the Spanish-ruled mainland).
- **From the 1690s** to the 1720s piracy was rife not only in the Caribbean, but around the world. Pirates sailed between Europe, North America, West Africa, Madagascar and the Indian Ocean.
- **The most notorious pirates** included Henry Avery, Bartholomew Roberts, Thomas Tew and 'Blackbeard' (Edward Teach), who attacked with smoking fuses tied in his beard to make himself as intimidating as possible.

▼ *Female pirates Anne Bonny and Mary Read sailed the seas with 'Calico' Jack Rackham.*

The slave trade

- **Slavery took on** a new global dimension in the 1500s, as Europeans established colonies in the Americas. Slavery had already existed in Africa and across the ancient world, but it now reached an industrial scale of inhuman brutality.
- **At first**, the settlers used Native Americans as slaves, but as numbers dwindled, they took slaves from Africa.
- **The trans-Atlantic** slave trade involved shipping hundreds of thousands of people across the Atlantic, either from the 'Slave Coast' of West Africa to the West Indies and North America, or from Angola to Brazil.
- **People captured to be slaves** were packed into small spaces and shackled during the voyage. Many died before they arrived. Once the ships had unloaded their slaves, they would return to Europe with cargoes of sugar, then sail for Africa with cotton goods and guns to exchange for the slaves.
- **Between 1500–1800**, Europeans shipped 10–12 million slaves from Africa to the New World. Of these, 40 percent went to Brazil, 30 percent to Cuba, Jamaica and Haiti, and 5 percent to North America.
- **Many Europeans ports**, such as Bristol and Liverpool in England, became very rich on the profits of the slave trade.
- **The American South** became dependent on a slave economy in the 1700s, where owners of large plantations needed cheap labour to grow first tobacco and then cotton.
- **In the Caribbean and Brazil**, there were more black than white people.

- **Slaves often revolted** against their harsh treatment. The greatest revolution was on French Haiti, where Toussaint l'Ouverture (1743–1803) led 500,000 slaves to take over the country in 1791. For a while Haiti was black-governed – but Napoleon's troops reasserted control in 1802.
- **By the 1790s**, a growing number of Europeans were speaking out against slavery.
- **Denmark banned** the Atlantic slave trade in 1792. William Wilberforce got Britain to ban the trade in 1807. The USA banned the import of slaves in 1808. Britain abolished slavery in its empire in 1833. In the USA, freedom for all slaves only came after the Civil War of 1861–1865.

▼ *African slaves process sugar cane on the Caribbean island of Hispaniola, the scene of the fierce Haitian revolt of 1791.*

New science

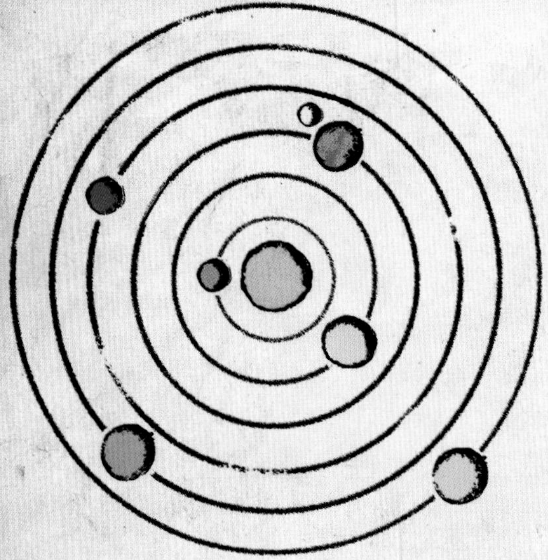

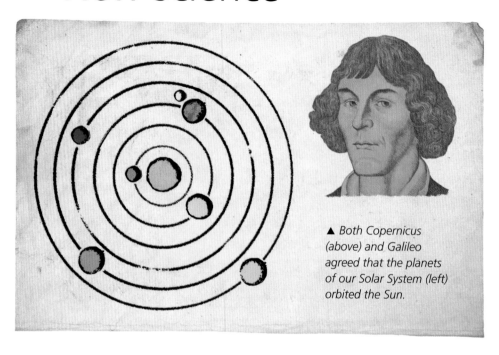

▲ *Both Copernicus (above) and Galileo agreed that the planets of our Solar System (left) orbited the Sun.*

- **The age of discovery** was not just about voyages of exploration and the New World, but also about scientific discoveries that changed our understanding of the world.
- **In the 1500s and 1600s**, Europe witnessed a sudden burst of energy and insight in the fields of astronomy, biology, chemistry, physics, optics, mathematics and medicine.
- **In Poland**, Nicolaus Copernicus (1473–1543) proposed that the planets, including the Earth, orbited the Sun. Italian scientist Galileo Galilei (1564–1642) supported this theory and as a result both of them clashed with traditionalists within the Roman Catholic Church.

- **Galileo used** the newly invented telescope to study the night sky, and experimented in physics. The German Johannes Kepler (1571–1630) calculated the motion of the planets.
- **English scientist** Isaac Newton (1642–1726) was a mathematical genius. He experimented with light and developed the reflecting telescope. He worked out the principles of mechanics.
- **Newton**, in competition with the German mathematician Gottfried Leibniz (1646–1716) invented calculus. Their work was based upon the mathematics of the French philosopher René Descartes (1596–1650).
- **An English doctor** called William Harvey (1578–1657) was the first to describe in detail the circulation of blood.

▲ *Commemorated on this stamp, the German philosopher and mathematician Gottfried Leibniz was fascinated by mechanical calculators.*

This was the age of global empires, of factories, cities, steam power and science – and revolution.

AFRICA

1720
The Sultan of Zanzibar gains control of the East African coast.

1806
Britain gains control of Cape Colony from Dutch settlers in South Africa.

1818
Shaka founds the Zulu empire in South Africa.

1822
Liberia is founded in West Africa as a colony for liberated slaves.

1869
Opening of the Suez Canal. European powers have growing influence in Egypt.

1881
Start of the 'scramble for Africa', rapid spread of the European empires.

1896
Ethiopian Emperor Menelik II defeats the Italians at Adowa.

1899
Start of the Boer War between the British and the Afrikaners (of Dutch descent).

EUROPE

1740
Frederick II becomes King of Prussia. Maria Theresa becomes Empress of Austria.

1789
Outbreak of the French Revolution. Louis XVI is executed in 1793.

1804
Napoleon Bonaparte is crowned Emperor of France, and draws up a new code of laws.

1832
Greece becomes independent from the Ottoman Turks.

1848
The Year of Revolutions: political unrest and rebellion sweeps across Europe.

1853–1856
Russia defeated by France, Britain and the Ottoman Turks.

1870
Italy unites as a single kingdom.

1871
Germany unites as single empire with Wilhelm I of Prussia as Kaiser.

ASIA

1757
The British East India Company effectively rules most of India.

1782
Start of rule by the Chakri dynasty in Siam (Thailand).

1800
The Dutch government takes over the Dutch East Indies from the Dutch East India Company.

1839–1860
The Opium Wars between Britain and China, growing influence of European traders in China.

1858
India comes under the rule of the British crown, with Queen Victoria as empress.

1858
The French start their rule of Indochina, in Southeast Asia.

1867
The Meiji Restoration: Japan modernzes under Emperor Mutsuhito.

1891
Work begins on Russia's Trans-Siberian Railway, linking the Pacific coast with Moscow.

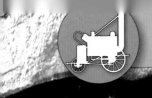

Industry and Empire

NORTH AMERICA

1718
The French found the port of New Orleans, Louisiana.

1759
The British capture the French Canadian city of Québec.

1776
Britain's North American colonists declare their independence.

1803
The USA purchases the vast French territory of Louisiana.

1861–1865
Civil war in the United States between the Unionist North and the Confederate South leads to abolition of slavery.

1867
The USA purchases Alaska from Russia.

1867
Canada becomes a self-governing Dominion within the British empire.

1876
Native Americans defeat US Cavalry at the Battle of Little Bighorn.

CENTRAL AND SOUTH AMERICA

1763
Rio de Janeiro becomes capital of Portuguese Brazil.

1780
Uprising of indigenous peoples in Peru under Tupac Amaru II.

1791
Revolution by slaves in the French colony of Saint-Domingue, and foundation of the Republic of Haiti.

1816–1826
Mexico, Argentina, Chile, Colombia, Venezuela, Ecuador, Peru and Brazil all break away as independent nations.

1838
Slavery ends in Jamaica and other British Caribbean colonies.

1848
The USA forces Mexico to cede its territories to the north of the Rio Grande.

1879
Conquest of the Desert: crushing of the last indigenous resistance in Patagonia.

1898
The Spanish-American War; the USA fights Spain over Cuban independence.

OCEANIA

1766–1788
French exploration of the Pacific under de Bougainville and La Pérouse.

1768–1771
British navigator James Cook visits Tahiti, New Zealand and Australia.

1779
James Cook is murdered at Kealakeku, Hawaii.

1788
British colonists and convicts arrive at Botany Bay, New South Wales, Australia.

1840
Treaty of Waitangi between Britain and Maori chiefs establishes New Zealand.

1845–1872
New Zealand Wars between the government and the indigenous Maoris.

1850–1856
Britain devolves powers of government to Australia and New Zealand.

1884
Germany and Britain divide the island of New Guinea.

The Hanoverians

- **The last ruler** of the Stuart dynasty in Britain was Queen Anne, sister of Mary II. She reigned from 1702–1714. In 1707, the parliaments of England and Scotland were united.
- **Anne died with no heir**, so the British throne passed to a very distant relative, George I, ruler of the German state of Hanover.
- **British politics** were already dominated by two political parties – the Tories, popular with Queen Anne and the aristocracy, and the Whigs, popular with the merchants and with the new king, George I.
- **Because George I** spoke little English, he relied on a Prime Minister to sort out government business. He in turn chose a working committee of ministers, the Cabinet. Politics was already taking on an appearance we would recognize today.
- **George II reigned** from 1727–1760. He was the last British monarch to lead troops into battle personally, at Dettingen in Bavaria, fighting the French in 1743.
- **George III was a very active ruler**, but a stubborn one. It was during his reign that Britain lost 13 North American colonies, which broke away to form the United States of America.

◀ *This medal was made in memory of the coronation of George I, the first Hanoverian ruler of Britain, in October 1714.*

▲ *George II's reign saw war and rebellion, bitter quarrels within the royal family, and the growing power of politicians.*

In 1810 George became mentally ill, and his son ruled as Regent before becoming king. George IV's brother ruled as William IV from 1830–1837.

DID YOU KNOW?

The Hanoverian era was one of great social change, of industrialization and of the creation of a global British empire.

Austria and Prussia

- **In 1711** Austria, Hungary, much of Germany and parts of Italy were all part of the Holy Roman Empire. The emperor was Charles VI, Archduke of Austria.
- **Charles VI** had no sons, but wanted his young daughter Maria Theresa to rule after him.
- **When Charles VI died** in 1740, three non-Austrians claimed they should be emperor. Maria Theresa rallied the Austrian people to defend her claim.

▲ *Maria Theresa was the only female Habsburg ruler. She was an ardent Catholic, and introduced educational and economic reforms.*

- **A War of the Austrian Succession** began with Britain, Hungary and the Netherlands backing Maria Theresa. Prussia, France, Bavaria, Saxony, Sardinia and Spain opposed her.
- **In 1742**, Maria Theresa was defeated and Charles of Bavaria became emperor. Charles, however, died in 1745. Maria Theresa's husband Francis I became emperor, although Maria was actually in charge.

- **The northeastern German kingdom** of Prussia was a growing power in the 18th century. Its ruling family was named Hohenzollern. This dynasty had been powerful ever since 1417, when Frederick Hohenzollern became Elector of Brandenburg. This meant he was one of the chosen few who could elect the Holy Roman Emperor.
- **By 1701**, Brandenburg had expanded to become the kingdom of Prussia. Frederick I became its first king and built up its army. Prussia was a land of very large agricultural estates owned by powerful aristocrats called *Junker*.
- **Frederick I's son**, Frederick II or Frederick the Great (1712–1786), was Prussia's greatest ruler. Frederick II was ambitious and manoeuvred Austria, France and Russia into wars that he used to gain territory.

▶ *As well as being a ruthless military leader, Frederick the Great played and composed flute music and exchanged long letters with the French philosopher Voltaire.*

Peter the Great's Russia

- **Peter the Great** (1672–1725) was the greatest of all the Russian tsars. He built a magnificent new capital at St Petersburg and turned Russia from an inward-looking country into a major European power.
- **Peter was a tall**, commanding figure. He had a burning interest in new ideas, but was impatient and often went into rages. When his son Alexei plotted against him, Peter had him put to death.
- **Peter became tsar** at the age of ten. His step-sister Sophia ruled for him until 1689, when her enemies drove her out and Peter took charge.
- **In 1697–1698** Peter travelled to the Netherlands and England disguised as a ship's carpenter, in order to learn about western European technology and culture. When Peter returned, he brought with him many western European craftsmen and teachers.
- **Peter insisted on** the nobles giving up their traditional robes and shaving off their long beards, which he thought looked old-fashioned.

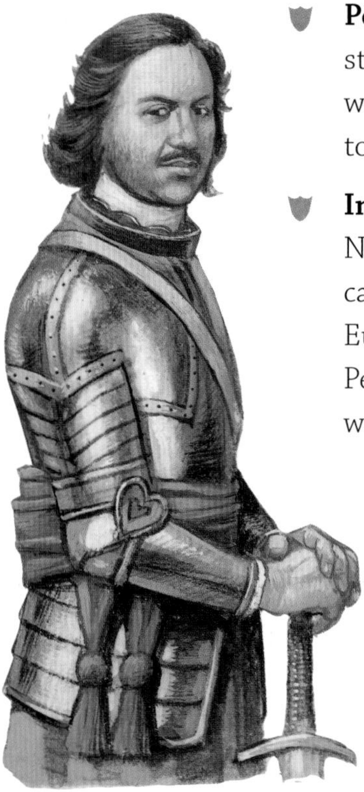

◄ *Peter the Great brought sweeping changes to Russia and carried many of them out with great brutality.*

▶ *The Cathedral of St Peter and St Paul in Petergof (Petrodvorets) on the Gulf of Finland.*

- **Peter loved ships** and boats. He built the first Russian navy, on the Volga River. His wars later ensured that Russia had, for the first time, a seaport on the Baltic.
- **He led Russia** to crucial victories in battle – notably against the Swedes at Poltava in 1709.

DID YOU KNOW?

Peter created the first Russian Academy of Sciences, started Russia's first newspaper, and founded many schools, technical institutions and art galleries.

The Seven Years' War

▲ *The Iroquois tribe lived in an eastern area of North America now known as New York State.*

- **Between 1756–1763** the continuing rivalry between the great powers in Europe boiled over yet again in a tangle of conflicts, known in Britain as the Seven Years' War.
- **With the overseas trading companies** and colonies of these nations spreading around the world, the fighting and the outcomes of the war affected not just Europe but North America, Central and South America, Africa, India and the Philippines, and disrupted global trade. It was a foretaste of world wars to come.
- **The European powers** had switched their previous alliances. On one side were Great Britain, Portugal, Prussia, Hanover and some other German states, and in North America the colonists and the Iroquois Confederacy of the Native Americans.

DID YOU KNOW?
Fighting on battlefields and in cities was often brutal, with perhaps over one million killed in Europe.

- **On the other side** were France, the Seven Nations of Canada's First Peoples, Austria, Russia, the Spanish empire, Sweden, Saxony and the Moghul empire.
- **As a result** of the Seven Years' War, Britain won a large amount of overseas territory, and France's naval power was reduced. Prussia emerged as the dominant German nation. However the years of fighting had badly damaged the British economy and created dangerous tensions in North America.

◄ *Frederick the Great suffered a major setback in 1757 when the Prussians were defeated by the Austrians at Kolín, today in the Czech Republic. The First Battalion of the Prussian guards prevented the defeat from becoming a rout.*

Who rules India?

- **Europeans had trading posts** in India ever since the Portuguese set up a base in Goa in 1510. In 1600, Elizabeth I of England had given a charter to the East India Company to trade in India. It set up posts at Surat, Madras, Bombay and Calcutta. The French had set up a base at Pondicherry, in 1668.
- **During the 18th century**, the Mogul empire was weakened by rebellions. The French and British, fighting against each other during the Seven Years' War, now vied to gain control.
- **In 1757**, 3000 British soldiers, led by the East India Company's Robert Clive, defeated the 62,000 strong army of the Nawab of Bengal, Siraj-ud-daulah, at the Battle of Plassey (Palashi). The Nawab's allies included a French artillery force.
- **After Clive's victory**, the British gradually gained control over much of India through a combination of bribes, bullying and making well-placed alliances. In 1803, the British captured the Mogul capital of Delhi – so completing their power base.
- **Rule by the British East India Company** was resented by many Indians. Hindus felt that the British were undermining their religion.
- **In 1857**, Indian soldiers revolted and other Indians joined them, but this 'mutiny' (now known as the Indian Rebellion) was crushed after 14 months.
- **In 1858**, the British decided to rule India directly. In 1876, Queen Victoria of Britain was named empress of India.

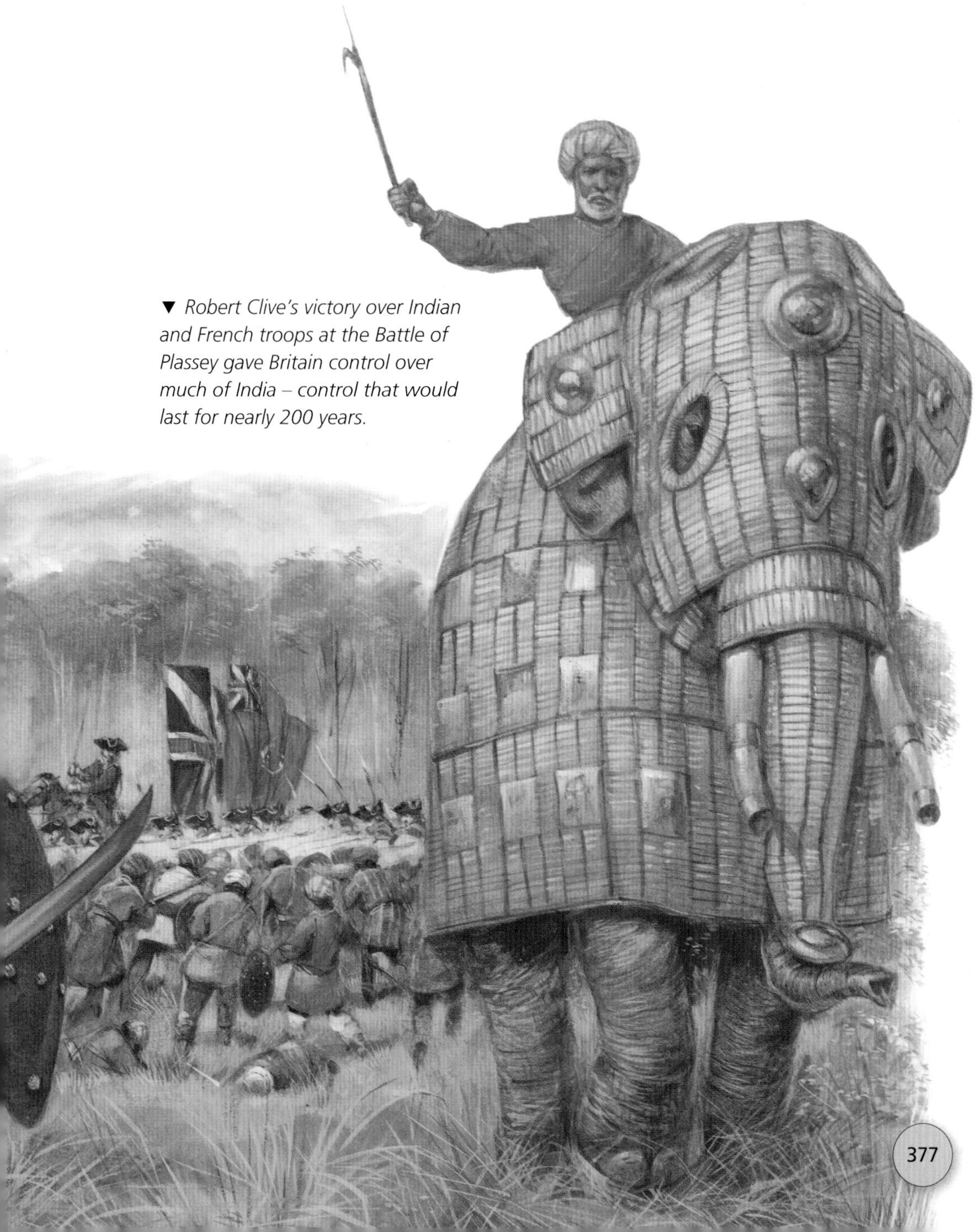

▼ *Robert Clive's victory over Indian and French troops at the Battle of Plassey gave Britain control over much of India – control that would last for nearly 200 years.*

French or British Canada?

- **In the 1500s and 1600s**, the French and English had competed in the exploration and settlement of Canada, and in its lucrative trade in fur.
- **Each side made alliances** with Canada's indigenous First Peoples. Thirty-eight Indian nations signed a peace treaty with the French in 1701.
- **During the Seven Years' War** the French and British armies battled with each other. In 1759 the British launched an attack on Québec, climbing cliffs to defeat the French and capture the city. Both the French commander, Louis-Joseph de Montcalm, and the British general, James Wolfe, died in the battle.

▼ *The building of railways encouraged settlement of Canada's prairie provinces and the far west. The Canadian Pacific Railway spanned the country coast-to-coast by 1885.*

▲ *Prospectors pose at a goldmine in British Columbia in about 1868.*

- **The British marched** on to Montréal, which surrendered. By 1760 the French had lost their foothold in Canada. However a 1774 law confirmed the rights of French Canadians regarding language and religion.
- **From 1776**, during the American War of Independence, many colonists who remained loyal to Britain moved from the east coast to settle in Canada.
- **The various Canadian provinces** were united as a self-governing Dominion in 1867.
- **Massive immigration** from Europe spread settlement westwards across the Prairies to the Pacific, aided by the Canadian Pacific Railroad from 1885.

The Agricultural Revolution

- **A transformation** of farming began in Britain in the 1700s. It became known as the Agricultural Revolution.
- **Before the 1700s**, wide open fields were cultivated in narrow strips by peasants growing food for themselves, using traditional methods.
- **Now smaller areas of land** were enclosed by hedges. Crops were grown and livestock were raised commercially, using scientific methods. Peasants were evicted from the land.
- **Crop-growing was improved** by techniques such as the four-field rotation system devised by Charles 'Turnip' Townshend and Thomas Coke. Turnips, clover, barley and wheat were grown in successive years, so that land was used all the time without becoming exhausted of nutrients.
- **Livestock farmers** improved methods of breeding cattle, pigs, horses and sheep in order to make them more suitable for the market.

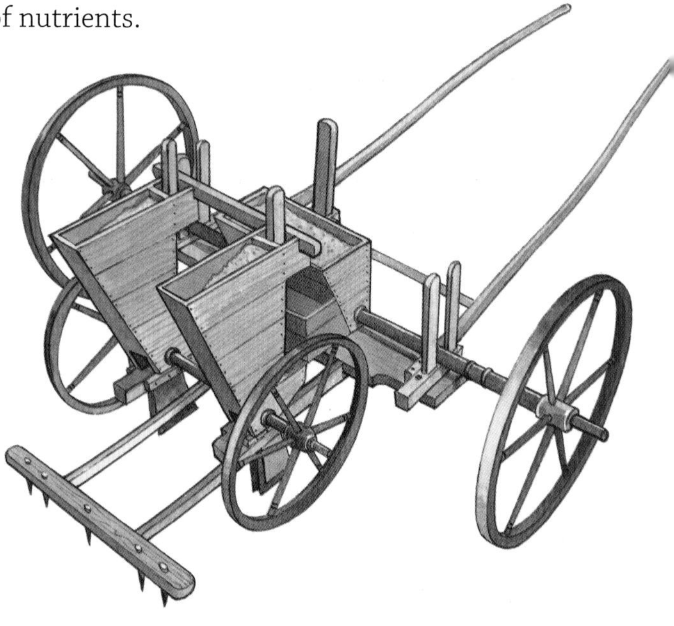

▶ *The seed drill invented by Englishman Jethro Tull in 1701 was more efficient than earlier models.*

▲ *As new machinery was brought into farming, labourers began to fear for their jobs.*

- **New machines were invented**, such as mechanical threshers and reapers.
- **In the 1800s** the agricultural revolution spread to North America and northern Europe, with new scientific theories applied to the land.

DID YOU KNOW?

In 1836 a combined reaping and threshing machine was designed in the USA – the first combine harvester.

The Age of Reason

- **The Age of Reason** is a period during the 1700s when many people began to believe that all-important questions about the world could be answered by reason.
- **This period** is also referred to as 'the Enlightenment'. The idea that human reason has the answers was revolutionary. It meant even the lowliest peasant was just as likely to be right as the highest lord. So why should a lord rule over a peasant?
- **In earlier times**, kings had ruled by 'divine right' – and their power over other people was God's will. The Age of Reason questioned this right.
- **As the 1700s** progressed, the ideas of the Age of Reason encouraged political revolutions in France and North America.

▶ *The French philosopher Diderot (1713–1784) spent much of his life compiling and writing* The Encyclopedia, *a work of reference that reflected his views on philosophy and science.*

▶ *American revolutionary leader and third US President Thomas Jefferson (1743–1826). Jefferson had a portrait of Newton before him when he drafted the USA's Declaration of Independence.*

- **The inspiration of the Age** was the English mathematician Isaac Newton (1642–1726). His theory of the Laws of Motion proposed that every single event in the Universe could be worked out mathematically.
- **In France**, the great ideas were discussed by philosophers such as Jean-Jacques Rousseau (1712–1778) and Voltaire (1694–1778). People discussed the ideas earnestly at fashionable 'salons' (supper parties).
- **In Britain**, thinkers like David Hume (1711–1776) showed how important it was to work things out for yourself – not just be told.

DID YOU KNOW?

By the 1800s, writers were inspired more by emotion than by reason. This became known as Romanticism.

The Industrial Revolution

- **The Industrial Revolution** refers to the dramatic growth in technology, mass-production, factories and cities that began in the 1700s and accelerated through the 1800s.
- **Farm labourers** living in rural villages poured into the cities in search of work in factories and mills. Others found dangerous work mining coal or tin.
- **The industrial age** began in Britain in the late 1700s, and spread across northern Europe and the USA in the early 1800s.
- **The economics** of this period depended on a pool of cheap labour. The spread of Europe's colonies around the world provided raw materials (such as cotton) as well as vast markets for manufactured goods.
- **It was with the invention** of machines for making cloth, like the 'spinning jenny' that the Revolution began.

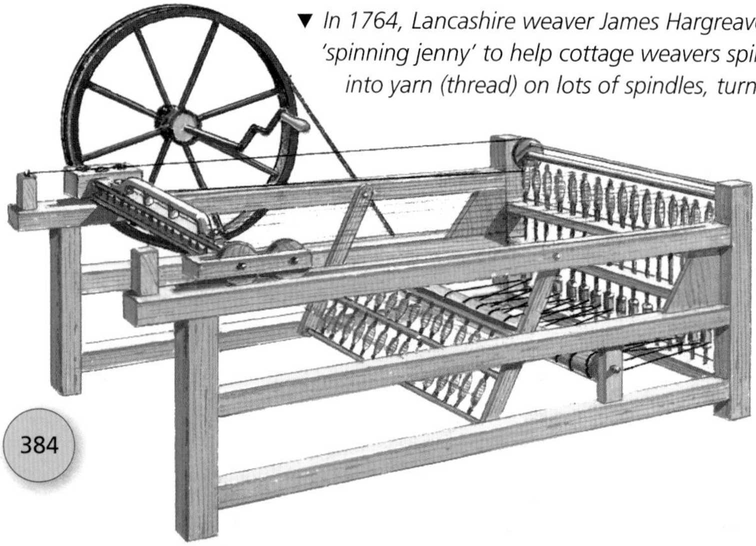

▼ *In 1764, Lancashire weaver James Hargreaves created the 'spinning jenny' to help cottage weavers spin wool or cotton fibres into yarn (thread) on lots of spindles, turned by a single handle.*

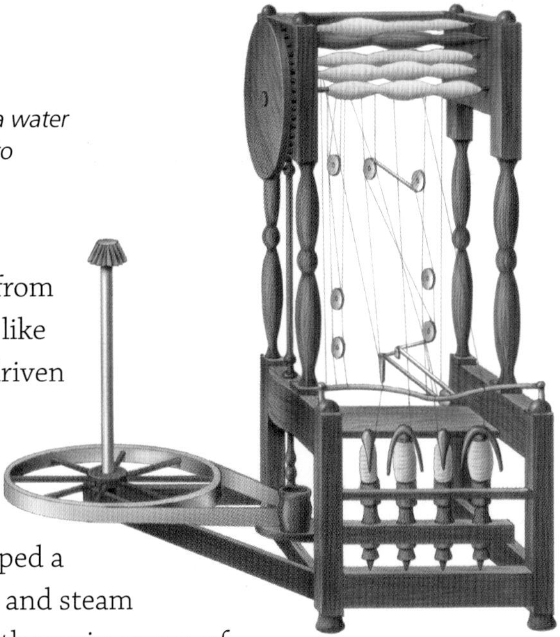

▶ *Arkwright's water frame, powered by a water wheel, used four pairs of rotating rollers to stretch fibres before they were spun.*

- **A turning point** was the change from the use of hand-turned machines like the spinning jenny, to machines driven by water wheels – like Richard Arkwright's water-powered spinning frame of 1766.
- **In the 1780s**, James Watt developed a steam engine to drive machines – and steam engines quickly replaced water as the main source of power in factories.
- **In 1713**, Abraham Darby discovered how to use coke, rather than charcoal, to make huge amounts of iron.
- **In 1784**, Henry Cort found how to remove impurities from cast iron to make wrought iron – and iron became the key material of the Industrial Revolution.

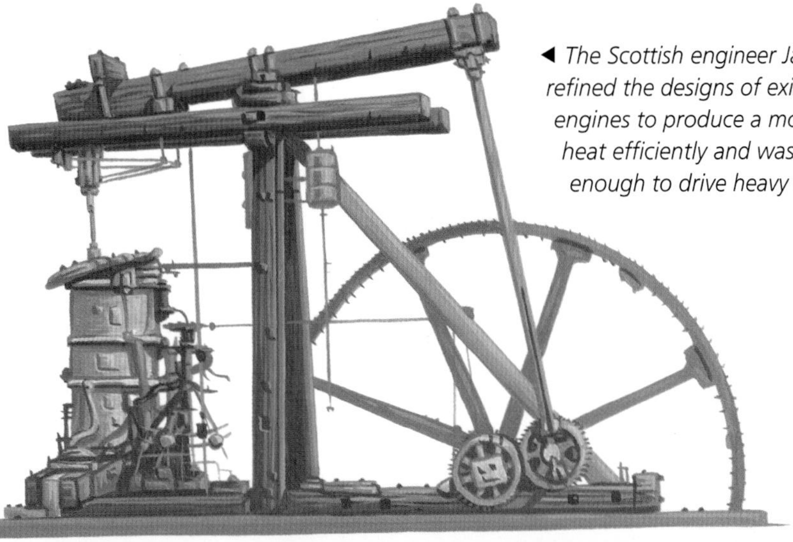

◀ *The Scottish engineer James Watt refined the designs of existing steam engines to produce a model that used heat efficiently and was powerful enough to drive heavy machinery.*

South to Australia

- **In 1770**, the English navigator James Cook charted the eastern coast of Australia and claimed it for Britain, although it had been home to Australian Aborigines for many thousands of years.
- **In 1788**, the British sent a fleet of 11 ships, carrying convicts, to start a prison colony in New South Wales.
- **The fleet landed** at Botany Bay, but the first governor, Arthur Phillip, settled in a new site that eventually became the city of Sydney.
- **Over the next 80 years** 160,000 convicts were sent to Australia, but by 1810 British settlers were arriving voluntarily.
- **After 1850**, settlers set up vast sheep farms in the interior. Many Aborigines were killed as they fought for their land.
- **In 1851**, gold was discovered in New South Wales and Victoria, and many thousands of people came to Australia to seek their fortune, tripling the population to 1.1 million in just nine years.
- **After the gold rushes**, ex-miners campaigned to 'unlock the lands' – that is, free up land from squatters and landowners for small farmers.
- **In the 1880s and 1890s**, Australians began to become aware of their own national identity – partly as Australian cricketers became heroes – and demand self-government.
- **In 1901**, Australia became the independent Commonwealth of Australia, with its own parliament.

▼ *The great Yorkshire-born navigator James Cook (1728–1779) made three voyages around the Pacific, charting New Zealand, Australia and several island groups. He was killed in an affray in Hawaii.*

The American Revolution

- **In 1763**, Britain finally defeated the French in North America, adding Canada to its 13 colonies – but wanted the colonists to help pay for the cost. The colonists resented paying taxes to a government 5000 km away.
- **To avoid costly wars** with Native Americans, George III issued a Proclamation in 1763 reserving lands west of the Appalachians for native peoples, and sent troops to keep settlers out, arousing colonists' resentment.
- **In 1764–1765**, British prime minister George Grenville brought in three new taxes – the Sugar Tax on molasses, which affected rum producers in the colonies; the Quartering Tax, which obliged the colonists to supply British soldiers with living quarters; and the Stamp Tax on newspapers, playing cards and legal documents.
- **Colonists tolerated** sugar and quartering taxes, but the Stamp Tax provoked riots. Delegates from nine colonies met in New York to demand a say in how they were taxed, demanding 'No taxation without representation.'

▶ (**1**) *Native American warriors were used by the British in their colonial wars with the French.* (**2**) *In 1776 Britain recruited about 29,000 Hessian troops (German mercenaries) to fight for them in North America.* (**3**) *A colonist militia, the Green Mountain Boys were formed in Vermont as early as 1770.*

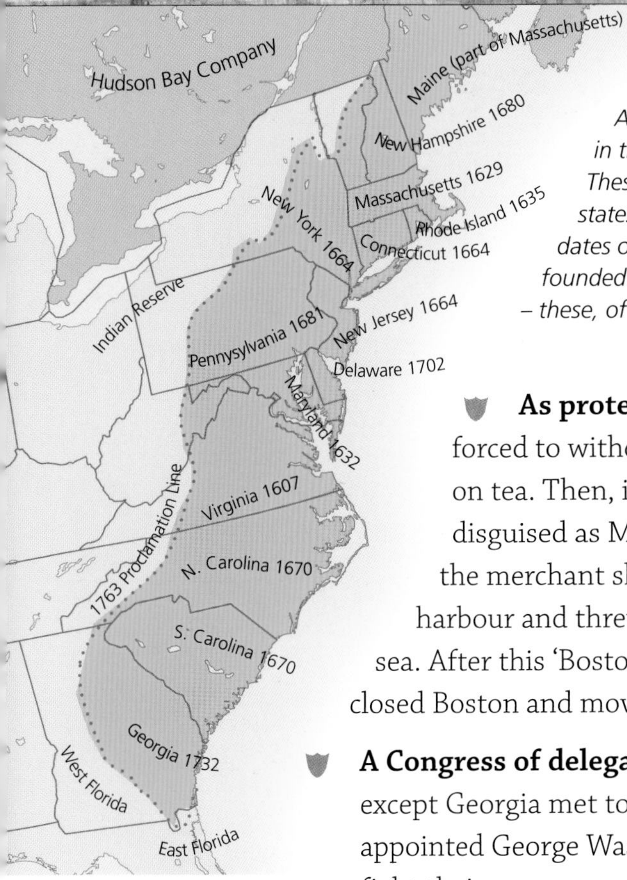

◀ *The original 13 colonies of North America stretched from Massachusetts in the north, 2500 km south to Georgia. These 13 colonies became the first 13 states of the United States of America. The dates on the map show when they were founded. The green lines show today's states – these, of course, did not exist in 1775.*

- **As protests escalated**, Grenville was forced to withdraw all taxes but one, the tax on tea. Then, in 1773, a crowd of colonists disguised as Mohawk Indians marched onto the merchant ship Dartmouth in Boston harbour and threw its cargo of tea into the sea. After this 'Boston Tea Party', the British closed Boston and moved troops in.

- **A Congress of delegates** from all the colonies except Georgia met to demand independence, and appointed George Washington to lead an army to fight their cause.

- **In April 1775**, British troops seized military stores at Lexington and Concord near Boston and the war began.

- **At first**, the British were successful, but the problems of fighting 5000 km from home told in the long run. In 1781, Washington defeated the British at Yorktown, Virginia, and they surrendered.

- **In 1776**, the colonists drew up a Declaration of Independence, written by Thomas Jefferson. The British recognized independence in 1783, and in 1787 the colonists drew up a Constitution stating how their Union should be run. In 1789, George Washington was elected as the first president of the United States of America.

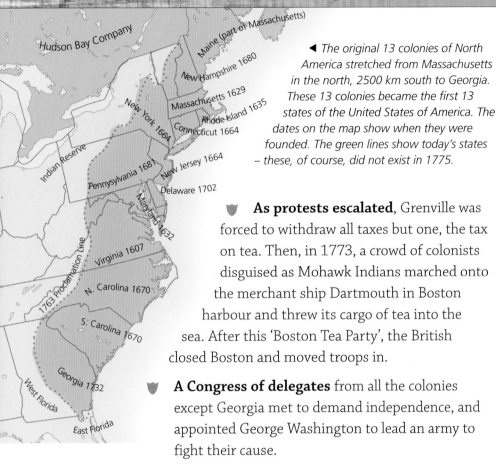

The French Revolution

- **In 1789**, French society was divided among three 'Estates' – the nobles, clergy and middle class – and also the peasants. Nobles owned all the land, but were exempt from paying taxes. The tax burden fell on the peasants.
- **In the same year**, France was bankrupt after many wars, and King Louis XVI was forced to summon Parliament, called the Estates-General, for the first time in 175 years.
- **The three Estates** had met separately in the past, but now insisted on meeting in a National Assembly to debate how to limit the power of the king. The Assembly was dominated by the Third Estate, the middle class.
- **On 14 July 1789**, the poor people of Paris, tired of debates, stormed the prison fortress of the Bastille.
- **Inspired by the fall** of the Bastille, peasants rose up all over the country and refused to pay taxes. Parisian women marched to Versailles and dragged the king back to Paris.

- **The National Assembly** became more radical, ending serfdom and attacking the nobles and the Church. Many nobles fled the country in panic.
- **Those Assembly speakers** who had the power to move the Paris mobs, like Georges Danton, came to the fore. The Assembly renamed itself the National Convention and set up the Committee of Public Safety, which governed France by terror.
- **Many nobles were sent** to the guillotine and in 1793 even Louis XVI and his queen, Marie Antoinette, were guillotined.
- **This Reign of Terror** was presided over by Maximilien de Robespierre, who sent more and more of his rivals to the guillotine, including the popular Danton. But in the end even Robespierre was guillotined, in July 1794.
- **With Robespierre gone**, conservatives regained control. Emphasis shifted to defending the revolution against foreign enemies.

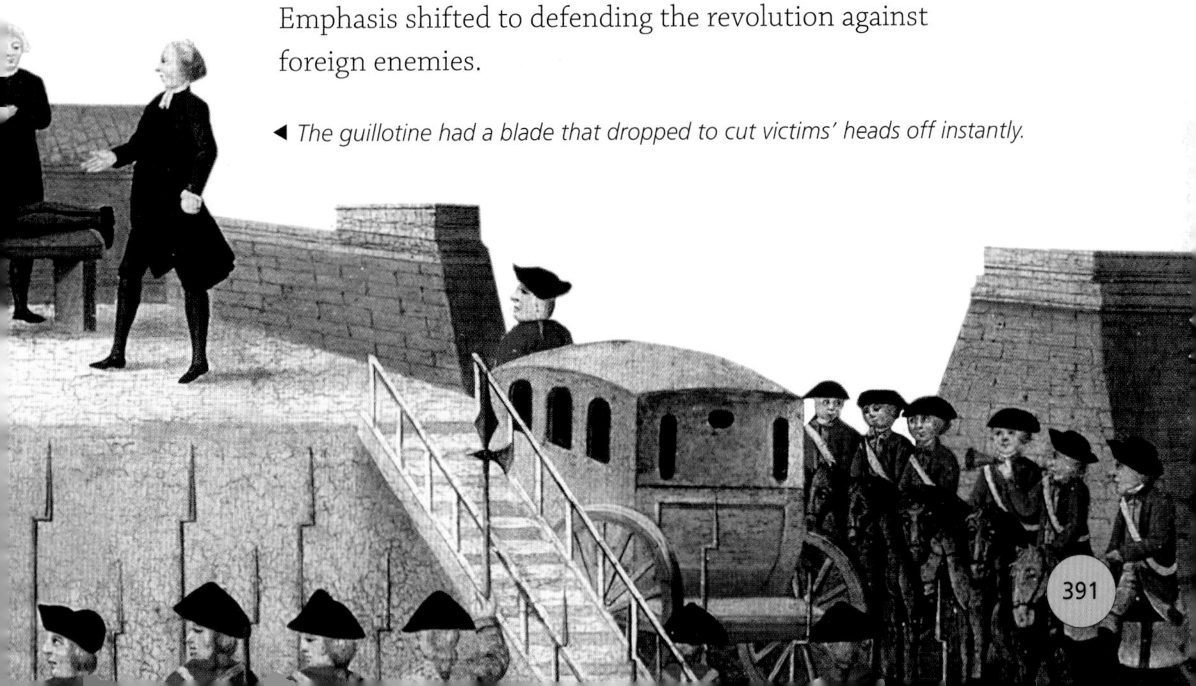

◀ *The guillotine had a blade that dropped to cut victims' heads off instantly.*

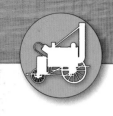

Napoleon

- **Napoleon Bonaparte** (1769–1821) was one of the greatest generals of modern times, creating a French empire that covered most of Europe.
- **Napoleon was an inspiring leader**, with a genius for planning and very strong will.
- **He was born** on the island of Corsica. At the age of nine he went to army school, and aged 14 he joined the French army.
- **The French Revolution** gave Napoleon the chance to shine and by 1794, at just 25, he was a brigadier-general.
- **In 1796**, days after marrying Josephine de Beauharnais, Napoleon was sent with a small troop simply to hold up the invading Austrians. Instead, he drove them back as far as Vienna and conquered much of Austria.

▼ *The Battle of Waterloo, in 1815, was a hard-won victory that finally ended Napoleon's bid for power. Leading the victors was the British general Arthur Wellesley, Duke of Wellington, aided by the arrival of Prussian troops and by some serious French errors.*

▶ *Napoleon's legacy included major legal reforms and a transformed map of Europe.*

- **The revolutionary period** finally ended in 1799, when Napoleon became First Consul, with dictatorial powers. By 1804, Napoleon's conquests had made him a hero in France, and he elected himself as Emperor Napoleon I.
- **By 1812**, Napoleon had defeated much of Europe. Britain remained undefeated.
- **Napoleon decided** to invade Russia with a huge army. It was a disaster. The French reached Moscow, but were forced to retreat through appalling winter weather.
- **Napoleon's power was broken**. Soon afterwards, he was defeated at Leipzig, Paris was occupied by his enemies, and he was placed in exile on the Italian island of Elba.
- **Napoleon escaped** from Elba in March 1815 to raise another army, but this was defeated by the British, Dutch and Prussian armies, at Waterloo, Belgium, that June.
- **After Waterloo**, Napoleon was sent to the island of St Helena in the mid-Atlantic, where he died, aged 51.

Napoleon's Wars

- **The French Revolutionary Wars** in which Napoleon Bonaparte rose to fame lasted from 1792–1802.
- **These wars began** with Napoleon's victories over the Austrians in Italy in 1796.
- **Napoleon wanted to destroy** British trade with the East, and so he invaded Egypt in 1798, defeating Egypt's rulers, the Mamelukes. Napoleon's fleet was destroyed by the British under Horatio Nelson at the Battle of the Nile.
- **The long and bitter European wars** Napoleon fought as sole ruler of France are called the Napoleonic Wars, and lasted from 1803–1815.
- **The French Revolution** had introduced a conscript system, which meant that every Frenchman had to serve in the army – Napoleon's army was 750,000 in 1799. Two million more had joined up by 1815.

▼ *Napoleon's retreat from Moscow in 1812 was one of the worst military disasters. The winter trek was so cold and food so scarce, only 30,000 of the army of 695,000 that set out made it back to France. However, the biggest cause of death was the spread of the disease typhus.*

- **In 1805**, Britain, Russia and Austria allied against Napoleon. Napoleon crushed the Austrians and Russians at Austerlitz. When Prussia joined Russia, Napoleon routed the Prussians at Jena and Auerstadt and the Russians at Friedland.

DID YOU KNOW?

Napoleon won many victories by holding much of his army in reserve until he had opened up a carefully chosen weak point in enemy lines.

- **In 1805** Nelson's ships destroyed the French and Spanish fleets at Trafalgar. Nelson died at Trafalgar, but his victory ended Napoleon's chances of invading Britain.
- **From 1807–1814** France was also battling with Britain, Spain and Portugal in the Peninsular War.
- **Napoleon tried to destroy** Britain with the 'Continental System', which banned any country from trading with it.
- **In 1812**, Napoleon captured Moscow, but the Russians burned everything as they fell back – leaving the French without food and victims of bitter winter storms.
- **After the 1812 disaster**, Napoleon's enemies moved in swiftly. Defeated at Leipzig, Napoleon abdicated. His brief comeback in 1815 ended in defeat at Waterloo.

Latin America revolts

▲ *South Americans under Bolívar fought hard against the Spanish in modern-day Colombia and Peru.*

- **By 1800**, the colonies of Spain and Portugal in Central and South America were ready to revolt after centuries of rule from Europe.
- **When the Napoleonic Wars** turned Spain and Portugal into a battleground, Latin American revolutionaries seized their chance.
- **Led by priests** Miguel Hidalgo y Costilla and José Maria Morelos, Mexicans revolted in 1810. The Spanish quelled the revolt and executed Hidalgo and Morelos. In 1821, however, Mexico gained independence.

DID YOU KNOW?
In 1824, San Martín left for Europe, saddened by disputes after Argentina's independence, and by his wife's death.

- **In 1810**, José de San Martín led Argentina to independence. In 1816, San Martín made an epic march across the Andes to bring Chile freedom, too – with the help of Bernardo O'Higgins.
- **In the north**, Venezuelans Francisco de Miranda, Simón Bolívar and Antonio de Sucre led a long fight against the Spanish in New Granada (now Colombia) and Peru. In 1819, after a victory at Boyacá in Colombia, Bolívar proclaimed the Republic of Gran Colombia (now Venezuela, Colombia, Ecuador and Panama).
- **In 1824**, Sucre won a crucial victory at Ayacucho in Peru, freeing all of north South America from Spanish rule.
- **The Republic of Bolivia** was named after Bolívar, who wrote its constitution. Sucre became its first president.
- **Brazil gained its freedom** from Portugal without a fight when its ruler Prince John fled. His son became emperor.
- **Miranda died** in a Spanish jail after Bolívar handed him over. Sucre was assassinated in 1830. Bolívar died in 1830, shortly after a failed assassination attempt.

Industrial unrest

▶ *Welshman Robert Owen did much to promote better conditions for workers.*

- **Wages in the new factories** of the Industrial Revolution were low and working conditions were very poor across Europe and the USA.
- **Luddites were English factory** workers who, in 1811–1812, smashed new machines that put people out of work.
- **High taxes** on imported corn meant that the poor were first to suffer in times of bad harvest, such as 1816–1819.
- **The 'Peterloo' massacre** of 16 August, 1819, was caused by a cavalry charge into a peaceful crowd gathered at St Peter's Fields, Manchester to hear radical leader Henry Hunt call for democratic reform. Fifteen were killed and hundreds were injured.
- **In the 1820s** there were violent uprisings in South Wales and in Scotland.
- **Welsh-born Robert Owen** (1771–1858) was the first great factory reformer and socialist. Owen set up 'ideal' communities at New Lanark in Scotland and New Harmony in Indiana, USA, where people might work together in good conditions.

DID YOU KNOW?
Thomas Paine's radical book The Rights of Man (1792) was the inspiration for many protesters.

- **Robert Owen's** Grand National Consolidated Trades Union of 1833 – the first national union – was instantly repressed by the government.
- **Trade unions were** banned by British 'Combination' Acts. These were partly removed in 1824. The Tolpuddle Martyrs were six Dorset farmworkers transported to Australia in 1834 for trying to form a trade union.

▼ *Sheffield, northern England, in 1879 – one of Europe's major centres during the Industrial Revolution, famed for its steel production. Cities such as this became hotbeds of social unrest.*

A century of revolution

- **The year 1830** saw revolutions break out across Europe, as revolutionaries and liberals sought political reform.
- **The troubles began** in France, which had restored the monarchy. King Charles X launched an attack on democracy, and was overthrown in a popular uprising.
- **The year 1848** saw a great wave of revolution spread like wildfire – in France, Germany, Italy, Austria and Hungary.

▼ *When rioters raged through Vienna, the feared Prince Metternich and many of his hated secret police were forced to flee.*

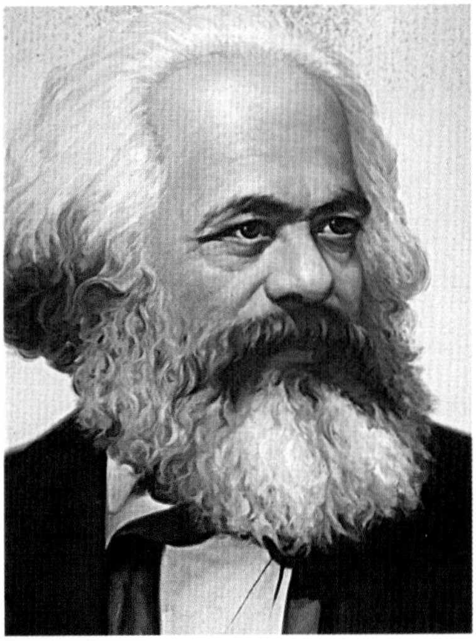

▶ *Karl Marx (1818–1883), founder of international communism. The ground-breaking pamphlet* The Communist Manifesto *that he wrote with Engels appeared during the 'Year of Revolution' – 1848.*

- **The revolutions** were not linked directly, but the revolutionaries shared many of the same grievances against repressive governments and the poverty suffered by industrial workers.
- **Many countries were fragmented** or ruled by foreign powers. Revolutionaries called for self-determination and nationhood.
- **In Paris**, revolutionaries shouting 'bread or death' stormed government buildings, threw out the king and restored the Republic.
- **In Vienna**, the Austrian emperor and his powerful Chancellor, Prince Metternich, were forced to flee as people created their own parliament and freed serfs.
- **In Hungary**, revolutionary leader Louis Kossuth established a short-lived Hungarian republic.
- **The desire for change** grew stronger over the century. *The Communist Manifesto*, written by Karl Marx and Friedrich Engels, called for workers to seize control of the factories and bring about a new social order.
- **In 1871** a socialist city government or Commune was elected in Paris. It refused to obey the national government and its supporters were brutally suppressed by the army.

Famine and emigration

▲ *This field on the west coast of Ireland, abandoned since the famine, still shows traces of potato ridges.*

- **During the 19th century**, millions of Europeans left behind poverty, hunger, religious persecution or political repression to seek a new life in the Americas. They included Italians, Germans, Russians, Jews, Scots and Irish.
- **The Irish potato famine** (1845–1849) was a tragic human disaster, in which over a million people starved to death.
- **Ireland became part** of the United Kingdom in 1800. Most Irish were poor farmers, working tiny plots of land rented from Anglo-Irish landlords.
- **Potatoes had been introduced** from America in the 1700s. They were such a successful crop that the Irish population grew to 8.4 million by 1844, but most remained very poor.
- **Half the Irish population** depended entirely on potatoes for food. English laws kept bread prices too high for the Irish to buy.

- **In 1845**, the potato crop was ruined by blight, a fungal disease.
- **When the blight** ruined even more of the 1846–1849 potato crops, millions of poor Irish farmers began to starve.
- **Many poor tenant farmers** were thrown off their land because they had no crop to sell in order to pay the rent.
- **Throughout the famine**, Irish farms exported grain, meat and vegetables too costly for the Irish to buy.
- **One and a half million** desperate Irish people packed up and left for America, leaving the country half-empty. Some were forced to emigrate by their landlords.

▼ *The great famine devastated Ireland's towns, its people and the Irish language.*

Land, sea and air

- **The period** from the late 1700s to the 20th century saw extraordinary changes in travel and transportation.
- **The 1700s and 1800s** saw a great new network of canals built across Europe in order to shift industrial goods by boat, from factories to cities and ports.
- **The improvement of steam power** transformed the landscape and the global economy.
- **The French inventor** Nicolas-Joseph Cugnot ran a steam-driven vehicle on the streets in 1769.
- **In 1804** the Cornish inventor Richard Trevithick designed the world's first moving steam locomotive, in order to haul carriages along a track at the Pen y Darren ironworks in South Wales.
- **The railway age** had begun in Britain, and thanks to pioneers such as George and Robert Stephenson, whose *Rocket* first ran in 1829, goods and passengers were being transported at undreamt of speeds.

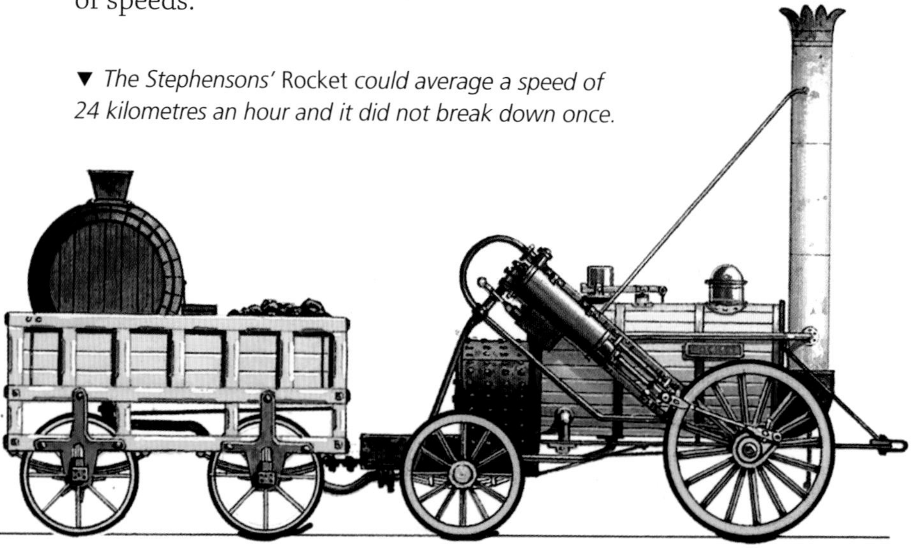

▼ *The Stephensons'* Rocket *could average a speed of 24 kilometres an hour and it did not break down once.*

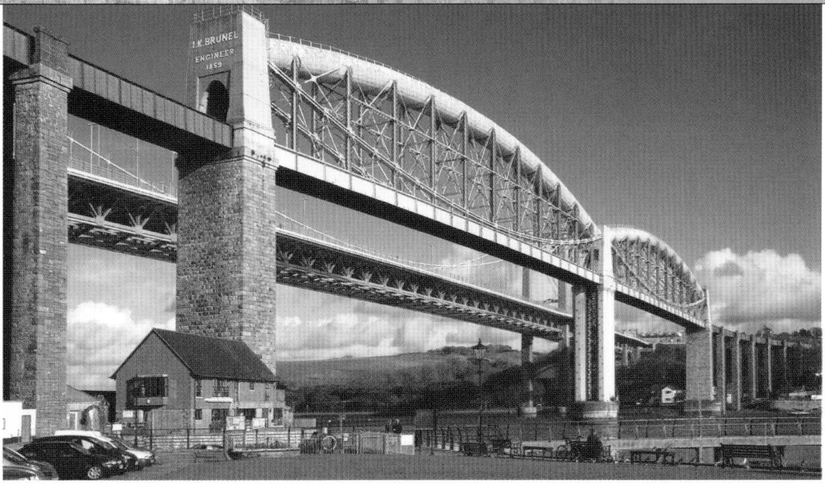

▲ *Brunel's magnificent railway bridge across the River Tamar, between Plymouth and Saltash, opened in 1859.*

- **Railway mania** soon spread across Europe, North America and the overseas empires of the European powers, encouraging the growth of industry and cities, settlement of remote areas, and tourism.
- **Steam power** also transformed shipping. The paddle steamer was invented in France in 1783, but it was the invention of the screw propeller in Britain in 1836 that made ocean-going iron steamships a reality.
- **The first petrol-driven** motor car was produced by Karl Benz in Germany in 1885, and in the 20th century road transport would have an even greater effect on society and the environment than the railways.
- **Air travel began in 1783**, with the first hot air balloon to carry passengers, designed by Joseph and Etienne Montgolfier in France. Gliders (1804), airships (1852) and hang-gliders (1890s) followed in Britain and Germany, but it was 1903 before Orville and Wilbur Wright brought about the first powered and controlled aeroplane flight at Kitty Hawk in the USA.

The rise of the USA

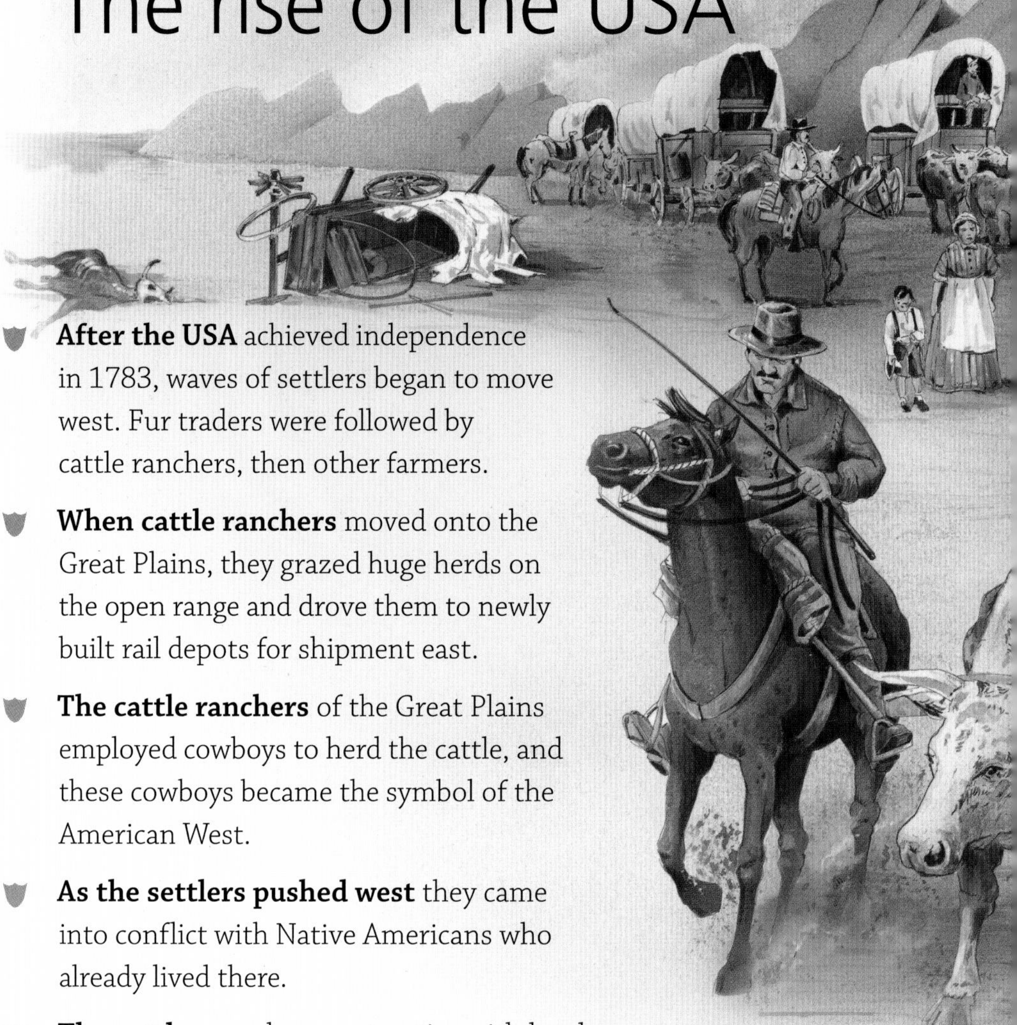

- **After the USA** achieved independence in 1783, waves of settlers began to move west. Fur traders were followed by cattle ranchers, then other farmers.
- **When cattle ranchers** moved onto the Great Plains, they grazed huge herds on the open range and drove them to newly built rail depots for shipment east.
- **The cattle ranchers** of the Great Plains employed cowboys to herd the cattle, and these cowboys became the symbol of the American West.
- **As the settlers pushed west** they came into conflict with Native Americans who already lived there.
- **The settlers** made many treaties with local peoples but broke almost all of them, and Native Americans were gradually driven from their lands or simply slaughtered.
- **In each decade**, new settlers struggled further west, facing great hardship in the hope of finding a new life.
- **Settlers often set out** with all their possessions in a covered wagon, travelling with other wagons in a convoy for safety.

▼ *The Oregon trail was the longest of the routes to the west, winding over 3000 km from Independence, Missouri to the Pacific northwest.*

The first group of 900 wagons set out on the Oregon trail in the Great Migration of 1843.

By 1869 the eastern states were linked with the Pacific coast by a Transcontinental Railroad. The United States now had access to a vast wealth of resources.

Industrialization was rapid around cities such as New York and Chicago, but the pioneering spirit of the West remained at the heart of the 'American dream'.

The American Civil War

▲ *The Union flag had stars for all the 13 original states (top). The Confederates had their own version of the flag, also with 13 stars.*

- **The American Civil War** (1861–1865) was fought between northern states (the Union) and southern states (the Confederacy). It split friends and families and resulted in the deaths of over 600,000 Americans.
- **The southern states** had an agricultural economy based upon slave labour. The northern states had a rapidly developing industrial economy, with a large pool of immigrant labour from Europe.
- **In 1850**, slavery was banned in the 18 northern states, but there were four million slaves in the 15 southern states, where they worked on huge plantations.
- **Conflicts developed** over whether new states, added as settlers pushed westward, should be 'slave' or 'free' states. In 1854, slavers gained legal victories with the Kansas-Nebraska Act, which let new states decide for themselves.
- **In 1860** a moderate Republican, Abraham Lincoln, was elected as president. He supported modernization of the economy and opposed the expansion of slavery.
- **The southern states** immediately broke away from the Union in protest, to form their own Confederacy.
- **As the war began**, the Confederates had the upper hand, fighting a mainly defensive campaign.

▶ *Lincoln was a tall, lanky man. His razor-sharp mind, calm manner and resolutely moral attitudes made him a hero to many Americans.*

- **The turning point** came in July 1863, when an invading Confederate army, commanded by Robert E Lee, was badly defeated at Gettysburg in Pennsylvania.
- **The extra industrial resources** of the north slowly began to tell, and General Ulysses S Grant attacked the south from the north, while General William T Sherman advanced ruthlessly from the west.
- **Lee surrendered** to Grant in Appomattox Court House, Virginia, on 9 April, 1865. Slavery was abolished, but a few days later Lincoln was assassinated.

▼ *The American Civil War has been described as the first 'modern war'. It utilized railways and industrial production and was recorded in photographs. It left a bitter legacy, which is still not forgotten today.*

The Victorian Age

- **In 1837**, 18-year-old Victoria became Queen of the United Kingdom of Great Britain and Ireland and reigned for 63 years until 1901.
- **In the Victorian Age**, Britain became the world's largest industrial and trading power, and the British Empire reached its peak.
- **British factories and towns** mushroomed and railways were built throughout the country.
- **In 1851**, London hosted the Great Exhibition. It opened in a huge building of glass and iron, known as the Crystal Palace, to show British skills to the world.

- **In 1861**, Victoria's German husband, Prince Albert, died. She went into mourning and wore black for the rest of her life.
- **The rapid expansion** of Victorian cities created vast slum areas where living conditions were appalling.

◀ *Under Victoria, Britain came to wield control over the largest empire the world had ever seen, and made astonishing artistic, scientific and manufacturing advances.*

▶ *Benjamin Disraeli, twice prime minister in Victorian England (1868 and 1874–1880), and one of Victoria's favourite statesmen. Under Disraeli, the British Empire gained even more status when Victoria became Empress of India.*

- **Social reformers and writers** such as Charles Dickens highlighted the problems of the slums. Slowly, Parliament passed laws to improve conditions for working people and to provide education for all.
- **The two greatest prime ministers** of the Victorian Age were the flamboyant Benjamin Disraeli (1804–1881) and the dour William Gladstone (1809–1898).

DID YOU KNOW?

Victorian middle-class life cultivated cosy moral values, but there was also a seamy side, with widespread prostitution and crime.

The Crimean War

- **The Crimean War** was mostly fought around the Crimea peninsula – on the north coast of the Black Sea – between 1854–1856.

▼ *Around a third of the British cavalrymen of the Light Brigade died making their charge.*

- **On one side was Russia**. On the other were Turkey's Ottoman empire, Britain, France, and Piedmont/Sardinia, while Austria gave political support.
- **The main cause** of the war was British, French and Turkish worries about Russian expansion in the Black Sea region.
- **The war began** when Russia destroyed the Turkish fleet.

- **Armies on both sides** were badly organized. Many British soldiers died of cholera before they even reached the Crimea and wounded soldiers suffered badly from cold and disease.
- **During the Battle of Balaclava**, on 25 October, 1854, a stupid mistake sent a gallant British cavalry charge straight onto the Russian guns. This charge of the Light Brigade was made famous in a poem by Lord Tennyson.
- **Conditions in the battle hospitals** were reported in the first-ever war photographs and in the telegraphed news reports of W H Russell.
- **Nurses like Florence Nightingale** and Jamaican Mary Seacole went to the Crimea to help the wounded. Lessons learned there helped to lay the foundations of modern nursing.
- **The war finally ended** in 1856 with the Treaty of Paris, with few gains on either side.

Nineteenth century France

- **After the First Empire of Napoleon**, French politics was balanced between monarchists on one side and radical republicans on the other.
- **In the 1840s**, the poverty of workers in French towns inspired men like Pierre-Joseph Proudhon and Charles Fourier to devise socialist ideas for solving social and economic problems.
- **In 1848**, protest and riots in Paris forced King Louis-Philippe to abdicate. After much wrangling, a new popular assembly set up the Second Republic and Louis-Napoleon Bonaparte was elected president.
- **Louis-Napoleon** (1808–1873) was the son of Napoleon's brother and his step-daughter Hortense. The Assembly proved conservative and, in 1852, Louis-Napoleon curbed their powers and had himself made Emperor Napoleon III by popular vote. His rule is called the Second Empire.
- **Napoleon III** gave state aid to industry, banks and railways. Industry boomed and France grew rich. French engineers became world-famous. Napoleon III's Spanish wife, Eugenie, set the style for beautiful, lavish fashions and decoration that was mimicked across Europe.

◀ *Louis-Napoleon, nephew of Napoleon I and ruler of the Second Empire.*

- **Gradually, Napoleon's rule** provoked more and more hostility among radicals, and the Franco-Prussian War of 1870–1871 led to his downfall, the declaration of a Third Republic and the defeat of France.
- **In the 19th century** literature, art and music flourished in Paris, as well as industry and the sciences.
- **France ruled** over a large colonial empire which took in Caribbean islands, French Guiana, much of North and West Africa, Indochina and Pacific islands.

▼ *The grand Palace of Commerce in Lyon contained not only shops and financial premises, but a museum of art and industry. It was opened in 1860 by Napoleon III and the Empress Eugenie.*

DID YOU KNOW?

The famous boulevards of Paris, with their grand houses, were created on Napoleon III's orders.

Italy united

- **After the Napoleonic Wars**, Italy was split into various kingdoms – some, like Naples, under French Bourbon kings, some under Austrian rule and Papal States under the Pope.
- **The Carbonari** (meaning 'charcoal burners') were a secret society working for Italian freedom.
- **In 1820, the Carbonari** got the Bourbon king of Naples to agree to a constitution, but the Austrians intervened to abolish it.
- **In 1831**, Giuseppe Mazzini founded 'Young Italy' to unite Italy. The drive to unite the country became known as the Risorgimento ('rising again').
- **In 1848**, revolutions broke out across Italy, but were put down.

▲ *The glittering city of Venice became part of a united Italy in 1866.*

▲ *Garibaldi was the hero who landed in Italy with just his thousand famous 'Red Shirts'. He went on to conquer all of southern Italy.*

- **In 1857**, Count Cavour, prime minister of Piedmont, asked France for help with evicting the Austrians.
- **In 1859**, France and Piedmont beat the Austrians at Magenta and Solferino. After political wrangling, northern Italy was joined to Piedmont under King Victor Emmanuel II.
- **The Battle of Magenta** was so bloody that a new purple-red colour was named after it.
- **In 1860**, the great hero Giuseppe Garibaldi (1807–1882) led a rebellion and conquered all of southern Italy. Only Cavour's intervention stopped Garibaldi from taking Rome.
- **In 1861**, most of Italy was united under Victor Emmanuel. Venice was added in 1866 and Rome as capital in 1870.

Germany united

- **In 1815**, Germany was divided among 38 different states of the German Confederation.
- **The most powerful** of the Germanic states were Prussia and Austria, who sparred for dominance.
- **In 1862**, Otto von Bismarck (1815–1898) became Chancellor of Prussia. He was known as 'the Iron Chancellor 'and it was through his determination and skilful diplomacy that Germany was finally united.
- **In 1864**, Denmark tried to annex the duchies of Schleswig and Holstein, whose duke was the Danish king. The Austrians and Prussians sent an army to drive the Danes out.
- **Austria and Prussia** could not agree on what to do with Schleswig-Holstein. Bismarck proposed a new North German Confederation, excluding Austria. Austria objected to Bismarck's plan, but was defeated by Prussia in a very swift war in 1866.
- **To complete Prussian** control over Germany, Bismarck provoked a war against France, which had been the main opponent to German unity. He used the trick of the Ems telegram – a version of a telegram reporting a conversation between the Prussian king and the French ambassador, skilfully edited to imply an insult to France.
- **France declared war** on Prussia, but was swiftly beaten by the Prussians, who marched into Paris in January 1871.
- **After the defeat of France**, all the German states agreed to become part of a united Germany under Prussian leadership. On 18 January, 1871, Wilhelm I was crowned Kaiser (emperor).

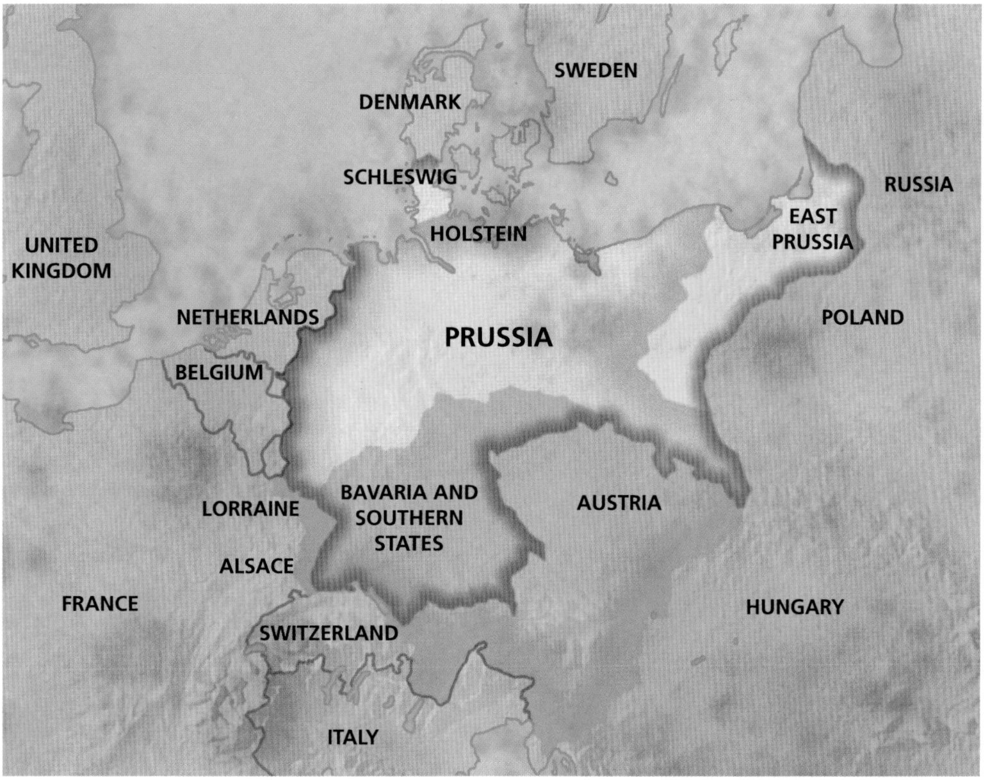

German Confederation

North German Confederation 1867

German Second Empire 1871

▲ *The North German Confederation was a union of states formed in 1867. Prussia dominated the confederation. Within this union, members were able to keep their own governments, but foreign and military policies were decided by a federal government.*

The British Empire

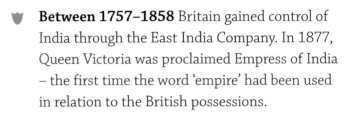

- **The British Empire** had begun with the colonization of North America in the 1500s and 1600s, but suffered a major setback when the United States won independence in 1783.

- **Between 1757–1858** Britain gained control of India through the East India Company. In 1877, Queen Victoria was proclaimed Empress of India – the first time the word 'empire' had been used in relation to the British possessions.

- **During the 19th century** the British came to rule the largest empire in history, competing with the other European powers.

- **Some British territories** attracted British settlement, such as Canada, South Africa, Australia and New Zealand. These colonies were given more and more freedom to govern themselves and came to be called 'dominions'.

- **Other important colonies** were located in the Caribbean, South America, Africa, Southeast Asia and the Pacific.

◀ *Indian brokers examine bales of cotton in Bombay. British cotton mills obtained about 20 percent of their cotton from India. However this changed when the civil war in the United States (1861–1865) interrupted supplies coming from America. The result was a boom in Indian cotton.*

DID YOU KNOW?
By 1920, 600 million people around the world were being ruled from London.

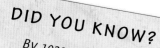

- **The territories** provided British factories with raw materials and also new markets for the export of manufactured goods. Roads, railways and towns were developed.
- **Colonial officials** were often motivated by high ideals. However indigenous labour was exploited, freedoms were limited and racism was common. Campaigns for independence soon took root.
- **The Empire** would reach its peak after World War I, when German and Turkish possessions were added. At its height, in 1920, the British Empire covered a quarter of the world and ruled a quarter of the world's population – more than any other nation.

◀ *One of China's chief exports was tea. Fast merchant ships called clippers raced back to Britain with their cargo. Clippers were the finest sailing vessels ever built. One of them, the* Cutty Sark, *can still be seen beside the River Thames at Greenwich, London.*

The scramble for Africa

- **Before the 1800s**, European knowledge of the African interior was limited. Explorers were deterred by deserts and dense forests, wild animals and hostile peoples.
- **After 1800**, many Europeans wanted to explore the interior of Africa.
- **Some were interested** in discovering new rivers, lakes and mountains. Some wanted to convert people to Christianity. Some wanted to find new lands where they could settle, or minerals that they could mine.
- **Famous explorers** included the Scottish missionary David Livingstone (1813–1873), the English traveller Richard Burton (1821–1890) and the German scholar Heinrich Barth (1821–1865).
- **In 1884** the Berlin Conference divided up the continent between the European colonial powers, and the feverish competition that followed was called 'the scramble for Africa'.
- **Boundaries were drawn** across the map with little knowledge of the land, or of the peoples who lived there. Some of these artificial divisions have caused conflict ever since.

▶ *David Livingstone (1813–1873) undertook several expeditions to Africa. Having gone missing while seeking the source of the Nile, he was famously found alive by H M Stanley, in 1871.*

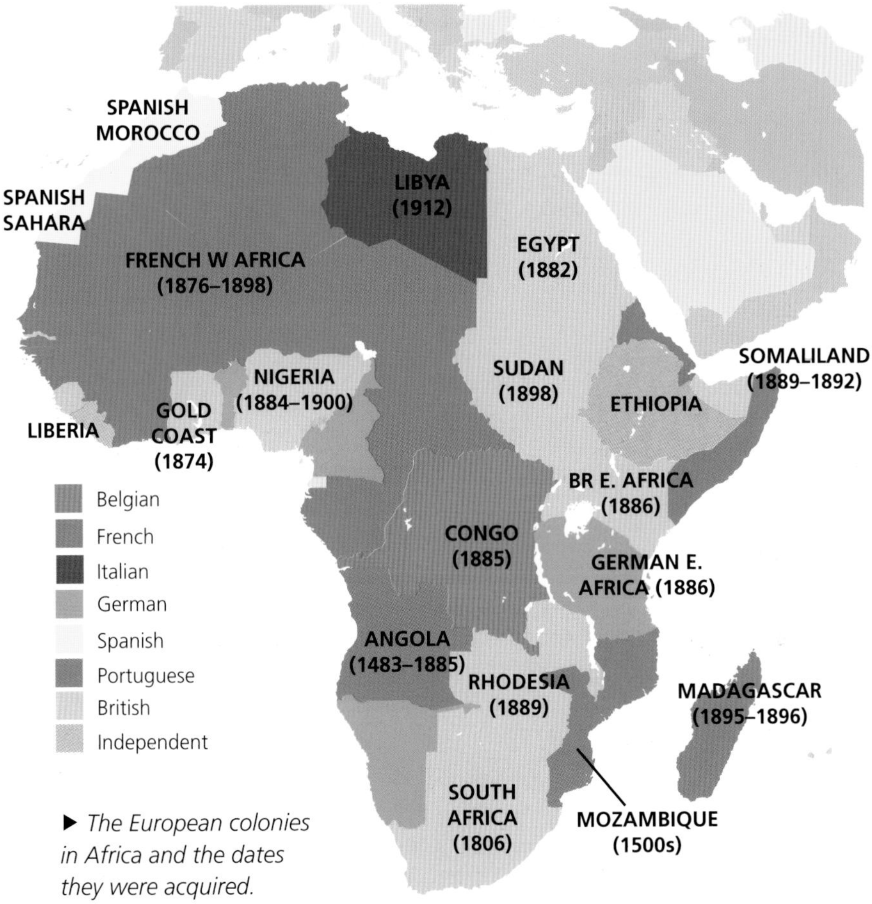

▶ *The European colonies in Africa and the dates they were acquired.*

- **In some parts of Africa**, colonial rule was established peacefully by agreement with indigenous peoples.
- **In Nigeria and Ghana**, many fought hard against the British, and in Tanzania and Namibia, they fought against German rule.
- **Ethiopia and Liberia** were the only countries in Africa to hold on to their independence.

China's troubles

- **By the end** of the 18th century, China's Qing dynasty was in decline. The population was increasing rapidly and there was a severe economic crisis.
- **The British East India Company** purchased tea and silk from China. It began to pay for these goods with opium grown in India, instead of with silver. More and more of this dangerous, addictive drug came onto the market in China.
- **When China tried to halt** this trade, Britain fought two 'Opium Wars' (1839–1842 and 1856–1860) against China to enforce it. By the 1842 Treaty of Nanjing, China lost Hong Kong to the British.
- **In 1860** British and French armies invaded China and occupied Beijing. At the Convention of Peking (Beijing), China opened more ports to western trade. More and more foreign traders now moved in to control China's trade.
- **In 1861** the new Chinese emperor was only six years old, so the Empress Dowager Cixi took control. She resisted any reform, but this only made the situation worse.

▶ *The Dowager Empress Cixi was Regent of China from 1861–1908. Her reign saw violent rebellions and foreign invasion.*

▲ *In 1900 foreign diplomats were trapped in Beijing by Chinese soldiers and by 'Boxer' rebels. An eight-nation international task force came to their rescue. Here, Japanese troops fight alongside the British against the Chinese.*

- **Poverty and hardship** had caused a violent civil war, the Taiping Rebellion, which lasted from 1850–1864 and killed about 20 million people.
- **Another great uprising**, known as the Boxer Rebellion, occurred in 1899. At first Cixi opposed it, but then decided to try to use it to rid China of its foreign occupiers. Foreigners in Beijing came under siege but were rescued by an international task force of 20,000 troops.

Turkey old and new

- **In 1774**, the Turkish Ottoman Empire was defeated by the Russians after a six-year war, and was forced to allow Russian ships to pass from the Black Sea to the Mediterranean.

- **During the 1800s**, the Ottoman Empire grew weaker. In 1829, the Greeks fought a successful war of independence. Other Balkan states followed suit.

- **During the 1800s**, the Turks fought four wars against Russia and lost three. Russia gained Bessarabia (now Moldova and Ukraine) and control of the Black Sea.

▲ *Abdülhamid visited Britain in 1867. He became sultan of the Ottoman empire nine years later, but was overthrown by the Young Turks in 1908.*

- **The Ottoman provinces** in the Near and Middle East were in decline. Trying to stop the empire's collapse, Sultan Abdülhamid II crushed opposition violently in the 1890s.

- **The Young Turks** were students and army officers who, in 1908, revolted against Abdülhamid and then ruled through his brother Mehmed V.
- **In November 1914** the Turks joined World War I on the German side, in a bid to regain lost territories.
- **After Turkey's defeat** in World War I, the Allies invaded and broke up the empire, leaving just modern Turkey.
- **The nationalist hero** Mustafa Kemal became the first president of the Turkish republic on 29 October 1923.
- **Kemal became known** as Atatürk (father of the Turks). He created modern Turkey by reforming education, law and language.

▼ *Modern Turkey was created by Mustafa Kemal Atatürk, shown here fighting for the Ottoman empire in the First World War.*

Many long-cherished dreams came true in the 20th and early 21st century – but there were also some terrible lessons to be learned.

AFRICA

1914–1918
World War I. Colonial troops fight in North, West, Southwest and East Africa.

1935
Italian fascists and Eritrean colonial troops invade Ethiopia.

1939–1945
World War II. Fighting in East Africa, major tank battles in the North African desert.

1956
Egypt nationalizes the Suez Canal and is invaded by Israel, Britain and France.

1957–1967
Thirty-one African countries gain their independence.

1963
Founding of the Organization of African Unity (OAU, from 2002 the African Union or AU).

1994
Apartheid (racist segregation) ends in South Africa. Nelson Mandela elected as the first black president.

2011
The 'Arab Spring'; governments overthrown in Tunisia, Egypt and Libya.

EUROPE

1914
Outbreak of World War I. France, the British Empire, Russia, Serbia and Romania fight Germany, Austria-Hungary, Ottoman Empire and Bulgaria.

1917
Revolution in Russia overthrows the Tsar. Civil war.

1918
Armistice ends World War I. Nine million troops and seven million civilians die.

1922
Founding of the USSR or Soviet Union, under Vladimir Ilyich Lenin.

1936–1939
The Spanish Civil War. Fascists under General Franco overthrow Spain's elected Republican government.

1939–1945
World War II and Holocaust. Nazi Germany invades much of Europe. Britain, the Soviet Union and the USA fight Germany, Italy and Japan.

1947–1991
The Cold War. Tension between communist Eastern and capitalist Western Europe. Germany divided.

1958
The Treaty of Rome establishes the European Economic Community (known as the European Union from 1993).

ASIA

1904–1905
Japan defeats Russia in the Russo-Japanese War.

1912
The Chinese empire is overthrown by nationalists under Sun Yatsen.

1939–1945
World War II: The Allies fight Japan across Burma, Southeast Asia and the Pacific. The USA drops atomic bombs on Hiroshima and Nagasaki.

1947–1949
Independence for India and Pakistan. Creation of the state of Israel. China becones a communist People's Republic.

1950–1953
The Korean War. United Nations' forces attack the communist North. Korea is divided into two nations.

1955–1975
The Vietnam War between communist North Vietnam and its allies, and anti-communist South Vietnamese regimes backed by the USA.

1979
Revolution overthrows the Shah in Iran, which becomes an Islamic republic.

2001–2014
Western powers fight in Afghanistan and Iraq.

The Modern World

NORTH AMERICA

1914–1918
Canada enters World War I in 1914. The USA enters in 1917.

1929
Global economic crisis starts in the USA. The Wall Street crash leads to the Great Depression.

1939–1945
World War II. Canada enters in 1939; the USA in 1941, following a Japanese air attack on Pearl Harbor, Hawaii.

1947–1991
The Cold War. The USA fights in Korea and Vietnam; arms race with the Soviet Union.

1963
Civil Rights movement marches on Washington, addressed by Dr Martin Luther King Jr.

1963
President John F Kennedy is assassinated in Dallas, Texas.

2001
A terrorist attack on the Twin Towers in New York City triggers a 'War on Terror'. The USA fights wars in Afghanistan and Iraq.

2009
Barack Obama becomes the first black US president.

CENTRAL AND SOUTH AMERICA

1910
Large oil reserves discovered in Venezuela.

1910–1920
Revolution and civil war in Mexico.

1946
Populist Peronist movement wins election in Argentina.

1962–1983
Independence for British territories in the region, including Jamaica and Trinidad (1962), Guyana (1966) and Belize (1981).

1973
Chile's elected government is overthrown, the Pinochet dictatorship.

1979
The Sandinista revolution in Nicaragua.

1982
The United Kingdom fights with Argentina over the Malvinas/Falkland Islands.

2010
Rapid growth of the Brazilian economy.

OCEANIA

1901
The Australian colonies federate as a Commonwealth.

1907
Australia and New Zealand become Dominions of the British Empire.

1914–1918
Australia and New Zealand forces fight in World War I.

1927
Australian parliament meets at Canberra, the new federal capital.

1939–1945
Australia and New Zealand fight in World War II. Japan invades New Guinea and many Pacific islands.

1967
Australian Aborigines granted citizenship rights in their own country.

1962–1980
Samoa, Nauru, Tonga, Fiji, Tuvalu and Vanuatu become independent nations.

2011
A severe earthquake hits Christchurch, New Zealand.

The Balkan crisis

- **The Balkan peninsula** is in southeastern Europe. Its lands have been home to many different peoples including Slovenes, Croats, Serbs, Bulgars, Greeks and Turks.
- **In the 19th century** the Balkan peoples were ruled over by two ageing and declining empires – Austria-Hungary and Ottoman Turkey. Many peoples dreamed of independence. European powers like Russia and Germany encouraged nationalist movements for their own purposes.
- **Austria refused** Slovenia and Croatia independence and held on to Bosnia-Herzegovina, which Serbia claimed.
- **In 1912**, various Balkan countries conspired to drive the Turks out of Europe in the First Balkan War, but rivalry between them led to a Second Balkan War in 1913, which left the Balkans highly unstable.

▼ *Within just four days of the assassination of Archduke Franz Ferdinand in 1914, World War I had started.*

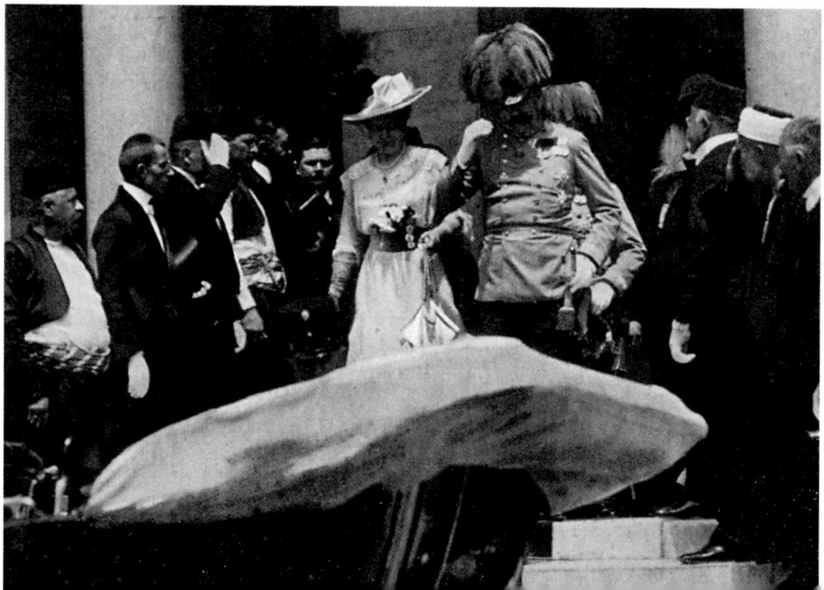

▲ *The first tanks appeared during World War I. The new century experienced warfare as it had never been known before.*

- **In June 1914**, Archduke Franz Ferdinand was assassinated in Sarajevo by Gavrilo Princip, a Serbian activist from Bosnia-Herzegovina.
- **The nations of Europe** were linked by a network of treaties and by related royal familes. However these alliances dragged everyone into conflict.
- **Austria believed** Serbs were behind the assassination and were encouraged by Germany to declare war. Russia sided with the Serbs, their fellow Slavs.
- **The Germans invaded** neutral Belgium in order to attack France, but Britain was pledged to protect Belgian neutrality.
- **Soon all of Europe** was engaged in the terrible global conflict of World War I.

World War I

- **World War I** (1914–1918), known as the Great War, was the worst the world had then seen, killing about nine million troops and seven million civilians.
- **The war was caused** by the rivalry between European powers in the early 1900s. The assassination of the Austrian Archduke Franz Ferdinand in Sarajevo in the Balkans, on 28 June 1914 was a trigger for catastrophe.
- **The Allied Powers** included Britain and France and their overseas empires and dominions, Belgium, Italy, Russia, Serbia, Montenegro, Romania, Greece, Portugal, Japan and Arab rebels.
- **The Central Powers** included Austria-Hungary, Germany, Bulgaria and the Ottoman empire.
- **The Germans** had the secret 'Schlieffen plan' for taking France by surprise, but their advance was halted by the Allies.
- **Both sides dug themselves in** along Germany's Western front, with a system of trenches stretching from the English Channel to Switzerland, killing-fields separated by mud and barbed wire.
- **The war soon developed** an Eastern front, where the Central Powers (Austria and Germany) faced the Russians. The deaths of millions of Russians provoked the 1917 revolution, which took Russia out of the war.
- **In the Alps**, the Central Powers were opposed by Italy. At Gallipoli in Turkey, British and Anzac (Australia and New Zealand) troops fought the Turks in another bloody campaign.
- **The war was also fought** in western Asia, in East and West Africa, in China and South America.

▲ *German troops on the Western front. The four-month Somme offensive in 1916 killed 600,000 Germans, 400,000 British and 200,000 French – and advanced the Allies just 7 km.*

- **The Allies relied** on supplies from North America, so the Germans used submarines to attack shipping. The sinking of RMS *Lusitania* in May 1915, brought the USA into the war in 1917.
- **By 1918**, there were 3.5 million Germans on the Western front and in March they broke through towards Paris. In July 1918, British tanks broke the German line at Amiens.
- **An Allied naval blockade** meant many people were starving in Germany. As more US troops arrived, the Germans were pushed back. At 11 o'clock on 11 November, 1918, the Germans signed an armistice to end the hostilities.
- **Had this really been** the 'war to end all wars'? Various peace agreements were drawn up, such as the Treaty of Versailles (1919), but some historians believe that the terms of the peace created even more problems, leading to World War II (1939–1945) and ongoing strife across the Middle East.

Wartime Britain and Ireland

- **All European countries** went through great social or political changes during World War I (1914–1918). Many families lost fathers, sons and brothers. A whole generation suffered, many from blindness, 'shellshock' (post-traumatic stress), from lost limbs or the terrible effect of poison gas.

▲ *A woman bus conductor stands on the platform of a Number 19 double-decker bus. The 20th century saw a revolution in women's role in society.*

- **From 1916** British troops were conscripted (called up) into the army. Those who refused to fight on grounds of their conscience ('conscientious objectors') faced hostility. Some were imprisoned, some worked in non-combat roles, such as ambulance driving.

- **In the United Kingdom**, the radical Suffragettes suspended their campaigns for women's voting rights during wartime, but women's role in society was changing fast. While men were away fighting, women took on many traditional men's jobs. They became teachers, typists, nurses and workers in munitions factories.

- **Women in Britain** aged over 30 finally got the vote in 1918, but it was 1929 before they, like the men, could vote at the age of 21. Women had won the vote in New Zealand as early as 1893.
- **Other long running problems** did not go away because of the war. The United Kingdom of Great Britain and Ireland had always had stresses and strains in its political union.
- **At Easter in 1916** an uprising took place in Dublin. Rebels seized the city's General Post Office and their leader, Padraig Pearse, proclaimed a republic. They were shelled by the British army and surrendered after five days.
- **The uprising** did not have mass support, but after 15 rebels were executed by the British, the republican party Sinn Féin ('Ourselves Alone') won the 1917 election. Ireland entered a long, often bitter and violent road to independence, which was fully achieved in 1949 (apart from in the six counties of Ulster, which experienced ongoing violence into the 1990s).

▼ *Irish rebels defend ruined buildings in Dublin against British troops armed with machine guns.*

The Russian Revolution

- **In 1861**, Tsar Alexander II had freed Russian serfs, but they stayed desperately poor. In towns, factory workers also suffered.
- **Unrest among factory workers** and peasants grew and by 1901 there were two revolutionary parties, the Socialist Revolutionary (SRP) and the Socialist Democrat (SDP).
- **In 1903**, the SDP split in two – the radical Bolsheviks (the 'majority'), led by Vladimir Ilyich Lenin, and the moderate Mensheviks (the 'minority').
- **In 1905**, the Imperial Guard fired on peaceful demonstrators in St Petersburg, killing 200 and wounding 800. Workers and peasants revolted and set up the first 'soviets' (workers' councils).

▼ *The Winter Palace in St Petersburg had been the official residence of the Russian tsars since 1732. In October (November in the Gregorian calendar) 1917 it was stormed by the Bolsheviks and became a museum. The city was renamed Leningrad.*

▲ *In 1918 the Bolsheviks shot Tsar Nicholas II and all his family at Yekaterinburg.*

- **Tsar Nicholas II** was forced to set up a Duma (parliament) but soon began to ignore it.
- **In 1914** Russia joined World War I, fighting against Germany on the Eastern front. In March 1917, terrible losses among Russian soldiers and hardship at home provoked mutinies, desertion and then a full-scale communist revolution.
- **The first 1917 revolution** is called the February Revolution, because this was the month in the old Russian calendar. Tsar Nicholas abdicated.
- **The moderate socialist** Alexander Kerensky became Prime Minister in a provisonal government, but more soviets were set up and the Bolseheviks gained support.
- **On 7 November** (25 October on the old calendar), the Bolsheviks seized the Winter Palace in St Petersburg. Lenin headed a new government in Moscow, while soviets took control of major cities.

Rise of the Soviet Union

- **Lenin** (Vladimir Ilyich Ulyanov, 1870–1924) was leader of the October Revolution in Russia in 1917. After the 1905 revolution, Lenin had lived in exile, but returned to Russia when the tsar was overthrown.

▲ *Lenin and Stalin in rare agreement.*

- **Like Karl Marx** (1818–1883), Lenin believed the world's workers would revolt and take over industry. Unlike Marx, he thought a small band of activists would need to lead the way.

- **After the revolution** in 1917, there was a civil war. The Bolsheviks' Red Army, led by Leon Trotsky, fought the Russian White Army, as well as foreign task forces, which intervened.

- **By 1922** all Russia was under Communist control. A new nation was founded, the Union of Soviet Socialist Republics (USSR, or Soviet Union). Lenin headed the government and introduced a pragmatic New Economic Policy.

- **In 1924** Lenin died and the ruthless Joseph Stalin (1879–1953) came to power. Stalin was from Georgia and his real name was Joseph Vissarionovich Dzhugashvili.

- **Stalin centralized** state control of the economy. The USSR was transformed into one of the world's great industrial and military powers, but at a terrible cost. Millions of Russian peasants starved in the 1930s as Stalin forced state control of farms.
- **Stalin used terror** to destroy all opposition. Trotsky was murdered in exile, in 1940. Russians lived in fear of the secret police NKVD (later the KGB), and millions went to their deaths in the gulags (prison camps).
- **Despite signing a pact** with Nazi Germany in 1939, the USSR entered World War II on the Allied side. The sacrifices of the Red Army assured the Allied victory in Europe in 1945.

▼ *Lenin's tomb in Red Square, Moscow. Over the years, countless thousands have queued to see the embalmed body inside.*

The Long March

- **In 1912**, the last Chinese emperor, six-year-old Puyi, gave up his throne in the face of rebellion and China became a republic, led by Sun Yatsen.
- **When Sun died** in 1925, leadership of his Guomindang (Nationalist) party fell to Jiang Jieshi (Chiang Kaishek) who allied with the Communist Party of China (founded in 1921) to defeat warlords in the north.
- **In 1927** Jiang Jieshi turned on the Communists and forced their leaders to flee to the Jiangxi hills as he took control in Beijing.
- **By 1931**, the Communists had regrouped enough to set up a rival government in the south, called the Jiangxi Soviet.

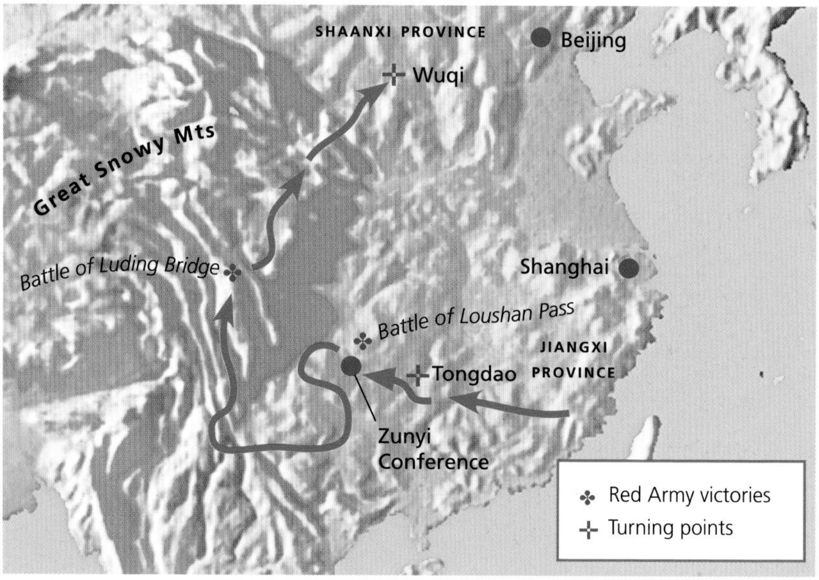

▲ *The Long March of the Red Army to escape the Nationalists – became a Chinese legend.*

- **In 1934**, Jiang Jieshi launched a massive attack on the Communists' Red Army, forcing them to begin their famous Long March to the north to escape.
- **On this 'Long March'**, the Red Army travelled 10,000 km through the mountains, covering up to 100 km a day, taking a year to reach the northern region of Shaanxi.
- **Almost 95,000** of the 100,000 who set out on the Long March died of cold and hunger on the way – but, crucially, the Red Army survived.
- **During the march**, Mao Zedong became the Red Army leader.
- **Both Jiang Jieshi's** Nationalists and Mao Zedong's Communists fought Japanese invading forces between 1937 and 1945.
- **After the war**, Mao drove out the weakened Guomindang party and took control. Jiang Jieshi and his government fled to Taiwan.

▲ *From 1934–1945 Puyi, the former emperor, served as puppet ruler of the Japanese-controlled state called Manchukuo.*

The Depression years

- **After World War I** the US economy boomed. People poured from the countryside into the cities. There was big money to be made. This was the age of jazz and the movies, a time of optimism nicknamed the 'Roaring Twenties'.
- **Soon, however**, the USA was in deep trouble. In October 1929 the US stock market collapsed. This disaster was named the 'Wall Street Crash', after the financial district of New York City.
- **Companies went bankrupt**, banks folded, investors lost all their money overnight. Some committed suicide. For the next decade, the economy was in a severe depression. Unemployment soared.
- **To make matters worse**, drought and unsustainable farming methods reduced the grain-producing prairies of the USA and Canada to a 'dustbowl' – a windblown semi-desert. Farm labourers and their families became migrants, seeking work wherever they could find it.

▶ *A migrant farm worker, hungry and exhausted, fears for her children. She was photographed in California, in 1936.*

▲ *The dignity and endurance of the Jarrow marchers impressed many people. It brought home to them the desperate poverty in Britain's industrial regions.*

- **The US economy** was by now so important to the wider world that a worldwide depression set in. International trade was halved.
- **In Britain** protests took the form of hunger marches by tens of thousands of people, held in Scotland, Wales and England. One of the most famous was from Jarrow, in the northeast, to London.
- **Economists still argue about** the causes of the Great Depression and remedies that were introduced. In the USA, President Franklin Roosevelt (1882–1945) introduced a series of regulations, work-creation schemes and reforms known as the New Deal.

DID YOU KNOW?

Tragically it took the outbreak of another World War (1939–1945) to finally end the Great Depression.

Rise of the Nazis

▲ *To boost their support, the Nazis held huge rallies at which their symbol, the swastika, was prominently displayed.*

- **Even before World War I ended**, Germans had risen in revolt against Kaiser Wilhelm II.
- **Marxists were establishing** workers' councils or Soviets. These were attacked by Freikorps, paramilitary volunteers who were mostly embittered ex-soldiers. The popular Social Democratic Party was opposed to revolution.
- **The Kaiser was exiled** and in 1919 Germany became a democratic republic. The new constitution had been drafted in Weimar, so this became known as the Weimar Republic.
- **Under the peace terms** of the Treaty of Versailles, Germany was forced to pay huge amounts of money for war damage. This ruined the German economy. Rising prices made people poor overnight.

- **In 1923**, the National Socialist German Workers Party, or Nazis, led by Adolf Hitler, tried to stage a rebellion in Munich. The rebellion failed, but support for the Nazis grew.
- **The Great Depression** threw six million Germans out of work, and in 1933 enough people voted for the Nazis to make them the strongest party. Hitler became Chancellor and set about destroying the opposition.
- **The Nazis were racists**, claiming German superiority over other races, including Jews and Slavs. They removed Jews from all government jobs and took away their rights.
- **On 9 November 1938**, Nazi thugs broke windows and burned down synagogues and Jewish businesses. This night became known as Kristallnacht ('Night of the Broken Glass').
- **The Nazis prepared** for war. In 1936, they marched into the French-occupied Rhineland. In 1938, they annexed Austria. In 1939 they invaded Czechoslovakia and then Poland.

▶ *Germany was already in a financial crisis during the war, and afterwards had huge reparations to pay to the Allies. Costs spiralled. By 1923, one loaf of bread could cost 200,000,000,000 Marks. This girl is playing with almost worthless banknotes.*

Adolf Hitler

- **Adolf Hitler** (1889–1945) was the dictator who turned Germany into the war machine that started World War II, and murdered six million Jews in what became known as the Holocaust.
- **Hitler was so angry** at the terms ending World War I that he joined the National Socialist German Workers' (Nazi) party, becoming its leader.
- **In 1923**, Hitler was put in prison after a failed Nazi coup, and there he wrote *Mein Kampf* ('My Struggle'). He claimed that Germany's problems were caused by Jews and communists, and that it needed a strong Führer (leader).
- **As the Great Depression** hit Germany in the early 1930s, Hitler's ideas gained support. In the 1933 elections, the Nazis got 37 percent of the vote and President Paul von Hindenburg asked Hitler to become Chancellor.

DID YOU KNOW?

Hitler was born in Braunau am Inn, Austria. A failed artist, he painted postcards before joining the German army in World War I.

▶ *Hitler was a mesmerizing speaker, with the power to get the whole audience at rallies shouting his praise.*

▲ *The Nazi concentration camps, such as Auschwitz, in Poland, became brutal death centres. Millions of Jews were killed in these camps, many of them sent to horrific gas chambers, where they were poisoned with toxic gas. Many Roma and other minorities and dissidents were also murdered.*

- **The Nazis established** the Gestapo (secret police) and used them to wipe out all opposition. When Hindenburg died in 1934, Hitler made himself Führer.
- **Hitler built up** Germany's army, rigidly organized all workers and sent millions of Jews to concentration camps.
- **By 1945** Germany lay in ruins. The Russians were advancing from the East, and the western Allies from the Rhine. Hitler married his mistress Eva Braun on April 29 in their bomb shelter in Berlin. They committed suicide the next day.

The Spanish Civil War

▲ *General Franco remained the extreme right-wing dictator of Spain until he died in 1975.*

- **In the 1920s and 30s**, extreme right-wing, anti-democratic political parties were on the rise across Europe.
- **In Italy**, Benito Mussolini (1883–1945) founded the National Fascist Party in 1921. He came to power glorifying militarism and suppressing human rights. In 1936 he formed an alliance called the Axis with Nazi Germany.
- **In Spain**, a civil war (1936–39) provided a testing ground for the weapons and tactics of the forthcoming World War.
- **In 1931** there was a popular vote for a Republican constitution, and King Alfonso XIII fled the country. Spain was split. On the Left were socialists, communists, anarchists and democrats who supported the Republic.
- **On the Right** was the fascist Falange party, allied with wealthy landowners, monarchists, army officers and the Catholic Church. Catalans and Basques wanted to break away from Spain.
- **The forces of the Right** ('Nationalists') were led by General Francisco Franco. They received practical support from Nazi Germany and Fascist Italy.

- **The forces of the Left** ('Republicans' or 'Loyalists') received support from the Soviet Union. Radicals from many other countries volunteered to join the 'International Brigades' fighting for the Loyalists.
- **In February 1936**, elections put the Popular Front, formed by all the left-wing groups, in power. In July 1936, a wave of army revolts threatened to topple the government. Its supporters armed themselves and a bitter civil war began, with terrible atrocities on both sides.
- **At first**, Loyalists held the northeast and the big cities, but they gradually fell back. In 1939 Franco's forces captured Madrid, the last Loyalist stronghold.

FALANGE OS LLAMA
AHORA O NUNCA

▲ *A recruiting poster for the fascist Falange party.*

World War II

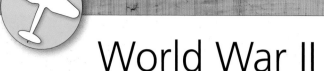

- **In World War II** (1939–1945), between 22–25 million soldiers were killed. About 38–50 million civilians also died. This was the most dreadful conflict in history.

- **The Axis powers** included Germany, Italy and Japan. They were opposed by the Allies, comprising the British Empire and Commonwealth troops, the USA, USSR and China. Many other nations also took part.

- **This was a truly global war**, fought on the plains of Europe, in the jungles of Southeast Asia, in the deserts of Africa, among the Pacific islands, and on and under the oceans.

- **It began** when Germany invaded Poland on 1 September 1939. Great Britain thought the USSR would defend Poland, but Hitler and Stalin made a pact. As Germany invaded Poland from the west, the USSR invaded from the east.

- **In May–June 1940**, the Germans quickly overran Norway and Denmark, then Luxembourg, the Netherlands, Belgium and France.

- **Northern France remained** occupied, while a collaborative regime ruled the south from Vichy. French Resistance fighters fought bravely against the occupiers and Free French forces assembled in exile.

◄ *Winston Churchill (1874–1965) was the British prime minister whose courage and inspiring speeches helped the British withstand the German threat.*

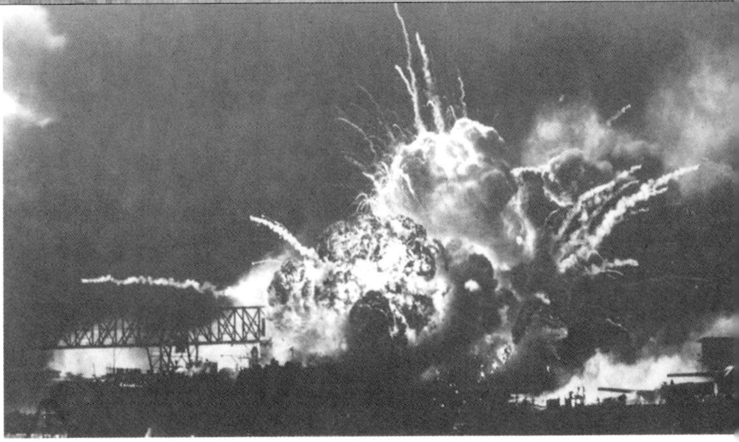

▶ *The bombing of Pearl Harbor by the Japanese forced the US to enter the war. Almost 4000 people were killed or injured by the attack, with the main targets being US warships.*

- **In the Battle of Britain** in August 1940, Germany launched wave after wave of air raids against Britain, to prepare for an invasion.
- **Fearing Stalin** would turn against him, Hitler launched a sudden invasion of the USSR on 22 June 1941. The fighting on this Eastern front was on a massive scale, killing 8.7 million Russian troops.
- **The USA joined the war** when Japan bombed its fleet without warning in Pearl Harbor, Hawaii, on 7 December 1941. Japan overran Southeast Asia and the Pacific. Many Allied prisoners-of-war suffered terribly in Japanese labour camps.
- **In 1942**, the Allies halted the Axis in Africa, invading Italy in 1943 and France in 1944. In 1945, the Allies invaded Germany from east and west. Germany surrendered on 7 May 1945.
- **The terrible Pacific conflict** ended when the USA dropped devastating atom bombs on the Japanese cities of Hiroshima and Nagasaki. Japan surrendered on 2 September 1945.
- **As the Allies moved** into Germany and Poland, they found the horror of Nazi death camps, where millions of Jews and others had been slaughtered by starvation and in gas chambers.

Japan in war and peace

▶ *Emperor Hirohito (1901–1989) was the first Japanese emperor to give up his god-like status, ruling after 1945 as a figurehead only.*

- **Japan suffered hardship** during the depression years. Right-wing extremists cracked down on civil rights and the army became ever more powerful.
- **Japan joined** the Axis powers in World War II, planning to dominate Southeast Asia. By 1942, Japanese conquests had succeeded in this aim. However in 1942 Japan lost the decisive naval Battle of Midway to the USA, and the tide was turned.
- **The final blow** for the Japanese was the devastating atomic bombs dropped by the USA on the cities of Hiroshima (6 August, 1945) and Nagasaki (9 August, 1945).
- **The Japanese accepted** the peace terms on 14 August, 1945, and surrendered to the USA on 2 September. The surrender brought a foreign occupying force to Japan, led by US general, Douglas MacArthur.
- **MacArthur drew up** a new constitution for Japan. Under this, Emperor Hirohito lost all real power. The Americans shared out farmland, legalized trade unions and improved women's and children's rights. The occupation force left in 1952.

- **Japan recovered** from the ruin of the war and launched itself on an amazing industrial boom, which turned it into the world's healthiest economy in barely 25 years. Japan has to import most of its energy, but it became a major producer of cars and electrical goods.
- **Japanese society changed** as people moved to the cities and the young began to behave independently.
- **An Asian financial crisis** in 1997 stalled the Japanese economy, and that was followed by the worldwide economic crisis from 2007. However Japan remains the world's third largest economy.

► *The devastating atomic blast at Hiroshima killed around 150,000 people, and many more suffered from chronic health problems.*

The United Nations

- **In the aftermath** of World War I, the great powers set up a League of Nations – a forum for nations to come together, discuss world problems and so avoid war.
- **This remarkable project** lasted from 1920–1946, but the USA did not join and the league failed to prevent World War II.
- **In February 1945**, US president Franklin D Roosevelt, British prime minister Winston Churchill and Soviet leader Joseph Stalin met at Yalta in the Crimea and announced that a United Nations conference would meet in San Francisco.
- **Fifty nations met** at San Francisco in April 1945 to draw up the Charter for the United Nations. Today there are 193 member states and two observer states. In 1971, the UN expelled Taiwan as China's representative and admitted the People's Republic of China instead.
- **The UN Charter** came into effect on 24 October 1945. The organization was made up of a General Assembly of member states, plus a Security Council, originally made up of just the leading powers, which had the power to veto (block) any UN measures.

◀ *The UN flag flies over the UN's permanent headquarters in New York City.*

▲ *Churchill, Roosevelt and Stalin (from left) established the UN at their Yalta Conference, in 1945.*

- **In 1948 the UN issued** a Universal Declaration of Human Rights outlining the global principles of social justice.
- **United Nations agencies** deal with a wide range of international issues, including world health, economics, culture and heritage, child protection, refugees, human rights, environment and food production.

DID YOU KNOW?

Blue-helmeted UN troops, seconded from member states, have helped to keep the peace in trouble spots around the world since 1945.

Mahatma Gandhi

- **The long years of struggle** against colonialism began to bear fruit in the years after World War II.
- **Many were inspired** by Mohandas K Gandhi (1869–1948), the non-violent campaigner who led India's fight for independence.
- **Gandhi is often called Mahatma**, meaning 'Great Soul'. He believed truth could only be known through tolerance and concern for others.
- **Gandhi was born** in Porbandar in India. At 13, he married a girl of 14 called Kasturbai. They later had four children. At 19 he went to study law in London.
- **Gandhi went to work** as a lawyer in South Africa in 1893, but soon after arriving was thrown out of a railway carriage because of the colour of his skin. He then stayed in South Africa for 21 years to fight for Indian rights.
- **Gandhi emphasized** non-violent protest. By imposing hardship on himself and showing no anger or hatred, he believed he could persuade his opponents he was right. This method of action was called *Satyagraha*.
- **In 1915** Gandhi returned to British India, and after troops had massacred many peaceful protestors at Amritsar, he led India's fight for independence.

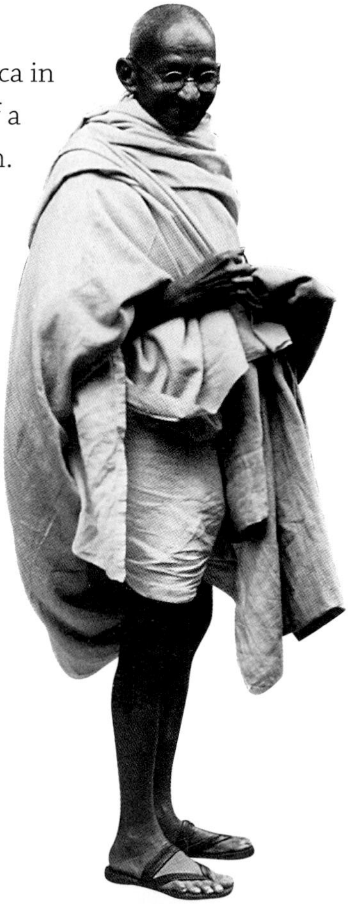

▶ *Gandhi dressed with extreme simplicity in traditional Indian clothes, with his feet bare or in sandals.*

▲ *A gathering of Indian Hindus. Gandhi campaigned to stop conflict between Hindus and Muslims.*

- **In 1920**, Gandhi began a programme of hand-spinning and weaving, traditional crafts that he believed could give Indians economic independence, so challenging the British.
- **Gandhi was jailed** again and again for his protests, and spent seven years in prison.
- **India became independent** in 1947, but tragically Gandhi was assassinated on 30 January 1948, by a Hindu who hated his tolerance of Muslims.

DID YOU KNOW?

In 1948, Gandhi persuaded Hindus and Muslims to stop fighting by going on a fast.

India and Pakistan

- **Indian troops** fought alongside the British in World War I. However, discontent with British rule began to boil after soldiers gunned down at least 379 Indian protestors at Amritsar in 1920.
- **In 1921**, Mohandas K Gandhi became the leader of a movement demanding independence for India. Gandhi led a series of non-violent protests against the British, such as boycotting British goods and refusing to pay taxes. He gained millions of supporters.
- **In 1935**, the British gave India a new constitution that allowed Indians more power. In 1940 the Muslim leader Muhammad Ali Jinnah (1876–1948) demanded that a separate country for Muslims should be created, called Pakistan.

▼ *The Indian Parliament building in New Delhi. Independent India's first Prime Minister was Jawaharlal Nehru (1889–1964).*

- **In World War II**, Indians said they would only fight on the British side if they were given independence. In 1942, Gandhi launched his 'Quit India' campaign.
- **In 1946**, Britain offered independence to all of India, but after terrible riots Indian and British leaders agreed to partition (divide) India and Pakistan. Pakistan became independent on 14 August 1947, India the next day.
- **About 7.2 million** Muslims immediately fled to Pakistan and 7.3 million Hindus and Sikhs to India.
- **In the following decades** there was ongoing hostility between the two nations, especially over the disputed region of Kashmir. In 1971 the western and eastern sections of Pakistan divided after a war, with East Pakistan becoming independent Bangladesh.

Israel and Palestine

- **In the 19th century** Palestine was part of the Ottoman empire. It was home to Arabs, both Muslim and Christian, and a small Jewish population.
- **Groups of Jewish nationalists** called Zionists began to move from other parts of the world to Palestine, wishing to settle in the ancient homeland of the Jewish people.
- **In 1917**, during World War I, Britain invaded Palestine and promised Zionists a 'national home for the Jewish people', provided it did not prejudice the rights of other peoples living there.
- **In 1922** the League of Nations gave Britain a 'mandate' (legal authority) to govern Palestine. After World War II and the horrors of the Holocaust, many Jews displaced from Europe wanted to settle in Palestine, to be free of persecution.

▼ *Palestinian students protest in Bethlehem, in the West Bank, against Israel's attack on Gaza in 2012.*

▶ *Israeli troops partially withdraw from the Palestinian territory of Gaza, as a ceasefire is announced in 2009.*

- **Jewish and Arab militants** fought against British rule and each other. Many dispossessed Palestinians fled to neighbouring lands and were never allowed to return. In 1947 the United Nations agreed to partition Palestine and in 1948 Jewish leaders proclaimed a new nation named Israel.
- **The new state** was immediately attacked by its Arab neighbours and further wars broke out in 1956, 1967, 1973 and 1982. Israel was strongly supported by the USA and acquired nuclear weapons.
- **Many Palestinians opposed** the state of Israel altogether. Some campaigned for their own nation state, comprising Gaza, the West Bank and East Jerusalem.
- **Israel successfully moved** from a farming economy to high-tech industries. However the nation was the centre of ongoing conflict.
- **Regional politics were dominated** by terrorism and uprisings ('intifadas'), by the illegal settlement of Palestinian land by Israelis, by Palestinan rocket attacks on Israel, by limited self-rule, by the blockading and bombing of Gaza by Israel, by the construction of a wall between Israel and the Palestinian West Bank. Peace seemed a distant prospect.

DID YOU KNOW?

In the 1967 Six-Day War, Israel occupied Egyptian Sinai, the Syrian Golan Heights, East Jerusalem and the Jordanian West Bank.

The Cold War

- **The Cold War** was a period of international tension lasting from 1947–1991. It was caused by rivalry between communist countries, headed by the Soviet Union, and capitalist countries, headed by the USA.
- **It was called the 'Cold' War** because there was no direct war between the two super powers. However both supported countries that did fight, as in the Korean War (1950–1953) and the Vietnam War (1955–1975).
- **The USA and USSR** waged an arms race to build up nuclear weapon stocks and keep ahead of each other.
- **Real war loomed** in 1962 when US president John F Kennedy (1917–1963) threatened the USSR as it attempted to build missile bases on Cuba.
- **The USSR dominated** Eastern and Central Europe, while Western Europe was allied with the USA. This East-West divide was nicknamed the 'Iron Curtain', a familiar term made famous by Winston Churchill in 1946.

▶ *Fidel Castro, prime minister of Cuba at the time of the 1962 missile crisis. The politics of Cuba's socialist revolutionary government was supported by the USSR but opposed by the USA.*

▲ *Glowing balloons mark the course of the former Berlin Wall, in 2014. Germans were celebrating the 25th anniversay of its fall, which led to the end of the Cold War.*

- **Berlin was an enclave** within the communist East, occupied by French, British, American and Soviet troops. In 1961 the West and East sectors were divided by the Berlin Wall. At least 136 people were killed trying to escape over the Wall.
- **Divided Berlin**, with its propaganda and its spies, became a symbol of the Cold War as a whole.
- **Tensions eased** after 1985, when Soviet leader Mikhail Gorbachev introduced reforms in the USSR and began a dialogue with the West.
- **In 1989** the Berlin Wall was demolished – and Berliners had a huge party on the ruins.

People's Republic of China

- **In 1949** Chinese communist leader Mao Zedong (1893–1976) declared China a People's Republic. People hoped communism would end centuries of poverty and oppression.
- **Mao spurred on peasants** to throw out landlords and work together on collective farms. Peasants who had starved in the war ate again. Healthcare and education improved.
- **In 1957**, Mao's 'Great Leap Forward' programme forced people to work on communes to develop farming and industry. This upheaval brought famine and economic disaster.
- **In the 1960s** there was a power struggle between those who wanted more economic freedom and hardline communists.
- **In 1966**, Mao launched a 'Cultural Revolution' to purge China of corrupting foreign ideas. Young 'Red Guards' rampaged as colleges and factories were shut down. Many people were killed or tortured.

▶ *The 'Little Red Book', properly called* The Thoughts of Chairman Mao, *became the 'bible' of communist China.*

▲ *Mao's picture taking pride of place at the Forbidden City, Beijing – a walled medieval palace that was once home to China's long line of emperors.*

- **In the 1970s** relations with the USA thawed, and the People's Republic was admitted to the UN in place of Taiwan.
- **Mao Zedong** died in 1976. Soon there were economic reforms, as China engaged with the rest of the world. The Chinese Communist Party now supported state-controlled capitalism. China remained under criticism for abuse of human rights.
- **The former colonies** of Hong Kong and Macau were returned to China in 1997 and 1999.
- **The 2000s** saw record economic growth and the rise of a prosperous middle class. Many poor rural workers became migrants, seeking work in the big cities. By 2014 growth was slowing.

Vietnam

- **From 1883**, Vietnam, Cambodia and Laos were ruled by France as 'Indochina'.
- **As Germany invaded France** in 1940, Japanese troops entered Vietnam. They were resisted by the Vietminh, a coalition of nationalist and communist forces, supported by the Allies.
- **When Japan surrendered** in 1945, the Vietminh, led by Ho Chi Minh, won control of much of Vietnam. Elections were held in 1946.
- **In 1947** the French invaded again and set up a new state in the south. In 1954 they were defeated by the Vietminh at Dien Bien Phu, and left Vietnam.

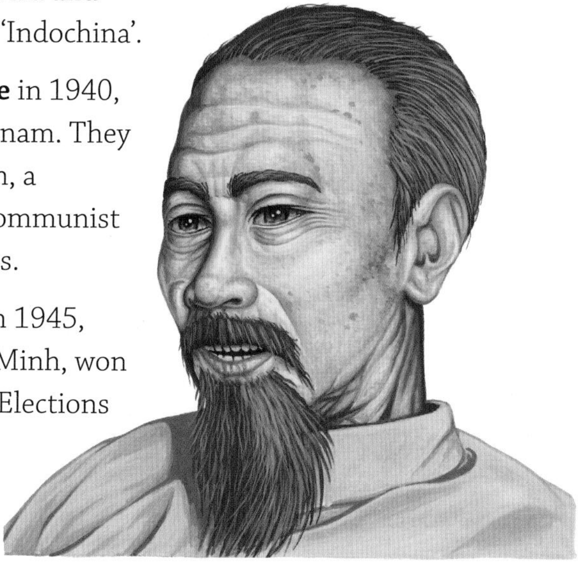

▲ *Ho Chi Minh (1890–1969), president of North Vietnam.*

- **In 1954** it was agreed to split Vietnam into North and South. South Vietnam and the USA promised all-Vietnamese elections.
- **In 1960 the North** established a National Liberation Front. In the South an insurgent force, the Viet Cong, was founded with northern support.

DID YOU KNOW?

The Vietnam War was the first war that was widely televised as it happened.

- **The USA sent troops** to support the South in 1963, and in 1965 began to bomb North Vietnam, which the USSR and China supplied with arms.
- **More and more US troops** and bombers were sent to Vietnam. There were anti-war protests in the USA and worldwide.
- **In 1968** northern and Viet Cong forces began a new offensive. In 1973 the USA withdrew. In 1975, the Viet Cong captured the southern capital Saigon (renamed Ho Chi Minh City).
- **The economy** of independent Vietnam slowly grew and today the USA is a major trading partner.

▶ *The USA used helicopters to devastating effect in the Vietnam War.*

The American century

- **The global power** of the European nations was finally exhausted during the two World Wars. The United States of America became the dominant global power.

- **US cities defined** the modern age, with their soaring skyscrapers, their mass-produced motorcars and their dance bands. Hollywood movies spread images of this new way of life around the world.

- **Not all was well**. Economic inequality was accentuated by the grim reality of the Great Depression. Gangsters and organized crime thrived in Chicago and New York.

▼ *Martin Luther King (third from left) and other civil rights campaigners meet with President John F Kennedy (third from right) in 1963.*

- **American politics** was dominated by two parties. The Republican Party, founded in 1854 on an anti-slavery ticket, was increasingly conservative. In the 1930s the Democratic Party (founded in 1828) looked more to liberal values and social intervention.
- **In the 1950s** there was fierce opposition to communism, at home and abroad, and a championing of capitalism and the free market. The 1960s saw many changes in the USA. A young, dynamic president called John F Kennedy was elected in 1961. Tragically he was assassinated in Texas in 1963.
- **African Americans** may have been freed from slavery, but they still faced segregation and racism. The Civil Rights movement of the 1950s attempted to remedy this injustice. It was inspired by the activism of Martin Luther King Jr, who was assassinated in 1968.
- **After the USSR** launched the first satellite in 1957, and the first man in space in 1961, the USA succeeded in landing astronauts on the Moon in 1969.
- **After the end** of the Cold War in 1991, the USA sought to maintain its power and influence worldwide. After severe terrorist attacks on the USA on 11 September 2001, it fought major wars in Afghanistan and Iraq.
- **The first African American** to become US president was Barack Obama, elected to office in 2009 and 2012.

Latin America

- **In the 1950s**, many Latin American countries sought to break their dependence on single agricultural products such as sugar and beef by undertaking major industrialization programmes.
- **'Populist' alliances** between workers and industrialists came to the fore.
- **In Argentina**, Juan Perón came to power and tried to build up industry at the expense of agriculture.
- **Landowners who were suffering** from the emphasis on industry began to form alliances with the army. Army coups took place in Argentina (1955), Brazil (1964) and Chile (1973).
- **Many of the military regimes** in the region were secretly backed by foreign powers such as the USA.
- **In the 1960s**, some Latin American groups resorted to guerrilla warfare to bring down the military dictatorships.
- **In 1959**, an Argentinian communist called Che Guevara helped overthrow the dictator of Cuba and bring Fidel Castro to power.

◀ *Eva Perón, also known as Evita (1919–1952), was the wife of Argentinian leader Juan Perón. A former actress, she became a popular politician in her own right.*

▶ *Activist Che Guevara played a major part in Cuba's revolution. Leaving Cuba for South America, he met an early death at the hands of political enemies and became an enduring hero, especially to young people in the 1960s and 1970s.*

- **In 1967**, Che Guevara was killed leading a guerrilla band trying to overthrow the dictator of Bolivia.
- **Under the dictators**, opposition was suppressed and many people were tortured, imprisoned or simply 'disappeared', as 20,000 did in Argentina.
- **In the 1980s and 1990s**, economic failure brought down most Latin American dictators, including Pinochet in Chile (1990) and Galtieri in Argentina (1983).
- **Many of the Latin American** nations became democracies in the 1990s.

DID YOU KNOW?

Brazil has become an economic giant, but the destruction of its rainforests worries scientists and environmentalists.

Winds of change

◀ *Young Caribbeans came to England in search of a decent wage, but found that there was little money left to save or send home.*

- **In 1960** the British Prime Minster Harold Macmillan spoke of a 'wind of change' blowing through Africa. He was referring to the end of Europe's global empires and the progress to independence.
- **The British Empire** had begun to change as early as 1931, with the creation of the British Commonwealth. This organization, today known as the Commonwealth of Nations, links former British territories and colonies.
- **Similar changes** were affecting the overseas colonies of Britain, France, Belgium, Portugal and the Netherlands around the world, from the Caribbean Sea to the Pacific Ocean.
- **In some countries**, such as Ghana or Jamaica, power was transferred peacefully. In others, such as Kenya or Algeria, independence was preceded by periods of violence or civil war.
- **In many cases** the Cold War (1947–1991) affected the struggles for independence, with the Soviet Union or the West backing rival insurgents or candidates.

- **Independence changed** many lives for the better. Some newly independent countries became wealthy and thrived.
- **Other new countries** faced problems from the start. The people may have never received proper education or healthcare from their rulers, or have had few resources for developing the economy. Often the changes favoured one ethnic group at the expense of another, leading to conflict. In some countries corrupt dictators seized power.
- **From the 1950s and 1960s** citizens of many colonies or former colonies migrated to Europe to work. Algerians brought their culture to Marseille and Paris, Surinamers to Amsterdam, and Caribbeans to London.

▼ *Caught up in Algeria's violent war of independence (1954–1962), Berber women hurry past a French tank.*

South Africa's challenge

- **In 1910**, four British colonies – Transvaal, Orange Free State, Cape Colony and Natal – joined to make the self-governing Union of South Africa.
- **White people** had almost complete power in the Union, while blacks had virtually no legal rights.
- **Mahatma Gandhi** campaigned for Indian rights in South Africa and had limited success.
- **Black South Africans** set up their own campaigning group in 1912, with the movement that was later called the ANC (African National Congress).
- **Afrikaners** – descended from the Dutch settlers – began to fight for control. Their National Party made headway and in 1948 came to power. It enacted 'apartheid' laws to keep all the races firmly apart.

▶ *Under the harsh rules of apartheid, blacks and whites were 'segregated' – kept apart from each other – in all kinds of public places and situations.*

- **The ANC fought** against apartheid – and especially against 'pass' laws that meant blacks had to carry passes.
- **In 1960**, police opened fire on protesting blacks at Sharpeville, killing 69. The government banned the ANC.
- **In the 1970s and 80s**, opposition to apartheid grew both in and outside South Africa, with many countries applying sanctions (trade restrictions).
- **In 1990**, President de Klerk released Nelson Mandela (1918–2013), an activist jailed since 1962, and repealed apartheid laws.
- **In 1994**, the ANC won the first open elections and Nelson Mandela became South Africa's first black president.
- **Under Mandela** (president 1994–1999), South Africa became a 'Rainbow Nation' in which different peoples cooperated. Court-like commissions investigated previous abuses of human rights and those guilty publicly sought forgiveness.

▲ *Nelson Mandela, South Africa's first black president. During his decades of imprisonment, Mandela provided a charismatic focus for ANC campaigns to end apartheid.*

The European Union

- **In 1945** a French diplomat called Jean Monnet promoted the idea of uniting Europe economically and politically.
- **In 1952**, six countries formed the European Coal and Steel Community (ECSC), to trade in coal and steel.

▼ *The European Commission building in Brussels. The Parliament is in Strasbourg. The Court of Justice is in Luxembourg.*

DID YOU KNOW?

The EU has 24 official and working languages. The three 'core' languages are English, French and German.

- **The success of the ECSC** led the member countries to break down all trade barriers between them as part of the European Economic Community (EEC), in 1958.
- **From 1973–1981**, six new countries joined the EEC, including the UK.
- **In 1992**, the 12 EEC members signed a treaty at Maastricht in the Netherlands to form the European Union (EU). The EU today has 28 members, including France, Germany and the UK.
- **The EU added cooperation** on justice and police matters, and on foreign and security affairs to the economic ties.
- **The EU has five governing bodies**: the European Council, the Commission, the Council of Ministers, the Court of Justice and the Parliament. The 27 Commissioners submit laws for the Council to make and put into effect.
- **In 1999**, the EU launched the Euro, a single European currency adopted in 18 of the member states (the 'Eurozone').
- **The European Council**, which is made up of the heads of state or of government in each country, meets four times a year. Since 2009, it includes an official called the President of the European Council who represents the EU.
- **Critics of the EU** claim that it is over-bureaucratic or too large. Some object to its principles, such as the free movement of labour. Supporters claim it is of great economic benefit to members and that after centuries of divisive conflict, it is time for close ties and peaceful cooperation.

Desert wars

- **For thousands of years**, Western Asia has seen warfare over resources, trade, international politics and religion.
- **In the 20th century** the discovery of oil brought fabulous riches to poor desert countries, but it also brought regional and global conflict.
- **From 1909** Britain exploited the oil reserves of Persia (known as Iran from 1935). In 1951 Iran's elected prime minister nationalized oil, and the Shah (king), fled the country. The USA and Britain returned the Shah to power to win back western control over the oilfields.
- **During the Cold War** the Shah was a staunch ally of the USA, as Iran bordered the USSR. He was overthrown in a revolution in 1979.
- **Power was seized** by a Shi'a Islamic cleric named Ruhollah Khomeini. He ruthlessly suppressed all opposition. There began decades of political tension between Iran and the Western powers.

▶ *The Ayatollah (cleric) Ruhollah Khomeini – Iran's head of state from 1979–1989. He led a revolution in Iran that saw a return to very strict Islamic principles.*

- **Iran's western neighbour**, Iraq, was another oil-rich nation. After years of wrangling, the dictatorial Saddam Hussein, at that point supported by the Western powers, became Iraqi president in 1979.
- **Saddam Hussein** was worried by the unsettling effects of the Islamic revolution in Iran and was eager to seize disputed border territory.
- **In September 1980**, Iraq invaded Iran to begin the eight-year-long Iran–Iraq War. This vicious war devastated both countries and killed 1.5 million people.
- **In 1990**, Iraq invaded and annexed Kuwait. In 1992, in the Gulf War, a US-led multinational force expelled Iraqi forces from Kuwait.
- **In 2003**, a US-led force invaded Iraq, ousting Saddam. They accused him of possessing 'weapons of mass destruction', but these were never found. Hundreds of thousands died. Saddam was captured in 2003, tried, and executed in 2006.
- **The country collapsed** in anarchy, as Iraqis fought each other and the foreign troops. The troubles re-ignited old divisions between Shi'a and Sunni Muslims.
- **In Afghanistan**, on Iran's eastern border, the USA and other western armies waged a deadly 13 year war against the Taliban movement, which had permitted the (chiefly Saudi) terrorist organization al-Qaeda to operate from their country.

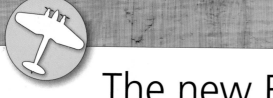

The new Russia

- **After Stalin died** in 1953, the USSR witnessed major reforms. However people remained restricted and fearful of the KGB secret police. Its new leader was the blunt-speaking Nikita Khrushchev (1894–1971).
- **The USSR's** pioneering space programme impressed the world, but by the 1980s, the Soviet economy was in decline. The decision of leader Leonid Brezhnev to invade Afghanistan (1979–1989) in support of its communist government, was a costly error.
- **In 1985 Mikhail Gorbachev** became Soviet leader and introduced *perestroika* (economic reform), *glasnost* (openness) and *demokratizatsiya* (increased democracy).
- **People in communist eastern Europe** demanded freedom too. New democratic governments were elected in Hungary, Poland, Czechoslovakia, Romania and Bulgaria.
- **Regional republics** within the Soviet Union also wanted independence. In 1991 the USSR was dissolved into 15 independent nations, changing the map of the Baltic region, the Caucasus and Central Asia.
- **Gorbachev's reforms** angered Communist Party leaders, who staged a coup and imprisoned him. He was freed, but Boris Yeltsin went on to become president of the new Russian Federation.

◄ *Mikhail Gorbachev (b 1931). He cut arms spending, improving relations with the West.*

▲ *Crowds in Vologda, in the Russian Federation, march in support of the pro-Russian eastern region of Ukraine and Crimea, in 2014.*

- **Yeltsin brought in** economic shock therapy and privatized state industries. The profits made instant millionaires of a few individuals. There was corruption, organized crime and rising food prices.
- **In 2000**, the Russians elected Vladimir Putin as president. Russia grew richer from oil and gas, and finally crushed a Chechen insurgency in the Caucasus.
- **Putin brought firm government** but restricted freedoms and intimidated the press. As Western powers extended their influence into former Soviet territories, Putin won popularity in Russia for hardline opposition.
- **In 2014** the Russian Federation annexed Crimea, part of Ukraine. The West imposed sanctions and many feared the start of a new Cold War.

The electronic revolution

- **Computers and electronic communications** transformed the way we live in the 20th and 21st centuries.
- **Mechanical calculating machines** have an ancient history. A mechanism found in a shipwreck off the Greek island of Antikythera is thought to be a kind of early computer, dating back to about 150 BC.
- **English polymath** Charles Babbage designed a remarkable calculating machine called an analytical engine in 1834.
- **The ENIAC electronic computer** (USA, 1945) could not store data or programs, but the Manchester Mark I (UK) 1948 was more like the real thing. In the 1950s large commercial computers began to appear in offices, made by companies such as IBM and Ferranti.

▼ *A vintage computer goes on display at a show in Milan, Italy. The pace of technological change has been very rapid.*

▶ *A mobile phone call is made in Tanzania. Electronic innovations have transformed communications in rural Africa, bypassing the need for costly land lines.*

- **The size of computers** was reduced greatly by a series of ingenious inventions. Transistors (1947) could replace valves. Circuits could be integrated with a single silicon chip (1958) and 1969 saw the first microprocessor.
- **Pocket calculators** were mass produced from 1971, and from 1975 the home computer began a real revolution, with Apple being founded in 1976.
- **The first email** was sent in 1971. In the 1980s and 90s email became popular not just in colleges, but in homes and offices. In 1991 an email was even sent from space, by an astronaut.
- **The Internet developed** out of many different computer networks that were amalgamated between the 1960s and 1990s. The World Wide Web was an invention of Sir Tim Berners-Lee and dates from 1989. It opened up unparalleled global access to all sorts of information and media.
- **In the 2000s** the game changed constantly, as computers, social media, smart phones and televisions interacted with each other. The electronic revolution changed education, research, medicine entertainment, social interaction, political protest, journalism communications, broadcasting, censorship, astronomy, commerce, banking, transport – almost every aspect of human life.
- **Electronics have shaped** and shrunk the modern world, but like all technological revolutions, cannot offer all the answers or promise happiness.

Globalization

- **We often say the world** is getting smaller, meaning that in the 21st century we can communicate instantaneously and travel around the planet at high speed. Nation states are more and more integrated through economics or common interests. This process is known as 'globalization'.
- **Globalization takes many forms**, such as the movement of people or traded goods around the world, the setting up of transnational corporations, electronic financial transactions, live satellite broadcasting or communication by Skype.
- **The urge towards globalization** has existed throughout human history, from the first migrations of *Homo sapiens*, to the first circumnavigation of the globe or the first international telephone cables. In every century the world has 'become smaller'. World Internet connectivity is just the latest example.
- **International organization** and cooperation makes it possible to tackle big problems on a global scale. The World Health Organization can tackle diseases such as ebola or malaria worldwide.
- **The International Monetary Fund** (IMF) aims to bring about international monetary cooperation, employment and trade. The UN's World Bank provides loans to developing countries.
- **Globalization has its critics**. International bodies may not be democratically accountable for their actions. The interest that poor countries have to pay on loans may actually hinder development.

- **Transnational corporations** may use their status to avoid paying taxes in countries where they operate. Electronic financial trading means that a financial crisis can spread around the world within minutes. International access to markets and cheaper prices sound like a good idea, but not if local farmers can no longer compete when they sell their produce at the nearest market.

- **Throughout most of history** the world has been home to a rich variety of regional cultures, languages, forms of dress and varieties of food. Globalization in the last 50 years has worn away many of these differences.

▼ *Colourful national flags flutter on a fine day. Sadly, the 21st century has also seen conflict and bloodshed, despite closer international relations.*

Planet Earth

- **In 2014** the European Space Agency landed a spacecraft on a 4 km-wide comet which was 518 million km from Earth.
- **Human development** over the last 200 years has changed the world we live in. Forests have been stripped away. Grasslands have been intensively farmed. Rivers and seas have become acidic, polluted with chemicals and filled with plastic waste. The air has been filled with toxic gases from factories and vehicle exhausts.
- **Many animals face extinction** as their habitats are destroyed or poisoned.
- **Most scientists believe** that human activity has surrounded the planet with layers of gases that trap reflected sunlight, making it warmer. They predict an increase in violent weather events and a rise in global temperatures and sea levels.
- **Some claim** that the planet is not warming. Others claim that it is, but that this is part of a natural cycle, rather than the result of human activity.

▶ *Planet Earth as seen from space. Does the future of humans belong on other, distant planets, which can support life?*

- **In 1992** the United Nations held a Conference for Sustainable Development in Rio de Janeiro, Brazil. It was attended by representatives of 172 nations and became known as the Earth Summit. Another summit was held there in 2012.

- **Many campaigners fear** that environmental action has been too little and too late. They say that the rapid advances being made in renewable energy production and storage must be made a priority.

- **In 35,000 BC** the world population was probably about 3 million. In 2011 the UN estimated the world population as having passed 7 billion. We cannot know what the future holds, but we can learn lessons from history.

DID YOU KNOW?

The more humans explore space, the more we look back at our own planet, with its blue oceans wreathed in cloud, and realize how precious it is.

Index

Index

Entries in **bold** refer to main entries; entries in *italics* refer to illustrations.

A

B

C

D

E

F

I

J

K

M

N

O

P

T

U

X

Y

Z

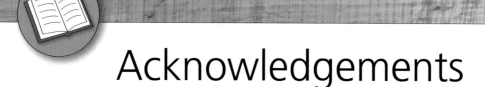

Acknowledgements

The publishers would like to thank the following sources for the use of their photographs:

Front cover: Anatoly Vartanov/Alamy

Alamy 83 North Wind Picture Archives; 277 The Art Archive; 309 Mireille Vautier

Corbis 195 Leemage; 245 Margaret Courtney-Clarke; 255 Bass Museum of Art; 263 Ira Block/ National Geographic Creative; 323 Philadelphia Museum of Art; 334 Asian Art & Archaeology, Inc; 355 Macduff Everton; 375 Bettmann; 390–391 Heritage Images; 400 Alfredo Dagli Orti/The Art Archive; 427 Ali Kabas; 449; 467 Bettmann; 468 Fred Ward; 473 Bettmann

Fotolia.com 196 Michelle Robek; 244 farbkombinat; 364 Georgios Kollidas; 421 Eli Coory

Glow Images 248 Werner Forman Archive/Beijing Museum

Robert Harding 76 Fabian von Poser; 79 Godong; 352 Bao; 357 Gunter Kirsch

Shutterstock.com 14–15 Phase4Studios; 37 Mono Collective; 41 Filip Fuxa; 46–47 Gurgen Bakhshetsyan; 61 Atthapol Saita; 81 Everett Historical; 86 barbar34; 102–103 Federico Rostagno; 110 Rudra Narayan Mitra; 119 Daniel J. Rao; 123 akkaradech; 124 jeff speigner; 125 Daniel Prudek; 139 Pyma; 142–143 milosk50; 152 Panos Karas; 154 wjarek; 155 claudio zaccherini; 161 JPF; 164 Vlad1988; 165 GhostKnife; 171 Reidl; 175 Brendan Howard; 176 Dave Head; 182 fulya atalay; 186–187 Ensuper; 193 matthi; 207 Albert Nowicki; 225 vladimir salman; 227 Kiev.Victor; 228 Doin Oakenhelm; 230 Zurijeta; 233 Andy Clarke; 238–239 James Michael Dorsey; 247 Meister Photos; 256–257 Henrik Winther Andersen; 259 KKulikov; 260 Bartosz Nitkiewicz; 272–273 LianeM; 280 IR Stone; 281 Andrea Danti; 282 Cathy Keifer; 286–287 karnizz; 294–295; 299 Veronika Galkina; 304 John Wollwerth; 306 trappy76; 308 Galyna Andrushko; 311 sunsinger; 313 Roberaten; 316 Georgios Kollidas; 317 Phant; 326 Paul Butchard; 330 Ekaterina Bykova; 333 cowardlion; 338 yuanann; 339 claudio zaccherini; 340 windmoon; 356 Kajano; 358 Kiev.Victor; 363 Everett Historical; 365 Neftali; 366–367; 371 Georgios Kollidas; 393 BVA; 402 Jane McIlroy; 405 Samot; 415 Morphart Creation; 428–429 Sean Pavone; 436 Art Konovalov; 458–459 Alexandra Lande; 460 Ryan Rodrick Beiler; 461 ChameleonsEye; 463 Jana Schoenknecht; 465 futureGalore; 481 Kichigin; 482 Stefano Tinti; 483 Lucarelli Temistocle; 485 ArtisticPhoto; 486–487

TopFoto 89 Fine Art Images/HIP; 237, 337, 341, 353, 424, 425, 426, 442 The Granger Collection

All other photographs are from:
digitalSTOCK, digitalvision, Dreamstime.com, ImageState, iStockphoto.com, John Foxx, PhotoAlto, PhotoDisc, PhotoEssentials, PhotoPro, Stockbyte

All artworks from the Miles Kelly Artwork Bank

Every effort has been made to acknowledge the source and copyright holder of each picture. Miles Kelly Publishing apologises for any unintentional errors or omissions.